SPARKNOTES™
5 Practice Tests for the SAT II U.S. History

2003 Edition

Editorial Director Justin Kestler

Executive Editor Ben Florman

Managing Editor Vince Janoski

Technical Director Tammy Hepps

Series Editor John Crowther

Editor Mike Hyatt

Contributing Editor Jen Chu

Copyright © 2003 by SparkNotes LLC

All rights reserved. No part of this book may be used or reproduced in any manner whatsoever without the written permission of the Publisher.

SPARKNOTES is a registered trademark of SparkNotes LLC.

This edition published by Spark Publishing.

Spark Publishing
A Division of SparkNotes LLC
120 Fifth Avenue, 8th Floor
New York, NY 10011

Please submit all comments and questions or report errors to www.sparknotes.com/errors

Library of Congress information available upon request

Printed and bound in Canada

ISBN 1-58663-870-X

SparkNotes is neither affiliated with nor endorsed by Harvard University.

Welcome to SparkNotes Test Preparation

IF YOU WANT TO SCORE HIGH ON THE SAT II U.S. HISTORY, YOU NEED TO KNOW more than just the material—you need to know how to take the test. Practice tests are the most effective method for learning the ins and outs of the test. But practice tests that accurately reflect the actual SAT II U.S. History have been hard to find—until now. *5 More Practice Tests for the SAT II U.S. History* is the first book anywhere dedicated to giving you accurate practice tests so you can perfect your test-taking skills. This book contains:

- **Five full-length SAT II U.S. History tests.** The practice tests in this book are the most accurate, true-to-life tests available. Our experts, who've been teaching the SAT II U.S. Historyfor years, researched the exam extensively so they could give you tests that reflect exactly what you'll see at the test center. Our tests replicate the format and content of the actual test so closely that nothing will catch you off guard on test day.

- **Clear, helpful explanations for every question—so you can study smarter.** Our explanations do more than tell you the right answer—they identify flaws in your thinking and show you exactly what topics you need to work on. We help you pinpoint your weaknesses, so you can make your studying more efficient by going straight to the stuff you need to review.

- **Specific, proven strategies for the SAT II U.S. History.** We give you smart, easy strategies on the best ways to guess, pace yourself, and find shortcuts to answers. These strategies help you maximize your score by showing you how to avoid the test's traps and turn the test's format to your own advantage.

Contents

Orientation

Introduction to the SAT II Tests **3**
    Colleges and the SAT II Subject Tests 4
    Scoring the SAT II Subject Tests 5
    Which SAT II Subject Tests to Take 6
    When to Take an SAT II Subject Test 8

Introduction to the SAT II U.S. History **11**
    Content of the SAT II U.S. History 11
    Format of the SAT II U.S. History 13
    Scoring and the SAT II U.S. History. 18

Strategies for the SAT II U.S. History **21**
    Basic Rules of SAT II Test-Taking. 21
    How the SAT II U.S. History Tests History 22
    Strategy and Multiple Choice Questions 25
    Guessing and the SAT II U.S. History 27
    Pacing: The Key to Scoring Well 29

Practice Tests

Practice Tests Are Your Best Friends 33
Using the Similarity of the SAT II U.S. History for Personal Gain . . . 33
Taking a Practice Test 36
Studying Your Practice Test. 37
The Secret Weapon: Talking to Yourself 39

SAT II U.S. History Practice Test 1 41
SAT II U.S. History Practice Test 1 Explanations 63

SAT II U.S. History Practice Test 2 77
SAT II U.S. History Practice Test 2 Explanations 99

SAT II U.S. History Practice Test 3 113
SAT II U.S. History Practice Test 3 Explanations 135

SAT II U.S. History Practice Test 4 149
SAT II U.S. History Practice Test 4 Explanations 173

SAT II U.S. History Practice Test 5 187
SAT II U.S. History Practice Test 5 Explanations 209

Orientation

Introduction to the SAT II Tests

THE SAT II SUBJECT TESTS are created and administered by the College Board and the Educational Testing Service (ETS), the two organizations responsible for producing the dreaded SAT I (which most people just call the SAT). The SAT II Subject Tests are meant to complement the SAT I. Whereas the three-hour-long SAT I tests your critical thinking skills by asking math and verbal questions, the one-hour-long SAT II Subject Tests examine your knowledge of specific subjects, such as U.S. history, writing, physics, or biology.

In our opinion, the SAT II Subject Tests are better tests than the SAT I, since they cover clearly-defined topics rather than some ambiguous critical thinking skills that no one can define. However, just because the SAT II tests do a better job of testing your knowledge of a useful subject than the SAT I does, they aren't necessarily easier. A "better" test isn't guaranteed to be "better for you," in terms of how easy it will be or how much you need to study.

In comparison to taking the SAT I, there are good things and bad things about taking an SAT II Subject Test.

The Good

- Because SAT II Subject Tests cover actual topics like U.S. History or Biology, you can study for them effectively. If you don't know a topic in U.S. history, such as the factors leading to the Louisiana Purchase, you can look it up and learn it. The SAT II tests are straightforward tests: if you know your stuff, you will do well on them.

- Often, the classes you've taken in school have already prepared you well for the test. If you've taken a U.S. history course, then you've probably already covered most of the topics that are tested on the SAT II U.S. History test.

- In studying for the History, Biology, and Chemistry SAT II tests, you really are learning history, biology, and chemistry. In other words, you are learning valuable, interesting knowledge. If learning is something you enjoy, you might actually find the process of studying for an SAT II test worthwhile and gratifying. It's hard to say the same about studying for the SAT I.

The Bad

- Because SAT II subject tests quiz you on specific knowledge, "beating" or "outsmarting" an SAT II test is much harder than outsmarting the SAT I. For the SAT I, you can use all sorts of tricks or strategies to figure out an answer. There are far fewer strategies to help you on the SAT II. Don't get us wrong: having test-taking skills *will* help you on an SAT II, but knowing the subject will help you much, much more. In other words, to do well on the SAT II, you can't just rely on your quick thinking and intelligence. You need to study!

Colleges and the SAT II Subject Tests

Stop for a second and think about why you would take an SAT II Subject test. Is it to prove to yourself how much you've learned in the year? That seems unlikely. Is it to prove to your teacher how much you've learned? No, you've got finals for that. Is it to win you a new car? You wish. No, there's only one reason to take an SAT II Subject Test: colleges want you to, and, sometimes, they require you to.

Colleges care about SAT II Subject Tests for two related reasons. First, the tests demonstrate your interest, knowledge, and skill in specific topics. Second, because SAT II tests are standardized, they show how your knowledge of U.S. history (or biology or math) measures up to the knowledge of high school students nationwide. The grades you get in high school don't offer such a measurement to colleges: some high schools are more difficult than others, meaning that students of equal ability might receive different grades from different schools. Since SAT II tests are national tests, they provide colleges with a yardstick against which they can measure every applicant's knowledge and skills.

When it comes down to it, colleges like the SAT II tests because the tests make the colleges' job easier. The tests are the colleges' tool. But because you know how colleges use the SAT II, you can make the tests your tool as well. SAT II tests allow colleges to easily compare you to other applicants. This means that the SAT II tests provide you with an excellent chance to shine. If you got a 93 percent in a U.S. history course and some other kid in some high school across the country got a 91 percent, colleges won't know what to make of it. They won't know whose class was harder, whose teacher was a tough grader, or whose high school inflates grades. But if you get a 720 on the SAT II U.S. History, and that other kid gets a 650, colleges will recognize the difference in your scores.

The Importance of SAT II Tests in College Applications

Time for some perspective: SAT II tests are *not* the primary tools that colleges use to decide whether to admit an applicant. High school grades, extracurricular activities, and SAT or ACT scores are all more important to colleges than your scores on SAT II tests. If you take a lot of AP tests, it's likely that those will also be more important to colleges than SAT II tests. But because SAT II tests do provide colleges with such a nice and easy measurement tool, they are an important *part* of your application to college. Good SAT II scores can give your application the extra shove that pushes you from the maybe pile into the accepted pile.

College Placement

Occasionally, colleges use SAT II tests to determine placement. For example, if you do very well on the SAT II U.S. History, you might be exempted from a basic history class. Though colleges don't often use SAT II tests for placement purposes, it's worth finding out whether the colleges to which you are applying do.

Scoring the SAT II Subject Tests

There are three different names for your SAT II U.S. History score. The "raw score" is a simple score of how you did on the test, like the grade you might receive on a normal test in school. The "percentile score" takes your raw score and compares it to the rest of the raw scores in the country for the same test. Percentile scores let you know how you did on the test in comparison to your peers. The "scaled score," which ranges from 200–800, compares your score to the scores received by all students who have ever taken that particular SAT II.

The Raw Score

You will never know your raw score on the SAT II that you take because the raw score is not included in the score report. But you should understand how the raw score is calculated, because this knowledge can affect your strategy for approaching the test.

A student's raw score is based solely on the number of questions that student got right, got wrong, or left blank. A correct answer is worth 1 point; a question left blank yields 0 points; a wrong answer results in the loss of ¼ of a point.

Calculating the raw score is easy. Simply add up the number of questions you answered correctly and the number of questions answered incorrectly. Then multiply the number of wrong answers by ¼, and subtract this value from the number of right answers.

$$\text{raw score} = \text{\# of correct answers} - \frac{1}{4} \times \text{\# of wrong answers}$$

In the next chapter, we'll explain how the way the raw score is calculated should influence your strategies for guessing and leaving questions blank on the test.

The Percentile Score

A student's percentile is based on the percentage of the total test-takers who received a lower raw score than he or she did. Let's say, for example, you had a friend named John Quincy Adams, and he received a score that placed him in the 37th percentile. This percentile score tells John that he scored better on the SAT II than 36 percent of the other students who took the same test; it also means that 63 percent of the students taking that test scored as well as or better than he did.

The Scaled Score

The scaled score takes the raw score and uses a formula to turn that raw score into the score from 200-800 that you've probably heard so much about. The curve to convert raw scores to scaled scores differs from SAT II test to SAT II test. For example, a raw score of 33 on the Math IC will scale to about a 600, while the same raw score of 33 on the Math IIC will scale to about a 700. In fact, the scaled score can even vary between different editions of the *same* test. A raw score of 33 on the February 2003 U.S. History test might scale to a 710, while a 33 in June 2003 might scale to a 690. These differences in scaled scores reflect differences in the difficulty level from edition to edition.

Which SAT II Subject Tests to Take

There are three types of SAT II tests: those you must take, those you should take, and those you shouldn't take.

- The SAT II tests you *must* take are those that are required by the colleges you are interested in.

- The SAT II tests you *should* take are tests that aren't required, but which you'll do well on, thereby impressing the colleges looking at your application.

- You *shouldn't* take unrequired SAT II tests that cover subjects you don't feel confident about.

Determining Which SAT II Tests are Required

To find out if the colleges to which you are applying require that you take a particular SAT II test, you'll need to do a bit of research. Call the schools you are interested in, look at their web pages, or talk to your guidance counselor. Often, colleges request that you take the following SAT II tests:

- The Writing SAT II test
- One of the two Math SAT II tests (either Math IC or Math IIC)
- Another SAT II in some other subject of your choice

Not all colleges follow these guidelines; you should take the time to research what tests you need to take in order to apply to the colleges that interest you.

Deciding Whether You Should Take an SAT II that isn't Required

To decide whether you should take a test that isn't required, know two things:

1. What a good score on that SAT II test is
2. Whether you can get that score or higher

Below, we have included a list of the most commonly taken SAT II tests and the average scaled score on each. If you feel confident that you can get a score that is significantly above the average (50 points is significant), taking the test will probably strengthen your college application. Please note that if you are hoping to attend an elite school, you might have to score significantly more than 50 points higher than the national average. The following list is just a general guideline. It's a good idea to call the schools that interest you; or talk to a guidance counselor to get a more precise idea of what score you should be shooting for.

TEST	AVERAGE SCORE
Writing	590-600
Literature	590-600
American History	580-590
World History	570-580
Math IC	580-590
Math IIC	655-665
Biology E/M	590-600
Chemistry	605-615
Physics	635-645

As you decide which test to take, be realistic with yourself. Don't just assume you're going to do well without at least taking a practice test and seeing where you stand.

It's a good idea to take three SAT II tests that cover a range of subjects, such as one math, one humanities (history or writing), and one science. However, there's no real reason to take *more* than three SAT II tests. Once you've taken the SAT II tests you need to take, the best way to set yourself apart from other students is to take AP courses and tests. AP tests are harder than the SAT II tests, and as a result they carry quite a bit more distinction. AP tests show that you're excited and able to take on responsibility, and that you want to challenge yourself. SAT II tests give you the opportunity to show colleges that you can learn when you want to; AP tests give you the change to show colleges that you *want* to learn as much as you can.

When to Take an SAT II Subject Test

The best time to take an SAT II subject test is, naturally, right after you've finished a year-long course in that subject. If, for example, you take U.S. History in eleventh grade, then you should take the SAT II U.S. History near the end of that year, when the material is still fresh in your mind. (This rule does not apply for the Writing, Literature, and Foreign Language SAT II tests; it's best to take those after you've had as much study in the area as possible.)

Unless the colleges to which you are applying use the SAT II for placement purposes, there is no point in taking any SAT II tests after November of your senior year, since you won't get your scores back from ETS until after the college application deadline has passed.

ETS usually sets testing dates for SAT II subject tests in October, November, December, January, May, and June. However, not every subject test is administered in each of these months. To check when the test you want to take is being offered, visit the College Board website at www.collegeboard.com or do some research in your school's guidance office.

Registering for SAT II Tests

To register for the SAT II test(s) of your choice, you have to fill out some forms and pay a registration fee. We know, we know—it's ridiculous that *you* have to pay for a test that colleges require you to take in order to make *their* jobs easier. But, sadly, there isn't anything we, or you, can do about it. It is acceptable for you to grumble here about the unfairness of the world.

After grumbling, of course, you still have to register. There are two ways: online or by mail. To register online, go to www.collegeboard.com. To register by mail, fill out and send in the forms enclosed in the *Registration Bulletin*, which should be available in your high school's guidance office. You can also request a copy of the *Bulletin* by calling the College Board at (609) 771-7600, or writing to:

College Board SAT Program
P.O. Box 6200
Princeton, NJ 08541-6200

You can register to take up to three SAT II tests for any given testing day. Unfortunately, even if you decide to take three tests in one day, you'll still have to pay a separate registration fee for each.

Introduction to the SAT II U.S. History

IMAGINE, FOR A MOMENT, two children playing tag in the forest. Who will win—the girl who never stumbles because she knows the placement of every tree and all the twists, turns, and hiding spots; or the kid who keeps falling down and tripping over roots because he doesn't pay any attention to the landscape? The answer is obvious. Even if the other kid is a little faster and more athletic, the girl will still win, because she knows how to navigate the landscape and use it to her advantage. This example of tag in the forest is extreme, but it illustrates the point: the structure of the SAT II is the forest; taking the test is the game of tag. And no one likes to lose at tag.

In this chapter we're going to describe the "landscape" of the SAT II U.S. History. In the next chapter, we will show you how to navigate and use the landscape to get the best score you can.

Content of the SAT II U.S. History

The SAT II U.S. History test covers 600 years of U.S. history, beginning with the period before Columbus' discovery of the New World and extending up to the present. There are two ways to organize and think about the 600 years of U.S. history covered on the test: by chronological eras, or by focusing on different aspects of history, such as political, social, or economic history.

Chronological Era

ETS breaks down the content of the test into three chronological eras, and tells how much of each the test covers:

Pre-Colombian to 1789	20%
1790–1898	40%
1899–present	40%

While these categories are helpful, they are overly broad. For example, the Pre-Colombian to 1789 category contains three distinct different time periods, each with its own characteristics: the Pre-Columbian period, the Colonial Period, and the American Revolution. The broad, chronological breakdowns provided by the ETS cover so much time that they aren't very sensible and won't be all that helpful in directing your study efforts.

We therefore created a test breakdown of our own in smaller, more cohesive chronological categories.

Pre-Columbian	1–3%
Colonial Period	10–14%
American Revolution and Constitution	8–12%
First Years of the New Nation	6–10%
Age of Jackson and Jacksonian Democracy	3–7%
Westward Expansion and Sectional Strife	6–10%
Civil War and Reconstruction	3–7%
Industrial Revolution	13–17%
American Imperialism	1–3%
Progressive Era	3–7%
Word War I	3–7%
The Roaring '20s	3–7%
The Great Depression and the New Deal	6–10%
World War II	5–9%
1950s: Cold War, Civil Rights	6–10%
1960s: Vietnam, Civil Rights, Social Movements	4–8%
1970s–Present	1–3%

Each question in the practice tests has been categorized according to this breakdown, so when you score the tests, you can very precisely identify your weaknesses.

Aspects of History

The second way to think about the content covered by the test is in terms of thematic focus, regardless of time period. The test targets five types of historical knowledge:

Political history	32–36%
Economic history	18–20%
Social history	18–22%
Intellectual, cultural history	10–12%
Foreign policy	13–17%

In our opinion, this second way of categorizing the test is not as helpful as the breakdown by chronological era. For example, studying the economic history of the Industrial Revolution would be pointless without knowing any political history of the period. You can't really understand one without the other. Instead, you should use this breakdown to get a sense of where you should focus while studying a chronological era. In effect, this list tells you that when you are studying, you need to learn more than just the dates of major political events. You should also be familiar with social movements, cultural trends, and intellectual and artistic achievements.

Format of the SAT II U.S. History

The SAT II U.S. History test is a one-hour long test composed of 90–95 multiple-choice questions. The instructions for the test are very simple. You should memorize them so you don't waste time reading them on the day of the test.

> Directions: Each of the questions or incomplete statements below is followed by five suggested answers or completions. Select the one that is best in each case and then fill in the corresponding oval on the answer sheet.

Have you read the directions? Have you memorized them? (Don't lie to us.) Have you memorized them? Good.

Basically, the instructions tell you two simple things: all the questions on the test are five-choice multiple-choice questions, and you will have an answer sheet on which to mark down your answers.

Now for the shocker: the instructions don't cover many of the important aspects of the format and rules of the test. We're going to remedy that flaw by providing you with a true understanding of the test's format.

- The questions on the test aren't organized by time period or difficulty. In other words, a difficult question about the Sherman Anti-Trust Act in the Industrial Revolution might be followed by an easy question about the causes of the War of 1812.

- You can skip around while taking the test. If, for example, you have a yearning to answer question 90 first, then question 1, then question 67, then 22… well, you could do that. But while it's silly to skip around for no reason, the ability to skip an occasional question can be very helpful.

- All questions are worth the same number of points, whether easy or difficult.

All of these facts can greatly affect your approach to taking the test, as we will explain in the next chapter on strategy.

The Four Types of Questions on the SAT II U.S. History

As the test directions imply, each question on the SAT II U.S. History follows the same basic format, involving a question and five possible answer choices. Within that basic format, though, there are four distinct types of questions:

1. Fact Questions
2. Trend Questions
3. EXCEPT Questions
4. Cartoons/Charts/Maps Questions

In order to avoid nasty surprises when you take the acutal test, you should become familiar with each question type now. Prepare to get familiar.

Fact Questions

Fact questions test your knowledge of names and definitions, as well as your ability to recognize, describe, and explain specific acts or events and the people associated with them. In this type of question, you might be asked about the ramifications of one particular act, rather than the effects of a general legislative policy. The questions will cover all people from presidents to social revolutionaries to authors, and all time periods and themes, from the Great Awakening to Jimmy Carter's foreign policy to women's rights.

Example Fact Questions:

The Haymarket Riot of 1886:

(A) helped rouse public support and sympathy for unions
(B) contributed to the Knights of Labor's success in demanding higher wages and shorter work days
(C) effectively ruined the Knights of Labor, temporarily crippling the labor movement
(D) was violent but effective, as it forced the police to give strikers more liberty to express their grievances
(E) had little effect, since "scabs" went to work in place of those striking

Answer: (C) In the Haymarket Riot of 1886, laborers met in Chicago to protest police cruelty against strikers. The riot turned violent when one member of the Knights of Labor threw a bomb, killing a police officer. In all, nine people were killed and close to sixty injured. Many leaders of the Knights of Labor were convicted of inciting the riot, and public support plummeted, effectively destroying the union. In the aftermath, anti-union hysteria spread through the American public, portraying unions as violent and lawless.

The first immigrants to be blocked from entering the U.S. were:

(A) Polish
(B) Italians
(C) Irish
(D) Russians
(E) Chinese

Answer: (E) The Chinese Immigration Act was passed in 1882, preventing more Chinese from immigrating for the next six decades.

Trend Questions

Trend questions cover basic themes regarding groups, movements, and time periods. These questions test your abilities to draw connections between the facts that you know and to display a more nuanced and longer view of U.S. history. For example, you might be asked to spot connections between three listed acts, or to identify key issues during a listed span of years. Some Trend Questions will include quotations, asking you to identify a speaker's attitude and to fit that speaker into a larger historical context by associating him or her with a relevant political or social movement.

Example Regular Trend Question:

Which of the following best characterizes the Transcendentalists?

(A) they aimed to transcend nature and overcome man's inherent flaws
(B) they believed that, through the church, man could unite with God and achieve perfection
(C) they urged enlightenment through reason and the close study of scripture
(D) they believed that man could personally connect with God through oneness with nature
(E) they preached church reform and encouraged women to join the clergy

Answer: (D) Transcendentalists called for an individualistic approach to faith, shunning the institutional church and its restrictive disciplines. They urged instead that man commune with God through nature, through a personal and emotional response rather than an intellectualization of faith.

Example Quote Trend Question:

"With malice toward none; with charity for all; with firmness in the right, as God gives us to see the right, let us strive on to finish the work we are in; to bind up the nation's wounds; to care for him who shall have borne the battle, and for his widow and his orphan—to do all which may achieve and cherish a just and lasting peace among ourselves."

These words from 1864 best describe which of the following political agendas?

(A) a war relief program to help Civil War veterans and their loved ones
(B) a moderate Republican plan, known as the Ten Percent Plan, to ease Reconstruction and reunite the nation
(C) a religious plan to unite the nation through faith in God
(D) a Southern appeasement plan, drafted by Southern Congressmen, to help rehabilitate the South without military supervision or Northern intervention
(E) the aims of the Radical Republicans to reunite the nation through a long and punishing reform of the South

Answer: (B) Lincoln finished his second inaugural address with these words, expressing his desire to reunite the nation smoothly and quickly, without harsh punishment of the South. His plan for reconstruction of the South was moderate, known as the Ten Percent Plan, which allowed southern states to reenter the Union so long as ten percent of their voters pledged an oath of loyalty to the Union. Radical Republicans condemned this plan as too mild; they wanted to punish the South for seceding.

EXCEPT Questions

EXCEPT questions can be either fact- or trend-related, and are characterized by the use of the words EXCEPT, NOT, LEAST, INCORRECT, INCONSISTENT or something similar. These words will always appear in all caps.

EXCEPT questions can be tricky because the right answer is actually the *wrong* answer; it is the one answer among the five that doesn't fit. Though the idea is simple, as you're moving quickly through the test, it can be easy to get confused. If you are careful not to fall into a trap, though, the trickiness of the question actually makes it easier. On other questions, if you aren't sure of the answer, you have to eliminate four answer choices in order to get to the right one; on except questions, all you have to do is eliminate one.

Example EXCEPT questions:

The Populist Party supported all of the following EXCEPT:

(A) graduated income tax
(B) immigration restriction
(C) public ownership of railroads, telephone, and telegraph systems
(D) maintaining the gold standard, countering inflation
(E) eight-hour work day

Answer: (D) The Populist Party vehemently opposed the gold standard, which served to limit the money in circulation and further aggravated farmers' debts and poverty. William Jennings Bryan, the Populist and Democratic candidate in the 1896 presidential election, condemned the gold standard as oppressive, declaring that the people, farmers and laborers in particular, should not be "crucified on this cross of gold." Bryan and the Populists pushed for a silver standard, which would create inflation and raise prices. They argued that increasing the money supply would help boost the struggling economy (and also make farmers' debts worth less).

Of the following, which was NOT a factor in the Panic of 1837?

(A) overspeculation
(B) inflation, followed by a tight contraction of credit
(C) the successful recharter of the Second National Bank
(D) recall of loans and Jackson's issuance of the Specie Circular
(E) possible bank mismanagement

Answer: (C) Jackson vetoed the recharter of the Second National Bank, considering it corrupt and unconstitutional.

Cartoons / Charts / Maps Questions

This type of question presents you with an image—whether political cartoon, chart, or map—and asks you to interpret it in order to answer the question. Since the charts and maps tend to hold more information than a single question can test, read the question first so you know what to look for in the image. When you do look at the image, pay attention to all the information given. Look for a title or date attached to the image. Such things can help you place the image into a historical context, which will make deciphering the question easier. There are usually about 5–7 of this type of question on the test. Here's an example:

THE SPANISH BRUTE—ADDS MUTILATION TO MURDER.
By Hamilton in "Judge."

The above cartoon suggests that

(A) the Spaniards used cruel guerilla tactics in the Spanish-American War
(B) the Spanish tried to demoralize Americans by desecrating their grave sites
(C) a disproportionate number of soldiers killed in the Spanish-American War were from Maine
(D) Spain was a brutish colonial power that had to be punished for sinking the Maine
(E) Americans attributed Spain's victory in the Spanish-American War to Spaniards' brutish, subhuman nature

Answer: (D) The cartoon shows Spain as a savage and brutal power hovering over a grave site for "Maine soldiers"—that is, for the 256 soldiers killed in the explosion of the U.S. naval ship, the *Maine*, off the coast of Havana in 1898. A 1976 investigation revealed that a fire onboard the ship had caused the blast, but in 1898 the U.S. government and general public were convinced that an underwater Spanish mine was to blame. Soon after the incident, the U.S. declared war on Spain to avenge both the loss of the *Maine* and Spain's well-publicized cruelty against Cuban nationalists, who had been fighting for independence from Spanish rule since 1895. The U.S. won the war within two months, securing Cuban independence.

Scoring and the SAT II U.S. History

Scoring on the SAT II U.S. History is the same as scoring for all other SAT II tests: for every right answer, you earn one point; for every wrong answer, you lose ¼ of a point; for every blank answer, you earn no points. Add all these points up, and you get your raw score. ETS then converts your raw score to a scaled score, according to a special curve tailored to the particular test that you take. We have included a generalized version of that table below. (Note that because ETS changes the curve slightly for each edition of the test, the table will be close to, but not exactly the same as, the table used by ETS.) You should use this chart to convert your raw scores on practice tests into a scaled score.

Raw Score	Scaled Score	Raw Score	Scaled Score	Raw Score	Scaled Score
90	800	55	650	21	450
89	800	54	640	20	440
88	800	53	640	19	440
87	800	52	630	18	430
86	800	51	630	17	430
85	800	50	620	16	420
84	800	49	610	15	420
83	800	48	600	14	410
82	800	47	600	13	410
81	790	46	590	12	400
80	790	45	590	11	400
79	790	44	580	10	390
78	780	43	570	9	390
77	780	42	570	8	380
76	770	41	560	7	380
75	770	40	560	6	370
74	760	39	550	5	370
73	760	38	540	4	360
72	750	37	540	3	360
71	740	36	530	2	350
70	740	35	530	1	340
69	730	34	520	0	340
68	720	33	520	–1	330
67	720	32	510	–2	320
66	710	31	510	–3	320
65	700	30	500	–4	310
64	700	29	490	–5	310
63	690	28	490	–6	300

Raw Score	Scaled Score	Raw Score	Scaled Score	Raw Score	Scaled Score
62	690	27	480	–7	300
61	680	26	480	–8	290
59	670	25	470	–9	290
58	670	24	470	–10	280
57	660	23	460		
56	660	22	460		

In addition to its function as a conversion table, this chart contains crucial information: it tells you that you can do very well on the SAT II U.S. History without answering every question correctly. In fact, you could skip some questions and get some other questions wrong and still earn a "perfect" score of 800.

For example, in a test of 95 questions, you could score:

- an 800 if you answered 87 right, 5 wrong, and left 3 blank
- a 750 if you answered 78 right, 10 wrong, and left 7 blank
- a 700 if you answered 72 right, 12 wrong, and left 11 blank
- a 650 if you answered 64 right, 20 wrong, and left 11 blank
- a 600 if you answered 56 right, 24 wrong, and left 15 blank

This chart should prove that when you're taking the test, you shouldn't imagine your score plummeting with every question you can't confidently answer. You can do very well on this test without knowing or answering everything. The key is to follow a strategy that ensures that you will get to see and answer all the questions you can answer correctly, and then intelligently guess on those questions about which you are a little unsure. We will discuss these strategies in the next chapter.

Strategies for the SAT II U.S. History

A MACHINE, NOT A PERSON, WILL SCORE YOUR SAT II U.S. History test. The tabulating machine sees only the filled-in ovals on your answer sheet and does not care how you came to these answers; it just impassively notes whether your answers are correct. So whether you knew the correct answer right away or just took a lucky guess, the machine will award you one point. It doesn't award extra points if you've spent a really long time getting the right answer. It doesn't award points if you managed to get a tricky question right. Think of this scoring system as a message to you from the ETS: "We care only about your answers, and not about any of the thought behind them."

So you should give ETS right answers, as many as possible, using whatever means possible. It's obvious that the SAT II U.S. History test allows you to show off your knowledge of U.S. history; but the test gives you the same opportunity to show off your fox-like cunning by figuring out what strategies will allow you to best display that knowledge. Remember, the SAT II test is your tool to get into college, so treat it as your tool. It wants right answers? Give it right answers by using whatever strategies you can.

Basic Rules of SAT II Test-Taking

There are some rules of strategy that apply to all SAT II tests. These rules are so obvious that we hesitate to even call them "strategies," but we're going to list them once, just to make sure that you've thought about them.

Avoid Carelessness

Avoiding carelessness probably sounds to you more like common sense than a sophisticated strategy. We don't disagree. But it is amazing how a timed test can warp and mangle common sense.

There are two types of carelessness, both of which will cost you points. The first type of carelessness results from moving too fast, whether that speed is caused by overconfidence or frantic fear. In speeding through the test, you make yourself vulnerable to misinterpreting the question, overlooking one of the answer choices, or simply making a logical mistake. As you take the test, make a conscious effort to approach it calmly, and not to move so quickly you become prone to making mistakes.

Whereas the first type of carelessness can be caused by overconfidence, the second results from frustration or lack of confidence. Some students take a defeatist attitude toward tests, assuming they won't be able to answer many of the questions. Such an attitude is a form of carelessness, because it causes the student to ignore reality. Just as the overconfident student assumes she can't be tricked and therefore gets tricked, the student without confidence assumes he can't answer questions and therefore at the first sign of difficulty gives up.

Both kinds of carelessness steal points from you. Avoid them.

Be Careful Gridding In Your Answers

The computer that scores SAT II tests is unmerciful. If you answered a question correctly, but somehow made a mistake in marking your answer grid, the computer will mark that question as wrong. If you skipped question 5, but put the answer to question 6 in row 5, and the answer to question 7 in row 6, etc., thereby throwing off your answers for an entire section . . . it gets ugly.

Some test prep books advise that you should fill in your answer sheet five questions at a time rather than one at a time. Some suggest that you do one question and then fill in the corresponding bubble. We think you should fill out the answer sheet whatever way feels most natural to you; just make sure you're careful while doing it. In our opinion, the best way to ensure that you're being careful is to talk silently to yourself. As you figure out an answer in the test booklet and transfer it over to the answer sheet, say to yourself: "Number 23, B. Number 24, E. Number 25, A."

How the SAT II U.S. History Tests History

Often, students think that studying history means memorizing lots of dates, names, and events. This sort of thinking will not serve you well on the SAT II U.S. History. Don't get us wrong: you do need to know facts, dates, and names for the SAT II U.S.

History. But to do well on the test, you need to understand these facts, dates, and names within the contexts of larger historical eras, movements, or trends.

Thinking of history in terms of eras and movements within U.S. history will help you on the SAT II U.S. History by directing your study, making it more efficient, and organizing your knowledge in such a way that is perfectly suited to answering the types of questions that the SAT II U.S. History asks.

Thinking in Eras Helps You Study

Thinking about history in terms of eras, movements, and trends provides organization for the information you learn. By thinking about history in terms of eras and trends, you create an outline in your mind. Then when you learn some new historical information, you can file it into that outline. Because this outline is structured, it will help you to remember and recall the things you learn, and to relate one era to another.

We'll make our point using an example. Imagine we had a box of 100 tacks, and we threw the tacks on the floor. Then we let you look at the tacks for 5 minutes. After that time, we ask you to go into another room and draw, on a piece of paper, where all of the tacks were. You probably wouldn't do a very good job of it, would you? But what if when you were looking at the tacks on the floor you noticed that they were organized into geometric shapes: 27 of the tacks were in a circle, 19 formed a triangle, another 28 formed a squiggly line, and 26 formed a hexagon. Then when you had to draw the tacks you'd do a pretty good job because though there are just as many tacks, now they're organized and easier to remember. All it would have taken was for you to notice the shapes in which the tacks were arranged. The same goes for history. All it takes is to always be aware of the trends the facts fit into.

Further, by always thinking of the facts you learn in terms of how they fit into an era or movement, you ensure that you remain engaged with the material you're studying. It's easy to read over a list of facts and think you've learned them, when really you've just looked at them and forgotten them. But if you are constantly trying to fit the facts you learn into an era or trend, you give yourself an active grip on those facts. You're not just reading them over; you're thinking about them. This engagement with the material will make your studying more efficient and fruitful.

Thinking in Eras Helps You Answer SAT II U.S. History Questions

Many questions on the SAT II U.S. History will test broad thematic knowledge. These questions ask you about the "big picture" of history, and test your general knowledge of an era or movement. For these questions, just knowing particular facts isn't going to help you all that much. To answer these questions, you have to have studied the trends of history. For example, look at the question below:

Which of the following best characterizes American foreign policy during the first half of Progressive Era, 1900 to 1910?

(A) aggressive intervention, through both military involvement and capitalist investment
(B) strict isolationism
(C) minimal diplomacy, as the U.S. focused almost exclusively on domestic reform
(D) primarily business-minded, aimed at expanding markets overseas
(E) alarmist and reactionary in nature, as the Red Scare swept the nation

This question doesn't care if you know a single fact or date. Instead, it tests to see if you understand the general situation of a particular era. Now, it is certainly true that in order to understand an era, you certainly have to know enough facts to understand the general trend, but you don't have to know *every* fact. There are a number of ways you could figure out the answer to this question. If you know that the U.S. won the Spanish-American War in 1898 and in the process arrived as a world power and took on an overseas empire, you would immediately know that the U.S. was heavily involved in foreign nations, sometimes through military means. Meaning the answer has to be (A). Alternately, you might have known that the president through many of those years was Teddy Roosevelt, who advocated "big stick" diplomacy. Again, that implies military intervention, giving you the answer (A). Note that you didn't have to know that one of the territories the U.S. gained in the Spanish American war was the Philippines, or that Roosevelt helped engineer a revolt in Panama.

Fact Questions Are Trend Questions in Disguise

But what about the more nitpicky questions that test you on precise facts and names? First, we've already discussed how thinking about history in terms of eras and trends will actually help you to remember individual facts. But knowing trends has an added importance: even if you aren't sure about a particular fact, understanding historical trends can still help you to answer a question that covers that fact. Let's say, for example, you are asked the following question, but don't remember the name John Calhoun:

John Calhoun most bitterly opposed Andrew Jackson's policies regarding

(A) American involvement in Europe
(B) slavery
(C) income taxes
(D) the nullification crisis
(E) the Supreme Court

If you approach the test as if it's testing only a collection of facts, you might think that this question is testing something very specific: John Calhoun's political beliefs as opposed to Andrew Jackson's beliefs. If you don't even know who John Calhoun was, then how are you supposed to answer this question? You might very well just skip this question and move on, assuming you can't answer it.

But if you approach the test with the understanding that all facts fit into trends, then knowing who John Calhoun was becomes secondary to answering this question. You know that Calhoun opposed Andrew Jackson on this issue. You therefore know that this issue took place during Jackson's presidency, and you should know the general trends of Jackson's presidency: an emerging two-party system that vastly increased popular interest and participation in government; the development of a strong executive branch that included a spoils system in which a party rewarded its followers with political posts; sectional strife over tariffs that led to the nullification crisis; removal of the Cherokee Indians from Georgia. When you think of the Jacksonian Era, these few issues and trends should immediately leap to mind. With them, you can see that the answer to this question must be (D), the nullification crisis.

The SAT II will ask questions in ways you won't expect, forcing you to be flexible with your knowledge of history. Knowing facts alone does not make you flexible; knowing facts *and* themes does. So, while studying, always keep the larger picture in mind, and try to fit the facts you are learning into this larger picture. In some ways, studying for the SAT II U.S. History test should be like writing a story in your head, where you don't just come up with lists of facts, but rather connect them.

Strategy and Multiple Choice Questions

When you look at an SAT II U.S. History question, the answer is always right there in front of you. Of course, the test writers don't just *give* you the correct answer; they hide it among a bunch of incorrect answer choices. The important thing to realize is that there are two methods by which you can try to come to the correct answer:

1. Find the right answer.

2. Eliminate wrong answers until there's only one answer left.

In a perfect world, you would always see the right answer. And for many of the questions on the test, you probably will be able to pick out the right answer from among the five answer choices. But if you can't decide which question is the right answer, then you might want to work in the other direction and try to figure out which choices *can't* be the right answer.

Eliminating Wrong Answers: Thinking Contextually

We've already explained how thinking in terms of eras helps your studying, and will help you answer SAT questions. It can also help you eliminate wrong answers. Let's say you come across a question:

26 • Strategy and Multiple Choice Questions

Between the 1860s and 1890s, the United States changed in all of the following ways EXCEPT:

(A) it became increasingly urban
(B) labor unions became a powerful force in politics and in business, and gained widespread popular support
(C) immigration significantly boosted the supply of workers
(D) big corporations and monopolies thrived, often unchecked by the government
(E) more women began to work outside of the home

What if you look at this question and just don't know the answer? Take a step back: identify the era the question covers to help you put the question into some historical context. In this case, knowing that "Between the 1860s and 1890s" roughly corresponds to the Industrial Revolution will help you remember the themes of that time period. What comes to mind when you ponder industrialization? Perhaps you think of big business and the rise in urbanization and immigration? If so, you can proceed to check off (A) and (C), since they're both clearly true. (Remember, for these EXCEPT questions, you are looking for the *wrong* answer, the answer that doesn't belong, so eliminate all the answers that are true.) The increased need for workers also likely had an effect on women, transforming some women from domestic to factory workers, allowing you to eliminate answer (E). Answer choice (D) might be a little trickier: yes, the first half of the answer is true because the Industrial Revolution spawned huge corporations like Carnegie's steel industry and Rockefeller's oil company, and the period is known as the "Era of Big Business"; but what about government regulation? Let's say you can't remember what government did with business during the Industrial Revolution, so you can't decide if (D) is true or false. As for (B), you may not know precisely what went on with unions during those years, so you can't say for sure whether that answer is right or wrong either.

So you are left with two possible answer choices: (B) and (D). You should be able to see that (B) and (D) are at odds with one another because if (B) were true, (D) would not be. If unions had been so politically powerful, they would have pushed for government to strictly regulate business and check the tyranny of monopolies (that is, the poor treatment of workers and the high prices of goods). In other words, if unions became so influential and popular during this period, then the Industrial Revolution would hardly be known as the "Era of Big Business," would it? Think again of what you remember about the trends of industrialization: big business was definitely a major one, whereas unions don't jar much in your memory. Armed with this knowledge of trends and eras, take a little leap of faith and guess that (B) is the right answer, the answer that doesn't fit with the other four.

Guess what? You guessed right!

Questions For Which You Can't Eliminate all Answers

Not all questions on the SAT II U.S. History test will work out quite as well as our last example. You might not always be able to use your knowledge of trends and eras to eliminate four answer choices, ensuring that you get the question right. But for almost every question you *will* likely be able to eliminate *at least one* answer. To see why this is important, move on to our discussion of guessing and the SAT II U.S. History.

Guessing and the SAT II U.S. History

Should you guess on the SAT II U.S. History? We'll begin to answer this question by posing a question of our own:

> Franklin Delano Roosevelt is holding five cards, numbered 1–5. Without telling you, he has selected one of the numbers as the "correct" card. If you pick a single card, what is the probability that you will choose the "correct" card?

The answer, of course, is one in five. But the answer is only important if you understand that the question precisely describes the situation you're in when you blindly guess the answer to any SAT II U.S. History question: you have a $1/5$ chance of getting the question right. If you were to guess on ten questions, according to probability you would get two questions right and eight questions wrong.

- 2 right answers gets you 2 raw points
- 8 wrong answers gets you $8 \times 1/4$ points = –2 raw points

Those ten answers, therefore, net you a total of *zero* points. This means that blind guessing is a complete waste of time, which is precisely what the ETS wants. They designed the scoring system so that blind guessing would be pointless.

Educated Guessing

But what if your guessing isn't blind? Here's a question about George Washington:

> George Washington was born in the year
>
> (A) 1730
> (B) 1731
> (C) 1732
> (D) 1733
> (E) 1977

You probably don't know what year George Washington was born (and you won't need to know such a minor fact for the SAT II test). But you probably do know that Washington was *not* born in 1977. Once you've eliminated "1977" as a possible answer, you have four choices from which to choose. Is it now worth it to guess? Probability states that if you are guessing between four choices you will correctly answer one question for every three you get wrong. For that one correct answer you'll get 1 point, and for the three incorrect answers you'll lose a total of ¾ of a point.

$$1 - \frac{3}{4} = \frac{1}{4}$$

This math indicates that if you can eliminate one answer, the odds of guessing turn in your favor: you become more likely to gain points than to lose points.

The rule for guessing on the SAT II U.S. History, therefore, is simple: *if you can eliminate even one answer-choice on a question, you should definitely guess.* And if you follow the above described contextual-thinking methods to eliminate answer choices, you should be able to eliminate at least one answer from almost every question.

Guessing as Partial Credit

Some students feel that guessing is similar to cheating, and that a correct guess is the same as getting credit where none is due. But instead of looking at guessing as an attempt to gain undeserved points, you should look at it as a form of partial credit. Take the example of the question about George Washington's birth. Most people taking the test will only know that Washington wasn't born in 1977, and will only be able to throw out that word as a possible answer, leaving them with a 1 in 4 chance of guessing correctly. But let's say that you also knew that Washington wasn't born in 1730. Don't you deserve something for that extra knowledge? Well, you do get something: you can throw out both "1977" and "1730" as answer choices, leaving you with a 1 in 3 chance of getting the question right if you guess. Your extra knowledge gives you better odds of getting this question right, exactly as extra knowledge should.

If You're Stumped

If you cannot eliminate even one answer choice and find yourself staring at a certain question with mounting panic, throw a circle around that nasty question and move on. If you have time, you can return to the question later. Remember, answering a hard question correctly doesn't earn you any more points than answering an easy question correctly. You want to be sure to see every question you can answer instead of running out of time by fixating on the really tough questions. While taking five minutes to solve a particularly difficult question might strike you as a moral victory when you're taking the test, you possibly could have used that same time to answer six other questions that would have vastly increased your score. Instead of getting bogged down on individual questions, you will do better if you learn to skip and leave for later the very difficult questions that you either can't answer or that will take an extremely long time to figure out.

Pacing: The Key to Scoring Well

Good pacing allows you to take the test, rather than letting the test take you. As we said earlier, the questions on the SAT II U.S. History test are not organized by difficulty or time period. You are as likely to come upon a question you can answer at the end of the test as you are at the beginning. Part of your job as you take the test is to make sure that you don't miss out on answering those questions near the end of the test that you could have answered if only you had more time.

By perfecting your pacing on practice tests, you can make sure that you will see every question on the test. And if you see every question on the test, then you can select which questions you will and won't answer, rather than running out of time before reaching the end of the test and letting the test decide, by default, which questions you won't answer.

In large part, pacing yourself entails putting into practice the strategies we've already discussed:

- Make sure not to get bogged down on one single question. If you find yourself wasting time on one question, circle it, move on, and come back to it later.

- Answer every question for which you know the answer, and make an educated guess for every question in which you can quickly eliminate at least two answer choices.

Learning to pace yourself is a crucial part of your preparation for the test. Students who know how to pace themselves take the test on their own terms. Students who don't know how to pace themselves enter the test already one step behind.

Setting a Target Score

You can make the job of pacing yourself much easier if you go into the test knowing how many questions you have to answer correctly in order to earn the score you want. So, what score do you want? Obviously, you should strive for the best score possible, but be realistic: consider how much you know about U.S. History and how well you do, generally, on SAT-type tests. You should also consider what exactly defines a good score at the colleges to which you're applying: is it a 620? a 680? Talk to the admissions offices of the colleges you might want to attend, do a little research in college guidebooks, or talk to your guidance counselor.

No matter how you do it, you should find out the average SAT II score of students attending the schools that interest you. Take that number and set your target score above it (you want to be above average, right?). Then take a look at this chart we showed you before.

You will get:

Score	Right answers	Wrong answers	Blank answers
800	83	5	2
750	74	8	8
700	66	12	15
650	59	16	15
600	52	20	18
550	44	24	22

So let's say the average score for the SAT II U.S. History, for the school you want to attend, is a 600. You should set your target at about 650. Looking at this chart, you can see that to get that score, you need to get 59 questions right, can absorb getting 16 wrong, and can leave 15 questions blank.

If you know all these numbers going into the test, you can pace yourself accordingly. You should use practice tests to teach yourself the proper pace, increasing your speed if you find that you aren't getting to answer all the questions you need to, or decreasing your pace if you find that you're rushing and making careless mistakes. If you reach your target score during preparation, give yourself a cookie or some other tasty treat and take a break for the day. But just because you hit your target score doesn't mean you should stop working altogether. In fact, you should view reaching your target score as a clue that you can do *better* than that score: set a new target to 50–100 points above your original, and work to pick up your pace a little bit and skip fewer questions.

By working to improve in manageable increments, you can slowly work up to your top speed, integrating your new knowledge of how to take the test and the subjects the test covers without overwhelming yourself by trying to take on too much too soon. If you can handle working just a little faster without becoming careless and losing points, your score will certainly go up. If you meet your new target score again, repeat the process.

Practice Tests

Practice Tests Are Your Best Friends

IN THIS CRAZY WORLD OF OURS, there is one thing that you can always take for granted: the SAT II U.S. History will stay the same. From year to year and test to test, the SAT II U.S. History will cover the same eras to the same degree. Obviously, there are different versions of the SAT II U.S. History. Individual questions will never repeat from test to test. But the topics that those questions test and the way in which the questions test those subjects *will* remain constant.

This constancy can be of great benefit to you as you study for the test. To show how you can use the similarity between different versions of the SAT II U.S. History to your advantage, we provide a case study.

Using the Similarity of the SAT II U.S. History for Personal Gain

One day, an eleventh grader named Molly Bloom sits down at the desk in her room and takes a practice test for the SAT II U.S. History. Because it makes this example much simpler, she takes the entire test and gets only one question wrong. Molly checks her answers and then jumps from her chair and does a little dance that would be embarrassing if anyone else were around to see her.

After her euphoria passes, she begins to wonder which question she got wrong and returns to her chair. She discovers that the question dealt with the Populist movement. Looking over the question, Molly at first thinks the test made a mistake and that she was actually right, but then she realizes that she answered the question wrong because she had mistakenly believed that the Populist Party wanted to raise protective tariffs, when in fact it wanted them lowered. Molly thinks about why she got the question wrong: she knew that the Populist Party arose among farmers in the 1890s, primarily because of falling prices for agricultural produce, and had assumed these falling prices were the result of foreign competition. Her logic made perfect sense, but it was wrong. In thinking about the question, Molly realizes she didn't have a good grasp of what was going on in the 1890s and looks in her books to figure out the truth. She studies up on the Populist Party, learns what policies they stood behind, and studies *why* they stood behind those policies. All this takes her about 10 minutes, after which she vows never to make a mistake about the Populists again.

Analyzing Molly Bloom

Molly's actions here seem like a minor thing. All she did was study a question she got wrong until she understood why she got it wrong and what she should have done to get it right. But think about the implications. Molly answered the question incorrectly because she didn't understand the topic it was testing. The practice test had pointed out her mistaken understanding in the most noticeable way possible: she got the question wrong. After doing her admittedly goofy little dance, Molly wasn't content simply to see what the correct answer was and get on with her day; she wanted to see *how* and *why* she got the question wrong and what she should have done, or needed to know, in order to get it right. So, with a look of determination, telling herself, "I will figure out why I got this question wrong, yes I will, yes," she spent a little while studying the question, discovered her mistaken understanding of the Populist movement and the issues facing 1890s America in general, and learned the truth of the historical situation. If Molly were to take that same test again, she definitely would not get that question wrong.

"But she never will take that test again, so she's never going to see that particular question again," some poor sap who hasn't read this guide might sputter. "She wasted her time. What a dork!"

Why That Poor Sap Really Is a Poor Sap

In some sense, that poor sap is correct: Molly never will take that exact practice test again. But the poor sap is wrong to call Molly derogatory names, because, as we know, the SAT II U.S. History is remarkably similar from year to year, both in the topics it covers and in the way it poses questions about those topics. Therefore, when Molly taught herself about the Populist movement and 1890s America, she actually learned how to answer the similar questions dealing with the Populist movement and 1890s

America that will *undoubtedly* appear on every future practice test, and on the real SAT II U.S. History.

In studying the results of her practice test, in figuring out exactly why she got her one question wrong and what she should have known and done to get it right, Molly has targeted a weakness and overcome it.

Molly and You

Molly has it easy. She took a practice test and got only one question wrong. Less than one percent of all people who take the SAT II U.S. History will be so lucky. Of course, the only reason Molly got so few questions wrong was because we wanted to use her as an easy example.

So, what if you take a practice test and get 15 questions wrong, and your errors span a number of different eras? Well, you should do exactly what Molly did. Take your test and *study it*. Identify every question you got wrong, figure out why you got it wrong, and then teach yourself what you should have done to get the question right. If you can't figure out your error, find someone who can.

A wrong answer on the SAT II U.S. History identifies a weakness in your test taking, whether that weakness is an unfamiliarity with a particular topic or a tendency to be careless. If you got 15 questions wrong on a practice test, then each of those 15 questions identifies a weakness in your ability to take the SAT II U.S. History or your knowledge about the topics the SAT II U.S. History tests. As you study each question you got wrong, you are actually learning how to answer the very questions that will appear in similar form on the real SAT II U.S. History. You are discovering your exact U.S. History weaknesses and addressing them, and you are learning to understand not just the knowledge behind the question, but also the way the test writers ask their questions.

True, if you got 15 questions wrong, studying your first practice test will take some time. But if you invest that time and study your practice test properly, you will be eliminating future mistakes. Each successive practice test you take should have fewer errors, meaning less time spent studying those errors. Also, and more importantly, you'll be pinpointing what you need to study for the real SAT II U.S. History, identifying and overcoming your weaknesses, and learning to answer an increasing variety of questions on the specific topics covered by the test. Taking practice tests and studying them will allow you to teach yourself how to recognize and handle whatever the SAT II U.S. History throws at you.

Taking a Practice Test

Through the example of Miss Molly Bloom, we've shown you why studying practice tests is an extremely powerful stratgey. Now we're going to explain how you should take practice tests in order to best put that tool to use.

Controlling Your Environment

Although no one but you needs to see your practice test scores, you should do everything in your power to make the practice test feel like the real SAT II U.S. History. The closer your practice resembles the real thing, the more helpful it will be. When taking a practice test, follow these rules:

Take the tests timed.

Don't give yourself any extra time. Be stricter with yourself than the meanest proctor you can think of would be. Also, don't give yourself time off for bathroom breaks. If you have to go to the bathroom, let the clock keep running; that's what'll happen on the real SAT II.

Take the test in a single sitting.

Training yourself to endure an hour of test taking is part of your preparation.

Find a place to take the test that offers no distractions.

Don't take the practice test in a room with lots of people walking through it. Go to a library, your bedroom, a well-lit closet, anywhere quiet.

Now, having stated the rules of practice test taking, we can relax a little bit: don't be so strict with yourself that studying and taking practice tests becomes unbearable. The most important thing is that you actually study. Do whatever you have to do in order to make your studying interesting and painless enough for you to actually do it.

Ultimately, if you can follow all of the above rules to the letter, you will be better off. But, if following those rules makes studying excruciating, find little ways to bend them that won't interfere too much with your concentration.

Practice Test Strategy

You should take each practice test as if it were the real SAT II U.S. History. Don't be more daring than you would be on the actual test, guessing blindly even when you can't eliminate an answer. Don't carelessly speed through the test. Don't flip through this book while taking the practice exam just to sneak a peek. Follow the rules for guessing and for skipping questions that we outlined in the chapter on strategy. The more closely your attitude and strategies during the practice test reflect those you'll employ during the actual test, the more predictive the practice test will be of your strengths and weaknesses and the more fruitful your studying of the test will be.

Scoring Your Practice Test

After you take your practice test, you'll no doubt want to score it and see how you did. When you score your test, don't just write down how many questions you answered correctly and tally your score. Instead, keep a list of every question you got wrong and every question you skipped. This list will be your guide when you study your test.

Studying Your ... No, Wait, Go Take a Break

You know how to have fun. Go do that for a while. Come back when you're refreshed.

Studying Your Practice Test

After grading your test, you should have a list of the questions you answered incorrectly or skipped. Studying your test involves going through this list and examining each question you answered incorrectly. When you look at each question, you shouldn't just look to see what the correct answer is, but rather why you got the question wrong and how you could have gotten the question right. Train yourself in the process of getting the question right.

Why Did You Get the Question Wrong?

There are three reasons why you might have gotten an individual question wrong.

- **Reason 1**: You thought you knew the answer, but actually you didn't.
- **Reason 2**: You managed to eliminate some answer choices and then guessed among the remaining answers; sadly, you guessed wrong.
- **Reason 3**: You knew the answer but made a careless mistake.

You should know which of these reasons applies to every question you got wrong.

What You Could Have Done to Get the Question Right?

The reasons you got a question wrong affect how you should think about it while studying your test.

If You Got a Question Wrong for Reason 1–Lack of Knowledge

A question answered incorrectly for Reason 1 identifies a weakness in your knowledge of the material tested on the SAT II U.S. History. Discovering this wrong answer gives you an opportunity to target your weakness. When addressing that weakness, make sure that you don't just look at the facts.

For example, if the question you got wrong refers to the election of 1912, which Woodrow Wilson won, don't just memorize the facts of the election; learn *why* Wilson won, study up on the split in the Republican party between Taft and Roosevelt, get some understanding of the ideological split between those two men and how the social and political realities of the U.S. at the time influenced this split. Remember, you will *not* see a question exactly the same as the question you got wrong. But you probably *will* see a question that covers the same topic as the practice question. For that reason, when you get a question wrong, don't just figure out the right answer to the question. Learn the broader topic of which the question tests only a piece.

If You Got a Question Wrong for Reason 2–Guessing Wrong

If you guessed wrong, review your guessing strategy. Did you guess intelligently? Could you have eliminated more answers? If yes, why didn't you? By thinking in this critical way about the decisions you made while taking the practice test, you can train yourself to make quicker, more decisive, and better decisions.

If you took a guess and chose the incorrect answer, don't let that sour you on guessing. As you go over the question and figure out if there was any way for you to have answered the question without having to guess, remind yourself that if you eliminated at least one answer and guessed, even if you got the question wrong, you followed the right strategy.

If You Got a Question Wrong for Reason 3–Carelessness

If you discover you got a question wrong because you were careless, it might be tempting to say to yourself, "Oh, I made a careless error," and assure yourself you won't do that again. That is not enough. You made that careless mistake for a reason, and you should try to figure out why. Whereas getting a question wrong because you didn't know the answer constitutes a weakness in your knowledge of the test subject, making a careless mistake represents a weakness in your *method of taking the test.*

To overcome this weakness, you need to approach it in the same critical way you would approach a lack of knowledge. Study your mistake. Reenact your thought process on the problem and see where and how your carelessness came about: were you rushing? Did you jump at the first answer that seemed right instead of reading all the answers? Know your error and look it in the eye. If you learn precisely what your mistake was, you are much less likely to make that mistake again.

If You Left the Question Blank

It is also a good idea to study the questions you left blank on the test, since those questions constitute a reservoir of lost points. If you left the question blank, a different thinking applies. A blank answer is a result either of:

1. Total inability to answer a question
2. Lack of time

In the case of the former, you should see if there was some way you might have been able to eliminate an answer choice or two and put yourself in a better position to guess. In the second case, look over the question and see whether you think you could have answered it. If you could have, then you know that you are throwing away points by working too slowly. If you couldn't, then carry out the steps above: study the relevant material (time period, movement, political leader, etc.) and review your guessing strategy.

The Secret Weapon: Talking to Yourself

Yeah, it's embarrassing. Yeah, you may look silly. But talking to yourself is perhaps the best way to pound something into your brain. As you go through the steps of studying a question, you should talk them out. When you verbalize something to yourself, it makes it much harder to delude yourself into thinking that you're working if you're really not.

SAT II U.S. History Practice Test 1

UNITED STATES HISTORY TEST 1 ANSWER SHEET

1. Ⓐ Ⓑ Ⓒ Ⓓ Ⓔ	31. Ⓐ Ⓑ Ⓒ Ⓓ Ⓔ	61. Ⓐ Ⓑ Ⓒ Ⓓ Ⓔ
2. Ⓐ Ⓑ Ⓒ Ⓓ Ⓔ	32. Ⓐ Ⓑ Ⓒ Ⓓ Ⓔ	62. Ⓐ Ⓑ Ⓒ Ⓓ Ⓔ
3. Ⓐ Ⓑ Ⓒ Ⓓ Ⓔ	33. Ⓐ Ⓑ Ⓒ Ⓓ Ⓔ	63. Ⓐ Ⓑ Ⓒ Ⓓ Ⓔ
4. Ⓐ Ⓑ Ⓒ Ⓓ Ⓔ	34. Ⓐ Ⓑ Ⓒ Ⓓ Ⓔ	64. Ⓐ Ⓑ Ⓒ Ⓓ Ⓔ
5. Ⓐ Ⓑ Ⓒ Ⓓ Ⓔ	35. Ⓐ Ⓑ Ⓒ Ⓓ Ⓔ	65. Ⓐ Ⓑ Ⓒ Ⓓ Ⓔ
6. Ⓐ Ⓑ Ⓒ Ⓓ Ⓔ	36. Ⓐ Ⓑ Ⓒ Ⓓ Ⓔ	66. Ⓐ Ⓑ Ⓒ Ⓓ Ⓔ
7. Ⓐ Ⓑ Ⓒ Ⓓ Ⓔ	37. Ⓐ Ⓑ Ⓒ Ⓓ Ⓔ	67. Ⓐ Ⓑ Ⓒ Ⓓ Ⓔ
8. Ⓐ Ⓑ Ⓒ Ⓓ Ⓔ	38. Ⓐ Ⓑ Ⓒ Ⓓ Ⓔ	68. Ⓐ Ⓑ Ⓒ Ⓓ Ⓔ
9. Ⓐ Ⓑ Ⓒ Ⓓ Ⓔ	39. Ⓐ Ⓑ Ⓒ Ⓓ Ⓔ	69. Ⓐ Ⓑ Ⓒ Ⓓ Ⓔ
10. Ⓐ Ⓑ Ⓒ Ⓓ Ⓔ	40. Ⓐ Ⓑ Ⓒ Ⓓ Ⓔ	70. Ⓐ Ⓑ Ⓒ Ⓓ Ⓔ
11. Ⓐ Ⓑ Ⓒ Ⓓ Ⓔ	41. Ⓐ Ⓑ Ⓒ Ⓓ Ⓔ	71. Ⓐ Ⓑ Ⓒ Ⓓ Ⓔ
12. Ⓐ Ⓑ Ⓒ Ⓓ Ⓔ	42. Ⓐ Ⓑ Ⓒ Ⓓ Ⓔ	72. Ⓐ Ⓑ Ⓒ Ⓓ Ⓔ
13. Ⓐ Ⓑ Ⓒ Ⓓ Ⓔ	43. Ⓐ Ⓑ Ⓒ Ⓓ Ⓔ	73. Ⓐ Ⓑ Ⓒ Ⓓ Ⓔ
14. Ⓐ Ⓑ Ⓒ Ⓓ Ⓔ	44. Ⓐ Ⓑ Ⓒ Ⓓ Ⓔ	74. Ⓐ Ⓑ Ⓒ Ⓓ Ⓔ
15. Ⓐ Ⓑ Ⓒ Ⓓ Ⓔ	45. Ⓐ Ⓑ Ⓒ Ⓓ Ⓔ	75. Ⓐ Ⓑ Ⓒ Ⓓ Ⓔ
16. Ⓐ Ⓑ Ⓒ Ⓓ Ⓔ	46. Ⓐ Ⓑ Ⓒ Ⓓ Ⓔ	76. Ⓐ Ⓑ Ⓒ Ⓓ Ⓔ
17. Ⓐ Ⓑ Ⓒ Ⓓ Ⓔ	47. Ⓐ Ⓑ Ⓒ Ⓓ Ⓔ	77. Ⓐ Ⓑ Ⓒ Ⓓ Ⓔ
18. Ⓐ Ⓑ Ⓒ Ⓓ Ⓔ	48. Ⓐ Ⓑ Ⓒ Ⓓ Ⓔ	78. Ⓐ Ⓑ Ⓒ Ⓓ Ⓔ
19. Ⓐ Ⓑ Ⓒ Ⓓ Ⓔ	49. Ⓐ Ⓑ Ⓒ Ⓓ Ⓔ	79. Ⓐ Ⓑ Ⓒ Ⓓ Ⓔ
20. Ⓐ Ⓑ Ⓒ Ⓓ Ⓔ	50. Ⓐ Ⓑ Ⓒ Ⓓ Ⓔ	80. Ⓐ Ⓑ Ⓒ Ⓓ Ⓔ
21. Ⓐ Ⓑ Ⓒ Ⓓ Ⓔ	51. Ⓐ Ⓑ Ⓒ Ⓓ Ⓔ	81. Ⓐ Ⓑ Ⓒ Ⓓ Ⓔ
22. Ⓐ Ⓑ Ⓒ Ⓓ Ⓔ	52. Ⓐ Ⓑ Ⓒ Ⓓ Ⓔ	82. Ⓐ Ⓑ Ⓒ Ⓓ Ⓔ
23. Ⓐ Ⓑ Ⓒ Ⓓ Ⓔ	53. Ⓐ Ⓑ Ⓒ Ⓓ Ⓔ	83. Ⓐ Ⓑ Ⓒ Ⓓ Ⓔ
24. Ⓐ Ⓑ Ⓒ Ⓓ Ⓔ	54. Ⓐ Ⓑ Ⓒ Ⓓ Ⓔ	84. Ⓐ Ⓑ Ⓒ Ⓓ Ⓔ
25. Ⓐ Ⓑ Ⓒ Ⓓ Ⓔ	55. Ⓐ Ⓑ Ⓒ Ⓓ Ⓔ	85. Ⓐ Ⓑ Ⓒ Ⓓ Ⓔ
26. Ⓐ Ⓑ Ⓒ Ⓓ Ⓔ	56. Ⓐ Ⓑ Ⓒ Ⓓ Ⓔ	86. Ⓐ Ⓑ Ⓒ Ⓓ Ⓔ
27. Ⓐ Ⓑ Ⓒ Ⓓ Ⓔ	57. Ⓐ Ⓑ Ⓒ Ⓓ Ⓔ	87. Ⓐ Ⓑ Ⓒ Ⓓ Ⓔ
28. Ⓐ Ⓑ Ⓒ Ⓓ Ⓔ	58. Ⓐ Ⓑ Ⓒ Ⓓ Ⓔ	88. Ⓐ Ⓑ Ⓒ Ⓓ Ⓔ
29. Ⓐ Ⓑ Ⓒ Ⓓ Ⓔ	59. Ⓐ Ⓑ Ⓒ Ⓓ Ⓔ	89. Ⓐ Ⓑ Ⓒ Ⓓ Ⓔ
30. Ⓐ Ⓑ Ⓒ Ⓓ Ⓔ	60. Ⓐ Ⓑ Ⓒ Ⓓ Ⓔ	90. Ⓐ Ⓑ Ⓒ Ⓓ Ⓔ

UNITED STATES HISTORY TEST I

Directions: Each of the questions or incomplete statements below is followed by five suggested answers or completions. Select the one that is best in each case and then fill in the corresponding oval on the answer sheet.

1. The Palmer Raids of 1919 were specifically designed to

    (A) attack German Americans who protested against United States involvement in World War I
    (B) eradicate communists and anarchists in the United States
    (C) end the progressive movement
    (D) crush strikes organized by the American Federation of Labor
    (E) oppose the League of Nations and the Versailles Treaty

2. Shaker communities in the United States practiced celibacy because they

    (A) were contemptuous of other utopian societies that flouted the sanctity of marriage
    (B) believed in eugenics and wanted only the fittest members of their society to procreate
    (C) believed Jesus' second coming was imminent and saw no reason to continue to populate the earth
    (D) were sexist and limited women to performing domestic chores
    (E) thought that raising children would take time away from religious rituals

3. The Supreme Court, in *Schechter Poultry Corp. v. The United States*, ruled that the

    (A) Agricultural Adjustment Act was unconstitutional because it prohibited farmers from making a profit
    (B) Tennessee Valley Authority was socialist in nature and violated the basic tenets of capitalism
    (C) Wagner Act was unconstitutional because it gave labor an unfair advantage in its negotiations with employers
    (D) Works Progress Administration was unconstitutional because it overstepped federal authority as delineated in the Tenth Amendment
    (E) National Recovery Administration was unconstitutional because Congress did not have the power to regulate intrastate commerce

4. The Navigation Acts of 1660–63 contained all of the following stipulations EXCEPT

    (A) no colonial products of any kind could be shipped to Europe or Asia without specific permission of the Crown
    (B) articles enumerated by the acts could be shipped only to English ports
    (C) ships involved in colonial trade had to be built and owned by English or colonial merchants
    (D) crews on ships trading with the colonies must be predominantly English or colonial
    (E) goods exported to the colonies from other European countries would be taxed by England

5. In response to the proliferation of trusts created in the late nineteenth century, the federal government

    (A) adopted a laissez-faire approach and passed no legislation to prohibit the growth of monopolies
    (B) waited for the president to act under his regulatory authority
    (C) mandated that any trust that restricted trade or commerce was illegal
    (D) passed legislation legalizing all trusts and exempting them from lawsuits
    (E) looked to the Supreme Court for guidance before taking action

6. All of the following were grievances that led to Bacon's Rebellion EXCEPT

    (A) class antagonisms
    (B) a nonresponsive government
    (C) the expansion of slavery
    (D) the falling tobacco prices
    (E) tensions between Native Americans and whites

GO ON TO THE NEXT PAGE

UNITED STATES HISTORY TEST—Continued

7. One of the earliest civil rights organizations established in the twentieth century to combat segregation and all forms of racial discrimination was the

    (A) Congress of Racial Equality
    (B) National Association for the Advancement of Colored People
    (C) Southern Christian Leadership Conference
    (D) Student Non-violent Coordinating Committee
    (E) Universal Negro Improvement Association

8. "But this act does not permit competition in the purchase of this monopoly. It seems to be predicated on the erroneous idea that the present stockholders have a prescriptive right not only to the favor but to the bounty of Government. It appears that more than a fourth part of the stock is held by foreigners and the residue is held by a few hundred of our own citizens, chiefly of the richest class. For their benefit does this act exclude the whole American people from competition in the purchase of this monopoly and dispose of it for many millions less than it is worth."

    In this particular message, Andrew Jackson was specifically addressing

    (A) internal improvements in Kentucky
    (B) Indian removal from state land in Georgia
    (C) the power of judicial review
    (D) South Carolina's nullification of the Tariff of 1832
    (E) the recharter of the Second Bank of the United States

9. Britain used the philosophy of virtual representation to

    (A) control the colonies through the employment of royal governors
    (B) explain why Britain could tax the colonies
    (C) calm colonial fears concerning the army's ability to protect them from Indian attack
    (D) underscore how highly prized the colonies were as part of the mercantile system
    (E) justify the development of the slave system in the American south

10. The Compromise of 1877, which formally ended the process of Reconstruction in the South,

    (A) gave the Democratic candidate the presidency despite the fact that he had not won the popular vote
    (B) rescinded the Wade-Davis Bill and allowed former confederate officers to vote
    (C) marked the beginnings of Ulysses S. Grant's political career
    (D) set the stage for a new era of harmonious race relations in the South
    (E) reflected growing northern disinterest in Reconstruction and in race relations in the South

11. The most significant problem affecting the railroad industry in America after the Civil War was

    (A) inefficiency and lack of coordination
    (B) a series of unfavorable Supreme Court rulings
    (C) intense congressional regulation and oversight
    (D) a lack of steel to expand railroad lines
    (E) low tariff policies

12. The Federalists enacted the Sedition Act of 1798 in order to

    (A) protect America from foreign invasion
    (B) stop England from continuing impressment of the high seas
    (C) weaken its political opposition
    (D) strengthen freedom of the press
    (E) prevent an alliance with Spain

13. Lyndon Johnson's Great Society program created all of the following EXCEPT

    (A) Medicare
    (B) Omnibus Housing Act
    (C) Air Quality Act
    (D) Model Cities Program
    (E) Soil Bank Act

GO ON TO THE NEXT PAGE

UNITED STATES HISTORY TEST—Continued

14. The critic who had the greatest influence on Franklin D. Roosevelt's decision to establish the Social Security System was

    (A) Francis Townshend
    (B) Father Caughlin
    (C) Huey Long
    (D) Louis Brandeis
    (E) Hugh Johnson

15. Jacob Riis, in his book *How the Other Half Lives* (1890), depicted the

    (A) wealth and leisure activities of the industrial elite
    (B) practice of segregation and its effects on blacks in the rural South
    (C) squalor and unsanitary conditions in America's urban slums
    (D) growth of labor unions in the northwest
    (E) domestic life and homemaking chores of the average American housewife

16. All of the following economic measures were part of the Mellon tax policies of the 1920s EXCEPT

    (A) reduction of personal income taxes for the wealthy
    (B) tax breaks for large corporations
    (C) high protective tariffs
    (D) excise taxes on automobiles and postal services
    (E) prohibition on margin buying of stocks

17. Slaves on antebellum Southern plantations found strength and comfort in singing spirituals because those songs

    (A) permitted them to ridicule their masters privately
    (B) identified them as God's children, who would eventually be freed
    (C) allowed them to avoid work on Sundays
    (D) convinced them that they were destined to be slaves and that they should accept their fate
    (E) were reminders that all workers suffered and that their circumstances were not different from other types of laborers

18. At the beginning of World War II, as a result of pressure from A. Philip Randolph, Franklin D. Roosevelt issued executive order 8802, which

    (A) merged the American Federation of Labor and Congress of Industrial Organizations into one large union
    (B) integrated the defense industries
    (C) converted former New Deal agencies into wartime agencies
    (D) ordered all munitions makers to begin overproduction
    (E) abandoned the Neutrality Acts

19. American citizens and their private property are protected against random intrusion by law enforcement officials through the

    (A) Fifth Amendment's protection against self-incrimination
    (B) Fourth Amendment's protection against unreasonable searches and seizures
    (C) First Amendment's guarantee of free speech
    (D) Eighth Amendment's protection against cruel and unusual punishment
    (E) habeas corpus provision in the Constitution

20. The secret documents detailing the history of American involvement in Vietnam, which were obtained by Daniel Ellsberg and later printed by the *New York Times*, were known as the

    (A) Watergate Tapes
    (B) Nixon memoranda
    (C) Pentagon Papers
    (D) Walker Report
    (E) Warren Commission findings

GO ON TO THE NEXT PAGE

UNITED STATES HISTORY TEST—Continued

21. In defending its decision to validate the constitutionality of racial segregation in the United States, the majority of the Supreme Court in *Plessy v. Ferguson* held all of the following to be true EXCEPT

    (A) segregation did not imply the inferiority of any race
    (B) the Fourteenth Amendment did not prohibit segregation
    (C) legislation could not equalize the races, if they were not equal in fact
    (D) the future of the country required that black and white Americans coexist and intermingle
    (E) if accommodations were separate but equal, they were not discriminatory

22. In attacking the arsenal at Harper's Ferry, Virginia, John Brown hoped to

    (A) abolish slavery in Virginia
    (B) convince Congress to prohibit slavery in the western territories
    (C) incite slave rebellions throughout the South
    (D) end the fugitive slave law
    (E) reverse the Supreme Court's Dred Scott decision

23. Soon after the Constitution had been ratified, two rival political parties developed. Which underlying principle was the center of disagreement between the Federalists and Anti-federalists?

    (A) Federal power versus states' rights
    (B) Slaveholding versus abolition
    (C) Interventionism versus isolationism
    (D) Balanced budget versus deficit spending
    (E) Internal improvements versus westward expansion

24. The Port Huron Statement, which delineated the frustrations and sense of alienation experienced by many young people in America in the 1960s, was written by

    (A) Black Panthers
    (B) Weathermen
    (C) the Student Non-violent Coordinating Committee
    (D) Students for a Democratic Society
    (E) the Chicago Eight

25. "The wealth of this land is tied up in a few hands. It makes no difference how many years the laborer has worked, nor does it make any difference how many dreary rows the farmer has plowed, the wealth he has created is in the hands of manipulators. They have not worked any more than many other people who have nothing. Now we do not propose to hurt these very rich persons. We simply say that when they reach the place of millionaires they have everything they can use and they ought to let somebody else have something. The people cannot ever come to light unless we share our wealth."

    Many critics took issue with Franklin D. Roosevelt's approach to solving the problems caused by the Great Depression. This statement reflects the solution offered by

    (A) Francis Townshend
    (B) Father Caughlin
    (C) Raymond Moley
    (D) Huey Long
    (E) Wendell Willkie

26. The British policy of mercantilism

    (A) relied on exporting more goods than were imported in order to maintain a favorable balance of trade
    (B) was designed to bolster the economy of the colonies at the expense of the mother country
    (C) led to King William's war
    (D) was irreparably damaged by the Navigation Acts
    (E) failed to provide England with sufficient revenue

27. Joseph McCarthy, the junior senator from Wisconsin, rose to political power in the 1950s by stressing

    (A) that America should begin space exploration
    (B) that farm subsidies were a critical part of economic policy
    (C) that communists were working for the U.S. government
    (D) that organized labor was becoming too powerful
    (E) that civil rights should be the Republicans' top domestic priority

GO ON TO THE NEXT PAGE

UNITED STATES HISTORY TEST—Continued

28. Marcus Garvey's Universal Negro Improvement Association was best known for

    (A) fighting for desegregation in American public education
    (B) lobbying Congress for antilynching legislation
    (C) instilling pride and self-sufficiency in working-class African Americans
    (D) pushing the National Association for the Advancement of Colored People to greater militancy during the 1920s
    (E) winning several notable Supreme Court cases in the 1920s and 1930s

29. Brigham Young was primarily associated with

    (A) the Whig party
    (B) transcendentalism
    (C) New Harmony
    (D) anti-Catholicism
    (E) the Church of Latter-Day Saints

30. The Trail of Tears refers to

    (A) Irish immigration to America
    (B) the removal of Cherokees from Georgia to the west
    (C) the deportation of Chinese from northeastern cities
    (D) the forced march of Africans to the sea after slave traders captured them
    (E) the migration west of unemployed workers in search of jobs

31. Woodrow Wilson's initial reaction to the beginning of World War I in Europe was to

    (A) support England and France
    (B) prepare immediately for war
    (C) send the U.S. Navy to the Mediterranean
    (D) declare American neutrality
    (E) enact Lend-Lease

32. In the immediate aftermath of the American Revolution, all states acted to

    (A) expand the right to vote to most white males
    (B) disestablish the Anglican Church
    (C) elect a national legislature
    (D) offer the franchise to women for the first time
    (E) abolish property holding qualifications for elective officeholders

33. From the end of the Civil War to the end of the nineteenth century, America's expanding economy was fostered by

    (A) agricultural consolidation
    (B) the organization of the railroads
    (C) the decentralization of the banking system
    (D) the growth of large-scale, heavy industry
    (E) consistent tariff policies

34. The philosophy of manifest destiny was prominently employed as a justification for America's westward expansion in the nineteenth century. The doctrine stated that

    (A) the United States had a god-given right to settle all the land in North America
    (B) farmlands needed to be settled so that America could fulfill its destiny of feeding Europe
    (C) American capitalism was the best system of trade and commerce for developing new territories
    (D) slavery was the best means of employing labor and required room to expand
    (E) Native American tribes should be permitted to remain on their lands while Americans settled the vacant lands to the west of the reservations

35. In his Farewell Address of 1796, George Washington cautioned the new nation to avoid all of the following potential problems EXCEPT

    (A) formation of political parties
    (B) divisive sectional issues
    (C) contentious criticism of the federal government
    (D) permanent alliances with foreign countries
    (E) excessive deficit spending on internal improvement

36. All of the following agencies were created during the New Deal EXCEPT

    (A) the National Recovery Administration
    (B) the Works Progress Administration
    (C) the Civilian Conservation Corps
    (D) the Reconstruction Finance Corporation
    (E) the Federal Emergency Relief Administration

GO ON TO THE NEXT PAGE

37. One major difference between the Pilgrims and the Puritans was that

    (A) Puritans were separatists, while Pilgrims welcomed all worshippers
    (B) Puritans left the Anglican Church, while Pilgrims remained attached to it
    (C) Pilgrims left the Anglican Church, while Puritans hoped to reform it
    (D) Puritans held slaves, and Pilgrims did not
    (E) Puritans were Catholics, and Pilgrims were Protestants

38. In 1955, the Supreme Court issued a ruling implementing its *Brown v. The Board of Education* decision of the previous year. The Brown II ruling, as it came to be known, did which of the following?

    (A) It required immediate integration of all public schools nationwide.
    (B) It integrated only totally segregated public schools in the South.
    (C) It suggested that public schools nationwide integrate as quickly as they could.
    (D) It integrated public schools through the forced busing of students from suburbia to urban centers.
    (E) It added private schools to its 1954 decision.

39. Theodore Roosevelt's decision to bust J.P. Morgan's Northern Securities Company in 1904 highlighted his

    (A) hatred of Morgan
    (B) determination to break up all monopolies under the Sherman Antitrust Act
    (C) inability to understand economic realities
    (D) aspirations to run for reelection to the presidency
    (E) determination to dissolve corrupt trusts, while leaving good ones intact

UNITED STATES HISTORY TEST—Continued

FEDERAL SUPERSTRUCTURE.

40. The picture above represents what specific event in the early years of the New Nation?

(A) The building of Federal City
(B) The beginnings of the abolition of slavery
(C) The ratification of the Constitution
(D) The growth of the Federalist party
(E) Federal assumption of state debts

GO ON TO THE NEXT PAGE

UNITED STATES HISTORY TEST—Continued

41. The Populist Party platform of 1892 contained all the following demands EXCEPT

    (A) bimetalism
    (B) direct election of senators
    (C) desegregation
    (D) referendum, initiative, and recall
    (E) government ownership of railroads

42. A major impediment to good relations between Europeans settling in North America and the native peoples already living there was

    (A) their different attitudes toward the land
    (B) language barriers
    (C) agricultural practices
    (D) religious differences
    (E) technology

43. The 1800 presidential election ended in a tie between

    (A) Thomas Jefferson and Alexander Hamilton
    (B) Alexander Hamilton and Aaron Burr
    (C) James Madison and John Adams
    (D) Thomas Jefferson and Aaron Burr
    (E) John Adams and John Jay

44. Franklin D. Roosevelt did not support federal antilynching legislation during the 1930s because

    (A) he believed local law was adequate to address that concern
    (B) he determined that lynching was not a major issue
    (C) he feared that supporting such a law would cause southern congressmen to turn against the New Deal
    (D) he was advised that such a law would be unconstitutional and would significantly weaken other New Deal measures
    (E) he was waiting for the National Association for the Advancement of Colored People to address the issue

45. The labor tension of post-World War I America, which culminated in a series of strikes in 1919, revolved around the issue of

    (A) collective bargaining
    (B) higher wages
    (C) socialist control of factories
    (D) segregation in defense industries
    (E) yellow dog contracts

46. Unlike Brazil and areas of the Caribbean, the American South experienced a dearth of slave rebellions in the colonial era primarily because

    (A) slaves in the American South had some political rights that allowed them room to negotiate demands
    (B) Africans who became slaves in the American colonies came from peaceful villages in West Africa where violence was unknown
    (C) the slave population was tightly controlled in America, and slaves spent little time away from their masters
    (D) the slave population was ordinarily not as large as the white population in any American colony, making rebellion difficult
    (E) slaves who worked diligently without rebelling were promised their freedom after a reasonable period of time

47. Alexis de Tocqueville visited the United States in the 1830s in an attempt to

    (A) study the concept and practice of American democracy
    (B) join the utopian community at Oneida
    (C) advocate for women's rights
    (D) determine whether slaves were well treated
    (E) become involved in prison reform

48. The U.S. Supreme Court, in the case of *Korematsu v. United States*, ruled that the forced internment of Japanese residents and citizens

    (A) violated the Fourteenth Amendment and was thus unconstitutional
    (B) applied only to Japanese visitors to the country
    (C) was acceptable based on prevailing laws concerning racial segregation
    (D) was illegal because only the states had the power to incarcerate citizens
    (E) was an appropriate wartime measure in light of fears of Japanese espionage

GO ON TO THE NEXT PAGE

1800 tie for president   Jefferson & Burr

Brown vs Board of Education

Korematsu vs US

A real puppy

Adopted sister

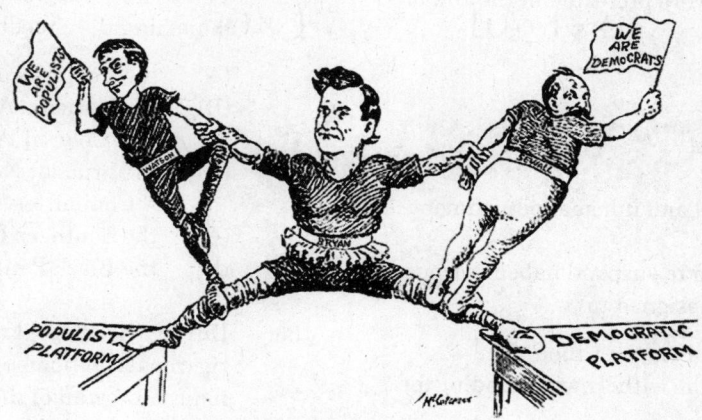

49. The cartoon above refers to William Jennings Bryan's fusion candidacy, which united Populists and Democrats over the issue of

(A) government ownership of the railroads
(B) antitrust legislation
(C) free silver
(D) initiative and referendum
(E) immigration restriction

50. All of the following rights were protected in the Bill of Rights EXCEPT

    (A) freedom of religion
    (B) universal suffrage
    (C) the right to bear arms
    (D) freedom of the press
    (E) protection from cruel and unusual punishment

51. Abraham Lincoln's decision to suspend habeas corpus during the Civil War was designed to

    (A) force the South back into the Union
    (B) prohibit Congress from withdrawing funding for the war
    (C) keep abolitionists from petitioning Congress to outlaw slavery in the South
    (D) silence his critics in the South who opposed the war
    (E) force his generals to be bolder in fighting the war

52. Political appointments in the second half of the nineteenth century were

    (A) rigidly controlled by strict rules on national, state, and local levels
    (B) decided primarily by state elections
    (C) difficult to make because of employment opportunities offered by industry
    (D) governed by property qualifications as they had been since the Constitution was first adopted
    (E) subject to patronage practices at all levels of government

53. The Mexican War initiated which of the following?

    (A) Northwest Ordinance
    (B) Missouri Compromise
    (C) Wilmot Proviso
    (D) James Polk's election
    (E) David Walker's Appeal

54. In the 1803 Supreme Court ruling, *Marbury v. Madison*, Chief Justice John Marshall

    (A) created the concept of checks and balances
    (B) gave the Supreme Court the implied power of judicial review
    (C) nullified the Atlantic Slave Trade
    (D) sanctioned the removal of Indians to western lands
    (E) authorized the establishment of a national bank

55. The civil rights group primarily responsible for launching the Freedom Rides in 1961 was

    (A) the Congress of Racial Equality
    (B) the National Association for the Advancement of Colored People
    (C) the Student Non-violent Coordinating Committee
    (D) the Southern Christian Leadership Conference
    (E) the Black Panthers

56. During the 1930s, Franklin D. Roosevelt adhered to a rigorous isolationist policy in foreign affairs, as indicated by all of the following EXCEPT

    (A) invoking the Stimson Doctrine
    (B) prohibiting Americans from traveling on ships of countries at war
    (C) refusing to allow American industries to sell weapons to countries at war
    (D) mandating that nations at war could buy non-military goods from America only by paying cash
    (E) disarming the American military forces to prevent intervention in European affairs

57. The Jamestown settlement in Virginia would most likely have failed financially had it not been for

    (A) the development of a shipbuilding industry
    (B) the discovery of gold
    (C) tobacco cultivation
    (D) the beginning of a timber industry
    (E) fur trapping

58. The concept of massive retaliation is best described as

    (A) industry's response to labor unrest
    (B) part of the containment policy in the 1950s
    (C) the Republican response to Democratic party criticisms
    (D) the strategy employed by Joseph McCarthy
    (E) an economic policy designed to combat inflation

59. The Progressive era can best be described as a

    (A) period of conservative politics and maintenance of the status quo
    (B) time of major civil rights activity and significant gains for African Americans
    (C) response to the industrialization of America
    (D) period in which Americans sought a return to traditional values
    (E) time of political instability and anarchy

60. Ralph Waldo Emerson had a profound impact on American intellectual thought because he stressed

    (A) that altruistic reform was largely unproductive
    (B) the value of capitalism for cultural and social development
    (C) Enlightenment principles of scientific inquiry into the working of the universe
    (D) values of religious devotion and obedience to the word of the Bible
    (E) the need for individuals to be self-reliant

61. President Harry Truman justified his decision to use the atomic bomb against Japan on the grounds that

    (A) a massive American ground invasion of Japan would result in millions of Japanese and American casualties
    (B) it was an appropriate retaliatory action after the attack on Pearl Harbor
    (C) Japan was rapidly developing its own bomb
    (D) the American electorate was growing tired of the war and demanded action
    (E) the British and Russian allies supported his action

62. Attempting to convince Americans to ratify the U.S. Constitution, Alexander Hamilton, James Madison, and John Jay wrote a series of essays that explained the advantages of the new form of government. Collectively, these essays were entitled

    (A) *Common Sense*
    (B) *The Federalist Papers*
    (C) *Notes on the State of Virginia*
    (D) *Democracy in America*
    (E) *The Suffolk Resolves*

63. In developing his steel industry, Andrew Carnegie relied on the concept of "vertical integration," which entailed

    (A) manipulation of low-interest bank loans to facilitate construction of his factories
    (B) working closely with local politicians and civic leaders to maintain favorable legislation
    (C) negotiation with labor unions to keep them content and to prevent strikes by bringing them into the industrial decision-making process
    (D) controlling all stages of his industry to keep him self-reliant
    (E) working with industrialists in other businesses to convince Congress to rationalize tariffs and to regulate all industries in an equitable and efficient manner

64. All of the following are accurate characterizations of the Free Soil Party EXCEPT:

    (A) They supported the abolition of slavery everywhere in the nation.
    (B) They wanted the land acquired in the Mexican War to be settled by small farmers.
    (C) They believed slaveowners were subverting democracy by impeding small farmers' ability to survive.
    (D) They opposed slavery's expansion into the territories.
    (E) They upheld the constitutionality of slavery where it already existed.

65. The Kentucky and Virginia Resolutions proposed that

    (A) states should abolish religious qualifications for officeholding
    (B) slavery should be gradually abolished and slaveowners should be compensated
    (C) Congress should be restricted in its ability to tax
    (D) states had the power to nullify federal law
    (E) political parties were the best means of insuring efficient government

UNITED STATES HISTORY TEST—Continued

66. The 1828 election between John Quincy Adams and Andrew Jackson was significant because it

    (A) focused on trenchant political issues that affected all Americans
    (B) opened up a far-reaching discussion of slavery's future in America
    (C) was limited to mudslinging and personal invective
    (D) dwelled overwhelmingly on foreign policy and the way in which the Monroe Doctrine could be applied to westward expansion
    (E) concentrated on internal improvements and the long range implementation of the American System

67. "No man shall be compelled to frequent or support any religious worship, place, or ministry whatsoever, nor shall be enforced, restrained, molested, or burthened in his body or goods, nor shall otherwise suffer on account of his religious opinions or belief; but that all men shall be free to profess, and by argument to maintain, their opinion in matters of religion, and that the same shall in no wise diminish, enlarge, or affect their civil capacities."

    Thomas Jefferson, in this excerpt from his 1786 Virginia Statute on Religious Liberty, had a significant impact on

    (A) the disestablishment of the Anglican Church in America after the Revolution
    (B) slaveholders' determination to prohibit their slaves from religious worship
    (C) office holding protections in the Constitution and freedom of religion in the Bill of Rights
    (D) the first Great Awakening, which criticized his ideas for secularizing the colonies and creating instability
    (E) Maryland's decision to allow religious tolerance for Catholics and all others persecuted for their religious beliefs

68. The Fifteenth Amendment, added to the U.S. Constitution in 1870,

    (A) abolished slavery
    (B) granted African Americans full citizenship rights
    (C) instituted a personal income tax
    (D) gave women the right to vote
    (E) gave African Americans the right to vote

69. The first large-scale labor union established in the post–Civil War era was the

    (A) American Federation of Labor
    (B) Knights of Labor
    (C) Congress of Industrial Organizations
    (D) American Railway Union
    (E) National Labor Union

70. The Kansas-Nebraska Act proposed to settle the issue of slavery's expansion into western territories by establishing

    (A) a Supreme Court case to mediate between the north and the south
    (B) a national referendum on expansion
    (C) popular sovereignty
    (D) a balance between slave and free states in Congress
    (E) a ban on slavery, conforming to the Missouri Compromise line

GO ON TO THE NEXT PAGE

OGRABME, or The American Snapping-turtle.

71. This political cartoon refers specifically to which event during the Jeffersonian presidency?

(A) Impressment
(B) The Orders in Council
(C) The Continental System
(D) The Embargo Act
(E) Jay's Treaty

UNITED STATES HISTORY TEST—Continued

ONE SEES HIS FINISH UNLESS GOOD GOVERNMENT RETAKES THE SHIP.

72. This cartoon suggests that

(A) the federal government should adopt a laissez-faire attitude toward monopolies
(B) the judicial branch was cooperating with big business
(C) the Sherman Antitrust Act was not employed effectively
(D) Congress needed to pass antitrust legislation
(E) the Interstate Commerce Commission was powerless

UNITED STATES HISTORY TEST—Continued

73. John F. Kennedy's determination to meet communist aggression with force led him to lend his support to

    (A) the deployment of ground troops in Vietnam
    (B) the Bay of Pigs invasion
    (C) the creation of the Peace Corps
    (D) the Cambodian incursion
    (E) the Tonkin Gulf Resolution

74. The English were the initial settlers of all of the following colonies EXCEPT

    (A) Pennsylvania
    (B) Rhode Island
    (C) Plymouth
    (D) New York
    (E) Virginia

75. All of the following contributed to the mounting federal deficit of the 1950s and 1960s EXCEPT

    (A) foreign aid
    (B) investment abroad
    (C) industrial exports
    (D) U.S. citizens' traveling abroad
    (E) military spending

76. "Now, the typical American citizen is the business man. The typical business man is a bad citizen; he is busy. If he is a "big business man" and very busy, he does not neglect, he is busy with politics, oh, very busy and very businesslike. ...He is a self-righteous fraud, this big business man. He is the chief source of corruption, and it were a boon if he would neglect politics. But he is not the business man that neglects politics."

    This criticism of American industrialists and their interference in American politics is most characteristic of

    (A) muckrakers
    (B) Marxists
    (C) Republicans
    (D) New Dealers
    (E) single taxers

77. As he considered intervening in World War II, Franklin Roosevelt relied most heavily on

    (A) his closest military advisors
    (B) the Brain Trust
    (C) the media
    (D) the American people
    (E) events in Europe

78. During the Spanish-American War, U.S. foreign policy consistently sought to maintain Cuba's independence rather than making it a colony because

    (A) Americans were uneasy about communism
    (B) no economic advantage would be gained by annexation
    (C) McKinley did not want the responsibility for assisting Cuba financially
    (D) many Americans saw similarities between the Cuban and American revolutions
    (E) slavery still existed in Cuba, which would raise fundamental constitutional issues

79. Before 1882, when the Chinese were prohibited from immigrating to the United States, most Chinese immigrants settled in

    (A) California
    (B) New York
    (C) Chicago
    (D) Boston
    (E) the midwest

GO ON TO THE NEXT PAGE

80. This cartoon about the 1860 presidential election suggests that

   (A) the four presidential candidates were attempting to prevent disunion
   (B) any of the candidates, other than Lincoln, could have held the country together
   (C) a coalition government was the country's best hope to avoid civil war
   (D) sectional politics were dividing the country and weakening the strength of the Union
   (E) the Republican primary would not produce a clear favorite

81. All of the following were accurate concerning American factory work in the 1840s EXCEPT

    (A) labor unions tried to represent workers in collective bargaining agreements with employers
    (B) factories were dangerous, unhealthy places
    (C) wages tended to decrease throughout the period
    (D) working hours increased, with some factories requiring twelve-hour shifts
    (E) women and children were exploited, and were paid less than men for the same work

82. The event that directly caused the United States to enter World War I was

    (A) the Zimmerman Telegram
    (B) anti-German propaganda promoted by the Yellow Press
    (C) Germany's violation of the Sussex Pledge
    (D) the German invasion of Belgium
    (E) the Russian Revolution

83. The individual primarily responsible for reorganizing American railroads in the wake of the depression of 1893 was

    (A) Andrew Carnegie
    (B) John D. Rockefeller
    (C) Samuel Gompers
    (D) Eugene Debs
    (E) J. P. Morgan

84. The center of the emerging African slave trade in colonial America was

    (A) Charleston
    (B) Philadelphia
    (C) Baltimore
    (D) Newport
    (E) Boston

85. All of the following were major aspects of Woodrow Wilson's Fourteen Points EXCEPT

    (A) the maintenance of European colonies in control of the Allied Powers
    (B) the self-determination of nations
    (C) the freedom of the seas
    (D) the establishment of a League of Nations
    (E) open covenants

86. "We do by these Presents, solemnly and mutually, in the Presence of God and one another, covenant and combine ourselves together into a civil Body Politick, for our better Ordering and Preservation, and Furtherance of the Ends aforesaid: And by Virtue hereof do enact, constitute, and frame, such just and equal Laws, Ordinances, Acts, Constitutions, and Officers, from time to time, as shall be thought most meet and convenient for the general Good of the Colony."

    The Pilgrims who signed the Mayflower Compact in 1620, from which this statement comes, created this document to

    (A) announce their intention to sever all ties with the Crown and the Anglican Church
    (B) exercise their right to self-government, as guaranteed in the Magna Carta
    (C) set an example for England by creating a "city upon a hill"
    (D) ensure that all individuals in Plymouth would be treated as equals
    (E) establish some authority in a land not covered by their charter from the Crown

87. Little Rock, Arkansas, in the 1950s is best identified with

    (A) suburban development
    (B) congressional redistricting
    (C) school integration
    (D) housing renewal
    (E) municipal governmental reform

88. The issue of slavery's expansion into the western lands acquired from Mexico became more urgent when

    (A) Congress passed the Wilmot Proviso
    (B) gold was discovered in California
    (C) the Supreme Court issued the Dred Scott decision
    (D) Nat Turner led a slave rebellion in Virginia
    (E) John Brown threatened to attack the South and abolish slavery

GO ON TO THE NEXT PAGE

UNITED STATES HISTORY TEST—Continued

89. "Middle Passage" refers to

 (A) Irish immigration in the 18th century
 (B) slaves being transported from Africa to the New World
 (C) travel between the New England colonies and the southern colonies
 (D) the conversion experience in Puritan theology
 (E) western routes over the Appalachian mountains

90. The Twenty-second Amendment to the United States Constitution, which placed a two-term limit on the presidency, was ratified in 1951 in direct response to

 (A) fears of communism in government
 (B) political corruption in government
 (C) a shift in political power from the executive to legislative branch
 (D) Franklin D. Roosevelt's four terms as President
 (E) a Supreme Court decision

91.

S T O P

IF YOU FINISH BEFORE TIME IS CALLED, YOU MAY CHECK YOUR WORK ON THIS TEST ONLY.
DO NOT TURN TO ANY OTHER TEST IN THIS BOOK.

SAT II U.S. History Practice Test 1 Explanations

Calculating Your Score

Question Number	Correct Answer	Right	Wrong	Question Number	Correct Answer	Right	Wrong	Question Number	Correct Answer	Right	Wrong
1.	B			31.	D			61.	A		
2.	C			32.	A			62.	B		
3.	E			33.	D			63.	D		
4.	A			34.	A			64.	A		
5.	C			35.	E			65.	D		
6.	C			36.	D			66.	C		
7.	B			37.	C			67.	C		
8.	E			38.	C			68.	E		
9.	B			39.	E			69.	E		
10.	E			40.	C			70.	C		
11.	A			41.	C			71.	D		
12.	C			42.	A			72.	C		
13.	E			43.	D			73.	B		
14.	A			44.	C			74.	D		
15.	C			45.	B			75.	C		
16.	E			46.	D			76.	A		
17.	B			47.	A			77.	D		
18.	B			48.	E			78.	D		
19.	B			49.	C			79.	A		
20.	C			50.	B			80.	D		
21.	D			51.	D			81.	A		
22.	C			52.	E			82.	C		
23.	A			53.	C			83.	E		
24.	D			54.	B			84.	D		
25.	D			55.	A			85.	A		
26.	A			56.	E			86.	E		
27.	C			57.	C			87.	C		
28.	C			58.	B			88.	B		
29.	E			59.	C			89.	B		
30.	B			60.	E			90.	D		

Your raw score for the SAT II U.S. History test is calculated from the number of questions you answer correctly and incorrectly. Once you have determined your composite score, use the conversion table on page 19 of this book to calculate your scaled score. To calculate your raw score, count the number of questions you answered correctly: _____
A

Count the number of questions you answered incorrectly, and multiply that number by $\frac{1}{4}$:

$$\underline{}_{B} \times \frac{1}{4} = \underline{}_{C}$$

Subtract the value in field C from value in field A: _____
D

Round the number in field D to the nearest whole number. This is your raw score: _____
E

1. **(B)** Roaring Twenties *Fact Question*

The Russian Revolution of 1917 threw the U.S. government into an anti-communist hysteria, known as the Red Scare. As part of the general panic, Attorney General A. Mitchell Palmer conducted these raids to round up and jail anarchists and communists suspected of advocating the overthrow of the government.

2. **(C)** Cultural Trends *Trend Question*

Certain of Jesus' imminent return to earth, the Shakers believed they had no reason to procreate. Their celibacy vow reflected their lack of interest in earthly concerns.

3. **(E)** The Great Depression & New Deal *Trend Question*

The Schechter brothers sued the U.S. government, arguing that industrial codes mandated by the National Recovery Administration, an administrative bureau established by Congress, conflicted with kosher law, thus impeding the Schechters' ability to conduct business. The Schechter Poultry Corp. conducted business only in New York, and the Supreme Court ruled that Congress had no constitutional authority to regulate intrastate commerce. Although the Court also ruled the Agricultural Adjustment Act unconstitutional, this ruling was not related to the Schechter case, and the ruling was not given for the reason stated in choice (A).

4. **(A)** The Colonial Period *Except Question*

Products not listed in the Navigation Acts could be shipped directly from the colonies to any port. These products included most food items and livestock. The Navigation Acts stipulated that certain products, including cotton, tobacco, fur, and rice, could be exported only to English ports.

5. **(C)** Industrial Revolution *Trend Question*

In 1890, Congress passed the Sherman Antitrust Act in an effort to curtail the power and reach of the trusts. The act specifically declared a trust illegal if it was found to "restrain trade or commerce."

6. **(C)** The Colonial Period *Except Question*

The expansion of slavery was not a factor behind Bacon's Rebellion. In 1676, Nathaniel Bacon and a group of poor Virginia farmers attacked Native Americans and then attacked Jamestown, Virginia. The uprising developed out of class tensions between the poor farmers and the wealthy Tidewater planters (A), who controlled the local government. Bacon and the farmers accused the governor of Virginia of failing to protect their interests (B) against falling tobacco prices (D) and Native American attacks (E).

7. **(B)** The Progressive Era *Fact Question*

The National Association for the Advancement of Colored People (NAACP) was created in 1909 in the wake of increased lynching cases throughout the South. The NAACP became the first twentieth-century civil rights organization to carry out widespread protest against racial discrimination.

8. **(E)** The Age of Jackson *Quotation Question*

Jackson opposed the recharter of the Second Bank of the United States. In his veto message, known as the Bank Veto, Jackson denounced the Bank as a corrupt monopoly. Later, Jackson removed federal deposits from the Bank and moved them to state banks; this policy effectively destroyed the Bank.

9. **(B)** Revolution & Constitution *Trend Question*

The concept of virtual representation held that all British citizens were "virtually" represented in Parliament, since members of Parliament represented not only their geographical constituencies but all of the British Empire. Under this argument, the British held that even though the colonists did not send representatives to Parliament, their interests were already represented there. Britain used this concept to defend itself against accusations that the colonies were taxed "without representation."

10. **(E)** Civil War & Reconstruction *Trend Question*

By 1877, northerners were growing tired of Reconstruction and race relations in the South. They no longer felt that civil rights in the South were their concern. In the 1876 presidential election, the Democratic candidate, Samuel Tilden, won more popular votes than the Republican candidate, Rutherford Hayes, but the Republicans negotiated a Hayes victory. In exchange for Democratic compliance, the Republicans promised to remove federal troops from occupied Southern states in what became known as the Compromise of 1877, or the Hayes-Tilden Compromise. The removal of federal troops allowed Democrats in those states to assume control of the legislature. Democratic control resulted in white supremacy, black oppression, and the end of Reconstruction.

11. **(A)** Industrial Revolution *Trend Question*

Although America had more miles of railroad track than any other nation after the Civil War, the railway system was highly inefficient and disorganized. Track sizes differed, making travel difficult, and carriers didn't coordinate their schedules or rates.

12. **(C)** A New Nation *Trend Question*

The Sedition Act made criticism of the federal government illegal and punishable by a prison sentence or deportation. Trying to maintain their political power, the Federalists enacted the Alien and Sedition Acts to prevent public criticism from the Anti-federalists.

13. **(E)** The 1960s *Except Question*

The Soil Bank Act of 1956 was not part of Johnson's Great Society program. Enacted under Dwight Eisenhower, the Soil Bank Act attempted to raise farm prices by paying farmers to keep land out of production.

14. **(A)** The Great Depression & New Deal *Fact Question*

Francis Townsend proposed a system in which the federal government would pay two hundred dollars a month to American citizens over the age of 60. In exchange for the monthly payment, these citizens would not work, thus opening up employment opportunities to younger citizens. Townsend's system would also lead to increased purchasing power, since these citizens would agree to spend that money within the month. Roosevelt responded to the Townsend Plan by creating the Social Security system.

15. **(C)** Industrial Revolution *Fact Question*

Riis, a muckraker, exposed the reality of tenement life in American cities. Focusing on New York City, he vividly illustrated the threats to human life posed by poor sanitation, cramped quarters, disease, and a lack of municipal services.

16. **(E)** The Roaring Twenties *Except Question*

The Mellon tax policies did not prohibit the margin buying of stocks, which continued until the stock market crash in 1929. The Mellon tax policies were designed to have a trickle-down effect on the economy: all Americans would benefit financially if the wealthy paid less in taxes and used their saved tax money to reinvest in the economy.

17. **(B)** Cultural Trends *Trend Question*

The words of slave spirituals often suggested that slaves were the chosen children of God and that eventually they would be freed from slavery.

18. **(B)** World War II *Fact Question*

At the start of World War II, job discrimination and segregation in the defense industry prevented African Americans from obtaining defense jobs. In response to this discrimination, A. Philip Randolph threatened to march on Washington with African Americans who had been refused defense jobs. This march would reveal the extent of racism in America. Rather than face the international embarrassment of such a march, FDR issued executive order 8802, which opened up all defense plants to black employment.

19. **(B)** Revolution & Constitution *Fact Question*

The Fourth Amendment protects citizens from unreasonable searches and seizures in their homes. Before entering a citizen's home to conduct a search, law enforcement officials must first demonstrate probable cause and obtain a search warrant from a judge.

20. **(C)** 1970s–2000 *Fact Question*

The documents Daniel Ellsberg gave to the *New York Times* were known as the Pentagon Papers. The federal government tried to stop the publication of the Pentagon Papers, but the Supreme Court ruled against the government in the landmark freedom of press case, *New York Times Co. v. The United States*, 1971.

21. **(D)** Industrial Revolution *Except Question*

The majority opinion of the Supreme Court stated that racial integration had no necessary place in American life. In his dissenting opinion, Justice John Harlan predicted that continuing segregation would create grave problems for America and argued that racial harmony was essential to the country's progress.

22. **(C)** Westward Expansion & Sectional Strife *Trend Question*

Brown believed that his raid would inspire slaves to rebel everywhere in the South, thus bringing about emancipation.

23. **(A)** A New Nation *Trend Question*

The Federalists and Anti-federalists disagreed on the role and power of the federal government. Federalists supported a strong centralized government and tended to interpret the Constitution broadly as calling for federal authority. Anti-federalists advocated the rights of the states and of the people. According to their interpretation, the Constitution curtails federal power and protects the rights of the states and citizens.

24. **(D)** The 1960s *Fact Question*

Students for a Democratic Society, a leftist organization, issued the Port Huron Statement in 1962. The statement articulated the growing sense of alienation among college students in the 1960s and urged the U.S. government to address international problems and to implement leftist policies.

25. **(D)** The Great Depression & New Deal *Quotation Question*

Huey Long proposed the "share our wealth" plan as a way of redistributing income and correcting the great imbalance of wealth in the country. As one of the New Deal's harsher critics, Long pushed FDR to act boldly during the planning of the Second New Deal.

26. **(A)** The Colonial Period *Trend Question*

The mercantilist theory of trade held that a nation must export more goods than it imports. Following that strategy would ensure a favorable balance of trade and would mean that more money would come into the country as payment for goods than left the country as payment for imports.

27. **(C)** The 1950s *Trend Question*

McCarthy rose to power by alleging that communists had infiltrated American institutions, including the federal government. By exploiting Americans' fear of communism and by using false accusations to intimidate opponents, he held considerable political power in the country for the first half of the 1950s.

28. **(C)** The Roaring Twenties *Trend Question*

Garvey advocated the separation of African Americans and whites. His heralded Back-to-Africa movement focused on making African Americans aware of their heritage and on promoting self-confidence and pride.

29. **(E)** Cultural Trends *Fact Question*

After the death of the Mormon leader Joseph Smith, Brigham Young rose to leadership in the Church of Latter-Day Saints. He led his followers to the Salt Lake region of Utah, where they established a settlement and the headquarters of their church.

30. **(B)** The Age of Jackson *Fact Question*

When the state of Georgia, with the backing of Andrew Jackson, began removing Cherokees from its land, the Indian nation was forced to march west. Several thousand Cherokees died during this journey, known as the Trail of Tears.

31. **(D)** World War I *Fact Question*

Wilson desperately wanted to keep the United States out of World War I. When the war broke out in Europe in 1914, he quickly pledged that America would remain neutral. He based his 1916 campaign for re-election around the slogan that he "kept us out of war."

32. **(A)** Revolution & Constitution *Trend Question*

All states significantly expanded their voting rolls by opening the franchise to most white males. While many states also moved to disestablish the Anglican Church (B), New England states resisted this change. Women were allowed to vote only in New Jersey (D), and most states retained property qualifications for officeholding (E).

33. **(D)** Industrial Revolution *Trend Question*

The growth of large-scale, heavy industry spurred the country's economic growth during the second half of the nineteenth century. Its impact accounted for a tripling of America's gross national product and an enormous rise in exports by the turn of the century.

34. **(A)** Westward Expansion & Sectional Strife — *Trend Question*

Americans explained westward expansion by stating that they had a divine right to settle the continent. This sense of manifest destiny allowed the government to justify land acquisition and its policy toward Native Americans, and it sparked the Mexican War over the territory of Texas.

35. **(E)** A New Nation — *Except Question*

Washington did not discuss deficit spending in his Farewell Address but instead left economic matters to his treasury secretary, Alexander Hamilton. Prophetically, Washington did warn about the other four issues, all of which were ignored as the nation grew.

36. **(D)** The Great Depression & New Deal — *Except Question*

During his presidency, Herbert Hoover created the Reconstruction Finance Corporation (RFC) to provide loans to banks and corporations suffering from the Depression. Hoover was criticized for proposing the RFC because it focused on helping the business sector rather than individuals who needed relief.

37. **(C)** The Colonial Period — *Trend Question*

The Pilgrims were a Separatist group who came to America to escape religious persecution and split from the Anglican Church. The Puritans, on the other hand, came to America intent on reforming and "purifying" the Anglican Church but did not want to break from it.

38. **(C)** The 1950s — *Fact Question*

In *Brown II*, the Court overturned its 1896 *Plessy v. Ferguson* decision and ruled that segregated schools were unconstitutional, advising that schools integrate at "all deliberate speed." Acknowledging that desegregation would meet with protest and delay in the southern states, the Court set forth a gradual implementation scheme designed to eliminate tensions. The wording of the *Brown II* ruling, however, allowed the southern states to avoid an immediate response and to delay integration for a long time.

39. **(E)** The Progressive Era — *Trend Question*

Although Roosevelt was known as the "trust-buster," he did not believe that trusts were inherently evil or corrupt. Invoking the Sherman Antitrust Act, he dissolved trusts that were dishonestly run and that unfairly restricted trade. Morgan's company was the first major trust Roosevelt dissolved.

40. **(C)** Revolution & Constitution — *Cartoon Question*

This cartoon depicts the ratification of the Constitution. As each state ratifies the Constitution, another pillar is erected in the "Federal Superstructure." The illustration is pro-Constitution, emphasizing the stability derived from a strong centralized government.

41. **(C)** Industrial Revolution — *Except Question*

Populists were not concerned about racial integration. The Populist Party represented agrarian interests and advocated for the free coinage of silver and for government control of monopolies.

42. **(A)** The Pre-Columbian Period — *Trend Question*

Native Americans valued the land as sacred ground that sustained and benefited the entire community. They did not believe in land ownership, whereas European explorers believed all land was available for purchase and ownership.

43. (D) A New Nation — *Fact Question*

The presidential election of 1800 ended in a tie between the Republicans Jefferson and Burr, even though Burr had intended to become vice-president to Jefferson's president. The decision between Jefferson and Burr fell to the House of Representatives, where Alexander Hamilton negotiated Jefferson's victory, primarily because Hamilton loathed Burr. The election resulted in the writing of the Twelfth Amendment, which changed the election process so that candidates running for president and vice-president were listed in separate categories on the ballot.

44. (C) The Great Depression & New Deal — *Trend Question*

FDR feared that backing any civil rights measure, such as the antilynching law, would alienate southern Democrats in Congress, whose support was essential to the New Deal coalition. He worried that those congressmen would retaliate against the antilynching law by voting against legislation crucial to the New Deal and financial recovery.

45. (B) The Roaring Twenties — *Trend Question*

In the postwar economy, wages did not keep pace with the price of consumer goods. Steelworkers around the Great Lakes, dockworkers in Seattle, and policemen in Boston went on strike over their wages. At the time, with the general anxiety about anarchism, many perceived these strikes to be more revolutionary in nature than they actually were.

46. (D) The Colonial Period — *Trend Question*

With the exception of South Carolina, which had a slave majority early in the colonial period, most colonies maintained large white majorities in their populations. These white majorities made it difficult for slaves to mount successful rebellions. One of the earliest slave uprisings in the American colonies, the Stono Rebellion, occurred in 1739 in South Carolina, where slaves outnumbered whites. Slave revolts were more likely in Brazil and the Caribbean, where slaves usually outnumbered whites.

47. (A) Cultural Trends — *Fact Question*

de Tocqueville was intrigued by the practice of democracy in America and wanted to compare it to the practice of democracy in France. He wrote his monumental work, *Democracy in America*, based on his studies of American democracy in the 1830s.

48. (E) World War II — *Trend Question*

In the 1844 *Korematsu* ruling, the Supreme Court upheld FDR's order to put Japanese Americans on the West Coast into internment camps, arguing that Americans' civil liberties could be suspended during times of war. American military leaders persuaded the Court that Japanese Americans presented a grave security threat on the West Coast, since some of them could be Japanese agents, so their internment was necessary to prevent sabotage and espionage.

49. (C) Industrial Revolution — *Cartoon Question*

Bryan was backed by both the Democrats and Populists in the 1896 presidential election. Bryan's advocacy of "free silver," the free coinage of silver, won him the support of Populists. This cartoon illustrates Bryan's attempt to unite the two parties.

50. (B) Revolution & Constitution — *Except Question*

The Bill of Rights did not grant universal suffrage. Women, African Americans, and many white males did not have the right to vote under the Constitution, and voting rights remained in control of the individual states.

51. (D) Civil War & Reconstruction — *Trend Question*

Concerned that Northern opponents of the war were lowering morale and dividing Union sentiment, Lincoln moved to suspend habeas corpus to silence his critics. Although Lincoln was criticized for breaching civil liberties, in the next century the Supreme Court validated the suspension of civil liberties during times of war.

52. (E) Industrial Revolution — *Trend Question*

Government jobs were viewed as rewards for party loyalty, for elected officials offered them to important supporters. Accordingly, with the election of a new administration, there were wholesale changes in the governmental workforce.

53. (C) Westward Expansion & Sectional Strife — *Fact Question*

David Wilmot proposed in Congress to prohibit slavery in all lands acquired by the United States from the Mexican War. The Wilmot Proviso did not pass, and sectional controversies mounted regarding the Mexican lands.

54. (B) A New Nation — *Trend Question*

The *Marbury* decision of 1803 significantly expanded the power and reach of the Supreme Court. Marshall ruled that Congress had overstepped its constitutional bounds in creating the Judiciary Act of 1789. With this ruling, Marshall established the Supreme Court's power of judicial review, which allowed the Court to interpret the Constitution and determine the constitutionality of laws passed by Congress or by the states.

55. (A) The 1960s — *Fact Question*

The Congress of Racial Equality (CORE) organized the freedom rides to test compliance with the Supreme Court's 1960 *Boynton v. Virginia* ruling, which integrated interstate transportation facilities. Members of the organization rode on public buses to protest illegal segregation. After meeting with violent attacks along routes in Alabama and Mississippi, CORE requested assistance from the Student Nonviolent Coordinating Committee.

56. (E) The Great Depression & New Deal — *Except Question*

FDR never advocated disarming the U.S. military forces. He carefully observed events in Europe and Asia throughout the 1930s but moved toward American involvement only when he sensed that he had public support. FDR did invoke the Stimson Doctrine in 1937 in the United States' refusal to recognize Japan's aggression in Shanghai. The stipulations in choices (B), (C), and (D) were part of the Neutrality Acts, passed by Congress between 1935 and 1937.

57. (C) The Colonial Period — *Trend Question*

Tobacco became the first important cash crop for Jamestown. John Rolfe, the Englishman who married Pocahontas, began growing a strain of West Indian tobacco as early as 1612 in Jamestown. This strain of tobacco grew well in the Virginia climate, and within a dozen years the tobacco crop yielded substantial profits for the colonists.

58. (B) The 1950s — *Trend Question*

The Eisenhower administration tried to contain communism using a policy of massive retaliation. Since enemy nuclear weapons posed a greater threat than armed forces, Eisenhower wanted the United States to amass a huge nuclear weapons arsenal. He believed such a stockpile would deter Soviet aggression because both the United States and the USSR would ultimately lose if they engaged in a massive nuclear war.

59. (C) The Progressive Era — *Trend Question*
The reformist impulses of the Progressive period were a reaction to the corruption and excesses of the Industrial Revolution. Progressives wanted to correct the problems of urban poverty and corrupt business practices, which resulted from modernization.

60. (E) Cultural Trends: 1781–Mid-1800s — *Trend Question*
A leading transcendentalist, Emerson instructed his readers to rely on themselves and to find knowledge and understanding in their inner selves. Transcendentalists believed in the supremacy of emotion and the senses over logic and analysis.

61. (A) World War II — *Fact Question*
Truman's military advisors estimated that one million Americans and millions of Japanese could die during a ground invasion of Japan. Truman thought that dropping an atomic bomb would result in fewer casualties and a quicker end to the war than invading would Japan.

62. (B) Revolution & Constitution — *Fact Question*
Hamilton, Madison, and Jay wrote the Federalist Papers, a collection of 85 essays that demonstrated the advantages of a strong federal government. They argued that a federal government would guarantee liberty for all Americans.

63. (D) Industrial Revolution — *Trend Question*
Carnegie controlled all stages of the steel production process, from mining the raw materials to producing the steel to owning the railroad that would ship the finished product out of his factory. Consolidating his power in this manner of vertical integration gave him independence and a full share of his profits.

64. (A) Westward Expansion & Sectional Strife — *Except Question*
The Free Soilers did not support the universal abolition of slavery. They opposed slavery's expansion into the western territories (D) primarily because they wanted to reserve western lands for small farmers (B). If slavery were allowed in the new territories, then rich slaveowners would take over most of the land, pushing out small farmers (C); however, Free Soilers never questioned slaveholders' constitutional rights in states where slavery already existed (E).

65. (D) A New Nation — *Fact Question*
In the Kentucky and Virginia Resolutions, Thomas Jefferson and James Madison argued that the Federalist Alien and Sedition Acts were unconstitutional. They asserted that states had the right to nullify those acts.

66. (C) The Age of Jackson — *Trend Question*
The 1828 presidential election focused on personal rather than political issues. Jackson and his supporters accused Adams of stealing the presidency in 1824 with a "corrupt bargain." Adams's supporters counterattacked, even vilifying Jackson's wife and mother. The campaign brought American politics to a new low and set an infamous precedent for future elections.

67. (C) Revolution & Constitution — *Quotation Question*
The Virginia Statute helped shape the Constitution, particularly regarding religious freedom and officeholding protections. Like the Virginia Statute, the Constitution states that religious preferences will have no bearing on the holding of government offices. Later, the First Amendment continued Jefferson's emphasis on freedom of religion for each individual.

68. **(E)** Civil War & Reconstruction *Fact Question*

The Fifteenth Amendment gave African Americans the right to vote by extending the franchise to citizens without regard to race, color, or "previous condition of servitude."

69. **(E)** Industrial Revolution *Fact Question*

Established in 1866, the National Labor Union (NLU) was the forerunner to both the Knights of Labor and the American Federation of Labor. The NLU ran candidates for the presidency in 1872. Two years later, the Union vanished.

70. **(C)** Westward Expansion & Sectional Strife *Fact Question*

Stephen Douglas, the author of the Kansas-Nebraska Act, proposed the implementation of popular sovereignty in the western territories. Under popular sovereignty, the settlers would decide for themselves whether to permit or abolish slavery in their state constitutions.

71. **(D)** A New Nation *Cartoon Question*

In this cartoon, the snapping turtle grabs the barrel away from a British merchant, who wants to load it on the ship moored in the distance. "Ograbme" (embargo spelled backwards) refers to Jefferson's disastrous attempt to stop trade with both Britain and France until both countries ensured the safety of American merchant ships on the ocean.

72. **(C)** Industrial Revolution *Cartoon Question*

This cartoon depicts the American government walking the plank as the trusts take charge of the ship. The implication of the cartoon is that, nine years after its passage, the Sherman Antitrust Act has not succeeded in controlling monopolies. The Act failed primarily because Congress adopted a laissez-faire attitude toward the trusts, permitting them to be "in restraint of trade."

73. **(B)** The 1960s *Trend Question*

JFK's fear of communism led him to approve the Bay of Pigs invasion of Cuba when the plan was proposed to him during his first days in office. His acceptance of the plan demonstrated his willingness to assassinate Cuban Premier Fidel Castro, whom Kennedy feared as a communist threat.

74. **(D)** The Colonial Period *Except Question*

The Dutch settled in New York, which they named New Netherland. It became New York colony when the English took control of it in 1664.

75. **(C)** The 1950s *Except Question*

Throughout the 1950s the United States continued to export far more goods than it imported. The favorable trade balance brought money and credit into the country. The budget deficit was caused by the outpouring of money to foreign aid (A), investment abroad (B), Americans traveling abroad (D), and military spending for American troops stationed abroad (E).

76. **(A)** The Progressive Era *Quotation Question*

The muckraker Lincoln Steffens penned this critique of big business's corrupt practice of using politics for its own purposes. Calling for reform, Steffens and other muckrakers published newspaper articles that reviled industry for its corrupt and exploitative practices.

77. (D) World War II — *Trend Question*
FDR rarely acted without first ascertaining public opinion. When World War II broke out, he gauged the American people's feelings about the war before deciding to join the Allies. His halfway war measures, such as the Destroyers for Bases deal and the Arsenal of Democracy, were designed to prepare the country for war in case the public came to support American participation.

78. (D) The Age of Imperialism — *Trend Question*
Cuba's revolt against the Spanish Empire reminded many Americans of their own colonial struggle against England. The similarity between those two events led prominent politicians to support Cuban independence, and the Senate passed the Teller Amendment, which stated that America would not annex Cuba.

79. (A) Industrial Revolution — *Fact Question*
Most Chinese immigrants settled in California, especially after work started there on the transcontinental railroad.

80. (D) Westward Expansion & Sectional Strife — *Cartoon Question*
While John Breckinridge tears off the lower south, which supported his strong expansionist, pro-slavery views, Abraham Lincoln and Stephen Douglas battle over the west. John Bell, trying to repair the rifts, attempts to glue the map together. The cartoon implies that each candidate represents the views of one geographical part of the country and that the lack of agreement among them tears the union apart.

81. (A) Cultural Trends — *Except Question*
Unions were virtually nonexistent during the 1840s. The concept of collective bargaining had not yet developed, and conditions in factories continued to deteriorate as industries increased in size.

82. (C) World War I — *Trend Question*
When Germany broke the Sussex Pledge and resumed unrestricted submarine warfare, the American government decided to join the Allied countries. Wilson's concern for the freedom of the seas could not co-exist with the resumption of German submarine activity.

83. (E) Industrial Revolution — *Fact Question*
J.P. Morgan oversaw the reorganization of the railroads after wasteful competition, poor management decisions, and the depression of 1893 drove the railroad system into bankruptcy.

84. (D) The Colonial Period — *Fact Question*
During the 1640s, Newport was the center of the African slave trade. At the time, the creation of large slave labor forces in the South made the slave trade increasingly lucrative.

85. (A) World War I — *Except Question*
Wilson wanted to rid the world of colonies; he believed that each nation should determine its own form of government and rule over its own people. He also believed that colonial competition was at least partially responsible for the outbreak of World War I.

86. **(E)** The Colonial Period *Quotation Question*

Since the *Mayflower* was blown off course during its voyage to the New World and landed outside the area designated in the charter from the Crown, the Pilgrims established rules, which they set down in the Mayflower Compact, before settling their colony. Their intention to create a "civil body Politick" spoke to their desire to create a government that would keep order and maintain the peace, since they believed they were not in lands governed by the charter.

87. **(C)** The 1950s *Fact Question*

Little Rock became nationally known in 1957, when nine black teenagers attempted to enroll in the previously segregated Central High School. An angry white mob threatened the black students and the Arkansas governor, Orval Faubus, called out the National Guard to prohibit the students from entering the school. Eisenhower was forced to send armed forces to Little Rock in an attempt to end the crisis.

88. **(B)** Westward Expansion & Sectional Strife *Trend Question*

The discovery of gold in California in 1848 quickly populated the territory and sped up its preparation for statehood. When California petitioned for admission to the Union, sectional tensions over slavery were renewed.

89. **(B)** The Colonial Period *Fact Question*

Middle Passage refers to the ocean voyage African slaves made to the New World. Africans were forced into large, crowded ships for the long trip across the Atlantic Ocean. Many died aboard these ships due to inhumane and unhealthy conditions.

90. **(D)** The 1950s *Trend Question*

When FDR ran for his third term as president in 1940, many critics accused him of striving for kingship. The Twenty-second Amendment was intended to prevent any individual from being elected to the presidency more than twice, in order to quell fears that the office could turn into a lifelong position for one individual.

SAT II U.S. History Practice Test 2

UNITED STATES HISTORY TEST 2 ANSWER SHEET

1. Ⓐ Ⓑ Ⓒ Ⓓ Ⓔ	31. Ⓐ Ⓑ Ⓒ Ⓓ Ⓔ	61. Ⓐ Ⓑ Ⓒ Ⓓ Ⓔ
2. Ⓐ Ⓑ Ⓒ Ⓓ Ⓔ	32. Ⓐ Ⓑ Ⓒ Ⓓ Ⓔ	62. Ⓐ Ⓑ Ⓒ Ⓓ Ⓔ
3. Ⓐ Ⓑ Ⓒ Ⓓ Ⓔ	33. Ⓐ Ⓑ Ⓒ Ⓓ Ⓔ	63. Ⓐ Ⓑ Ⓒ Ⓓ Ⓔ
4. Ⓐ Ⓑ Ⓒ Ⓓ Ⓔ	34. Ⓐ Ⓑ Ⓒ Ⓓ Ⓔ	64. Ⓐ Ⓑ Ⓒ Ⓓ Ⓔ
5. Ⓐ Ⓑ Ⓒ Ⓓ Ⓔ	35. Ⓐ Ⓑ Ⓒ Ⓓ Ⓔ	65. Ⓐ Ⓑ Ⓒ Ⓓ Ⓔ
6. Ⓐ Ⓑ Ⓒ Ⓓ Ⓔ	36. Ⓐ Ⓑ Ⓒ Ⓓ Ⓔ	66. Ⓐ Ⓑ Ⓒ Ⓓ Ⓔ
7. Ⓐ Ⓑ Ⓒ Ⓓ Ⓔ	37. Ⓐ Ⓑ Ⓒ Ⓓ Ⓔ	67. Ⓐ Ⓑ Ⓒ Ⓓ Ⓔ
8. Ⓐ Ⓑ Ⓒ Ⓓ Ⓔ	38. Ⓐ Ⓑ Ⓒ Ⓓ Ⓔ	68. Ⓐ Ⓑ Ⓒ Ⓓ Ⓔ
9. Ⓐ Ⓑ Ⓒ Ⓓ Ⓔ	39. Ⓐ Ⓑ Ⓒ Ⓓ Ⓔ	69. Ⓐ Ⓑ Ⓒ Ⓓ Ⓔ
10. Ⓐ Ⓑ Ⓒ Ⓓ Ⓔ	40. Ⓐ Ⓑ Ⓒ Ⓓ Ⓔ	70. Ⓐ Ⓑ Ⓒ Ⓓ Ⓔ
11. Ⓐ Ⓑ Ⓒ Ⓓ Ⓔ	41. Ⓐ Ⓑ Ⓒ Ⓓ Ⓔ	71. Ⓐ Ⓑ Ⓒ Ⓓ Ⓔ
12. Ⓐ Ⓑ Ⓒ Ⓓ Ⓔ	42. Ⓐ Ⓑ Ⓒ Ⓓ Ⓔ	72. Ⓐ Ⓑ Ⓒ Ⓓ Ⓔ
13. Ⓐ Ⓑ Ⓒ Ⓓ Ⓔ	43. Ⓐ Ⓑ Ⓒ Ⓓ Ⓔ	73. Ⓐ Ⓑ Ⓒ Ⓓ Ⓔ
14. Ⓐ Ⓑ Ⓒ Ⓓ Ⓔ	44. Ⓐ Ⓑ Ⓒ Ⓓ Ⓔ	74. Ⓐ Ⓑ Ⓒ Ⓓ Ⓔ
15. Ⓐ Ⓑ Ⓒ Ⓓ Ⓔ	45. Ⓐ Ⓑ Ⓒ Ⓓ Ⓔ	75. Ⓐ Ⓑ Ⓒ Ⓓ Ⓔ
16. Ⓐ Ⓑ Ⓒ Ⓓ Ⓔ	46. Ⓐ Ⓑ Ⓒ Ⓓ Ⓔ	76. Ⓐ Ⓑ Ⓒ Ⓓ Ⓔ
17. Ⓐ Ⓑ Ⓒ Ⓓ Ⓔ	47. Ⓐ Ⓑ Ⓒ Ⓓ Ⓔ	77. Ⓐ Ⓑ Ⓒ Ⓓ Ⓔ
18. Ⓐ Ⓑ Ⓒ Ⓓ Ⓔ	48. Ⓐ Ⓑ Ⓒ Ⓓ Ⓔ	78. Ⓐ Ⓑ Ⓒ Ⓓ Ⓔ
19. Ⓐ Ⓑ Ⓒ Ⓓ Ⓔ	49. Ⓐ Ⓑ Ⓒ Ⓓ Ⓔ	79. Ⓐ Ⓑ Ⓒ Ⓓ Ⓔ
20. Ⓐ Ⓑ Ⓒ Ⓓ Ⓔ	50. Ⓐ Ⓑ Ⓒ Ⓓ Ⓔ	80. Ⓐ Ⓑ Ⓒ Ⓓ Ⓔ
21. Ⓐ Ⓑ Ⓒ Ⓓ Ⓔ	51. Ⓐ Ⓑ Ⓒ Ⓓ Ⓔ	81. Ⓐ Ⓑ Ⓒ Ⓓ Ⓔ
22. Ⓐ Ⓑ Ⓒ Ⓓ Ⓔ	52. Ⓐ Ⓑ Ⓒ Ⓓ Ⓔ	82. Ⓐ Ⓑ Ⓒ Ⓓ Ⓔ
23. Ⓐ Ⓑ Ⓒ Ⓓ Ⓔ	53. Ⓐ Ⓑ Ⓒ Ⓓ Ⓔ	83. Ⓐ Ⓑ Ⓒ Ⓓ Ⓔ
24. Ⓐ Ⓑ Ⓒ Ⓓ Ⓔ	54. Ⓐ Ⓑ Ⓒ Ⓓ Ⓔ	84. Ⓐ Ⓑ Ⓒ Ⓓ Ⓔ
25. Ⓐ Ⓑ Ⓒ Ⓓ Ⓔ	55. Ⓐ Ⓑ Ⓒ Ⓓ Ⓔ	85. Ⓐ Ⓑ Ⓒ Ⓓ Ⓔ
26. Ⓐ Ⓑ Ⓒ Ⓓ Ⓔ	56. Ⓐ Ⓑ Ⓒ Ⓓ Ⓔ	86. Ⓐ Ⓑ Ⓒ Ⓓ Ⓔ
27. Ⓐ Ⓑ Ⓒ Ⓓ Ⓔ	57. Ⓐ Ⓑ Ⓒ Ⓓ Ⓔ	87. Ⓐ Ⓑ Ⓒ Ⓓ Ⓔ
28. Ⓐ Ⓑ Ⓒ Ⓓ Ⓔ	58. Ⓐ Ⓑ Ⓒ Ⓓ Ⓔ	88. Ⓐ Ⓑ Ⓒ Ⓓ Ⓔ
29. Ⓐ Ⓑ Ⓒ Ⓓ Ⓔ	59. Ⓐ Ⓑ Ⓒ Ⓓ Ⓔ	89. Ⓐ Ⓑ Ⓒ Ⓓ Ⓔ
30. Ⓐ Ⓑ Ⓒ Ⓓ Ⓔ	60. Ⓐ Ⓑ Ⓒ Ⓓ Ⓔ	90. Ⓐ Ⓑ Ⓒ Ⓓ Ⓔ

UNITED STATES HISTORY TEST 2

Directions: Each of the questions or incomplete statements below is followed by five suggested answers or completions. Select the one that is best in each case and then fill in the corresponding oval on the answer sheet.

1. Which of the following practices did American industry use to attract cheap labor until 1885?

    (A) Industry leaders visited European slums and promoted the American "good life."
    (B) Factories improved working conditions and instituted nine-hour days.
    (C) Companies placed their immigrant workers in settlement houses.
    (D) Companies paid for the passage of immigrants to the United States.
    (E) Factories permitted workers to join unions.

2. Which of the following people constituted the 1960s counterculture?

    (A) Feminists
    (B) Communists
    (C) Alienated youth
    (D) Opponents of economic reform
    (E) Supporters of segregation

3. The Embargo Act of 1807

    (A) effectively ended tensions with England
    (B) demonstrated Thomas Jefferson's shrewd economic judgment
    (C) severely impaired the American economy
    (D) cemented a political alliance with France
    (E) was the major cause of the War of 1812

4. "It is for us the living, rather, to be dedicated here to the unfinished work which they who fought here have thus far so nobly advanced. It is rather for us to be here dedicated to the great task remaining before us— that from these honored dead we take increased devotion to that cause for which they gave the last full measure of devotion—that we here highly resolve that these dead shall not have died in vain, that this nation, under God, shall have a new birth of freedom, and that government of the people, by the people, for the people shall not perish from the earth."

   In addition to consecrating the cemetery at Gettysburg after the three-day battle there in 1863, Lincoln's address

    (A) called for the abolition of slavery
    (B) offered the South a chance to surrender
    (C) blamed the Confederacy for starting the war
    (D) stated his vision for the rebirth of American democracy
    (E) announced his decision to run for reelection in 1864

5. Harry Truman won the support of organized labor in the 1948 election because he

    (A) was known as a trust-buster
    (B) vetoed the Taft-Hartley Act
    (C) approved the merger of the American Federation of Labor and the Congress of Industrial Organizations
    (D) suported the use of loyalty oaths
    (E) supported the Marshall Plan

6. The major difference between the Articles of Confederation and the Constitution is that the Constitution

    (A) gives more power to the federal government than the Articles do
    (B) gives more power to the states than the Articles do
    (C) specifically recognizes the legality of slavery
    (D) takes away the power of the states to raise taxes
    (E) calls for a two-party system to make the political process more efficient

GO ON TO THE NEXT PAGE

UNITED STATES HISTORY TEST—*Continued*

7. Historical research on antebellum slavery has revealed that all of the following were part of slave culture on large plantations EXCEPT

    (A) secret religious services
    (B) education for children
    (C) stable black families
    (D) songs, music, and folktales
    (E) open political gatherings to debate abolition

8. The 1925 "monkey trial" in Dayton, Tennessee, was significant because it

    (A) exposed the xenophobia that pervaded southern society
    (B) destroyed the political strength of the Ku Klux Klan
    (C) weakened the Democratic Party's white supremacist base
    (D) revealed the clash between traditional religious beliefs and modern, scientific values
    (E) led to the repeal of the prohibition amendment

9. John Adams appointed the "midnight judges" in an effort to

    (A) ensure an equitable court system
    (B) prevent the newly elected Jeffersonians from controlling the courts
    (C) assist the courts in handling the high volume of cases they heard
    (D) carry out his presidential mandate
    (E) respond to his critics who charged that the courts were ineffective

GO ON TO THE NEXT PAGE

UNITED STATES HISTORY TEST—Continued

10. The National Recovery Administration poster above was placed in companies that

   (A) adhered to the industrial codes established by the New Deal
   (B) did not have a union representing the workers
   (C) had integrated African Americans into the workforce
   (D) took an active role in preventing communist infiltration
   (E) pledged campaign contributions to the Franklin D. Roosevelt administration

February 18, 1871

THE CHINESE QUESTION
COLUMBIA.—"Hands off gentlemen! America means fair play for all men."

11. The cartoon above illustrates rising anti-Chinese sentiment, which led to the passage of the

(A) Pendleton Act
(B) Exclusion Act
(C) Immigration Restriction Act
(D) National Origins Act
(E) Dawes Severalty Act

UNITED STATES HISTORY TEST—Continued

12. Which of the following groups was the most responsible for challenging the constitutionality of segregated public education before the Supreme Court?

    (A) Americans for Democratic Action
    (B) The Congress of Racial Equality
    (C) The Southern Christian Leadership Conference
    (D) The National Urban League
    (E) The National Association for the Advancement of Colored People

13. The Jacksonian Democratic party was formed in response to

    (A) the re-emergence of the Federalists in 1824
    (B) the economic depression caused by aggressive federal tax policies
    (C) the federal government's policy on Native Americans
    (D) corruption during the 1824 presidential election
    (E) the establishment of the Second Bank of the United States

14. The Harlem Renaissance refers to

    (A) urban renewal in New York City's largest African-American ghetto
    (B) civil rights activity stressing desegregation
    (C) the emerging political power of African Americans on the municipal level
    (D) an African-American literary and cultural awakening
    (E) Marcus Garvey's desire to separate the African-American community from the white community and to create independent African-American institutions

15. In the mid-nineteenth century, the phenomenon of domesticity in American society resulted in

    (A) a shift from women working outside the home to staying at home to oversee domestic chores
    (B) the raising of livestock on the Great Plains for sale to eastern markets
    (C) an attempt to improve slave conditions on large plantations
    (D) the improvement of working conditions in factories
    (E) the federal government's attempt to "civilize" Native Americans and assimilate them into American society

16. Which of the following describes the process necessary to amend the Constitution?

    (A) The president must propose a new amendment, and Congress must ratify it by a two-thirds vote in each house.
    (B) Congress must propose a new amendment and pass it by a two-thirds vote in each house; then the Supreme Court must rule the amendment constitutional and ratify it.
    (C) Congress or the state legislatures must propose an amendment, which must be ratified by three-quarters of Congress or of the state legislatures.
    (D) U.S. citizens must propose an amendment through a national referendum, and the president and Congress must ratify it.
    (E) The Supreme Court must use its enumerated powers of amendment.

17. South Carolina seceded from the Union in December 1860 because

    (A) a Republican had been elected president
    (B) Congress was overwhelmingly antislavery
    (C) the Supreme Court reversed its *Dred Scott* ruling
    (D) protective tariffs were at levels higher than the Tariff of Abominations
    (E) the U.S. Army had fired on Fort Sumter

18. In the early years of the American republic, the principal source of funding for the federal government came from

    (A) income taxes
    (B) bond sales
    (C) loans from the states
    (D) custom duties
    (E) excise taxes

GO ON TO THE NEXT PAGE

UNITED STATES HISTORY TEST—Continued

19. The Congress of Industrial Organizations was established in 1933

    (A) because the American Federation of Labor was no longer attracting skilled labor
    (B) to organize unskilled laborers, especially women and African Americans, in addition to skilled laborers
    (C) to demand the overthrow of the industrial order
    (D) to return the Republican party to the White House
    (E) to lobby Franklin D. Roosevelt for labor's right to collective bargaining

20. The last and most significant of the colonial wars was

    (A) King William's War
    (B) Queen Anne's War
    (C) the French and Indian War
    (D) King George's War
    (E) King Philip's War

21. Which of the following was a primary cause of the Gulf War?

    (A) Iraq's invasion of Kuwait
    (B) A communist threat to expand into Iraq
    (C) Israel's invasion of Iraq
    (D) An Iraqi threat to attack the United States
    (E) Retaliation for Iraq's treatment of American hostages

GO ON TO THE NEXT PAGE

REAR VIEW.
—Orr in the Chicago *Tribune*.

22. What does the 1919 cartoon above suggest about Woodrow Wilson as a diplomat?

(A) He successfully reconciled the differences between World War I combatants.
(B) His peace plan received careful consideration because the United States had been invaluable in winning the war.
(C) He was politically sophisticated and knew how to deal with each combatant's desires within the structure of world peace.
(D) His former allies were turning against him and planning to break all diplomatic relations with the United States.
(E) His peace plan was destined to fail because it conflicted with the Allies' hidden agendas.

UNITED STATES HISTORY TEST—*Continued*

23. Between 1840 and 1860, population increases due to immigration were most dramatic

    (A) in rural parts of the South
    (B) along the Canadian border
    (C) in major urban centers
    (D) on the Great Plains
    (E) in the Northwest

24. The American Federation of Labor did all of the following EXCEPT

    (A) focus on obtaining shorter hours, higher wages, and better working conditions for its members
    (B) oppose the unionization of African Americans
    (C) get involved in national politics to force its demands
    (D) unionize only skilled workers
    (E) go on strike only if negotiations between labor and management failed

25. The Kitchen Debates of 1959 can best be described as

    (A) advertising strategies to attract Americans to purchase new home appliances
    (B) subcabinet-level policy discussions in the executive branch
    (C) discussions about American imperialism in Latin America
    (D) arguments for women to join the domestic workforce
    (E) conversations between Nixon and Khrushchev concerning communism and capitalism

26. Jay's Treaty of 1794 contained all of the following provisions EXCEPT that

    (A) Britain would agree to evacuate forts in western regions of the United States
    (B) the United States would agree to pay debts it owed to Britain prior to the Revolution
    (C) Britain would promise to end the practice of impressment
    (D) the United States would stop discriminating against English shipping
    (E) Britain would compensate American merchants for ships it had previously seized

27. Prohibition forces successfully ratified the Eighteenth Amendment during World War I because

    (A) the war added a moral and practical justification for prohibition
    (B) Woodrow Wilson was firmly in favor of banning alcohol
    (C) progressives were no longer a strong enough political force to challenge the amendment
    (D) imports from Germany ceased, so alcohol was no longer available in America
    (E) public attention was focused on developments overseas, and few people noticed the amendment's ratification

28. Many of Lyndon Johnson's Great Society programs suffered in the later years of his administration because

    (A) the Supreme Court ruled them unconstitutional
    (B) the Republicans took control of Congress and rejected many of his social programs
    (C) the money originally allocated to social programs was spent on Vietnam
    (D) the civil rights movement depleted the government's financial resources
    (E) the Democrats grew tired of Johnson's programs and his advisors suggested that he scale them back significantly

29. Herbert Hoover refrained from providing relief to American citizens during the Depression because he

    (A) believed such relief was unconstitutional
    (B) was told by his advisors that the government did not have the needed resources
    (C) thought that financial relief should be handled on a local level
    (D) believed that Americans' rugged individualism would help them survive hardship
    (E) was a Social Darwinist who believed that only the strong should survive

GO ON TO THE NEXT PAGE

UNITED STATES HISTORY TEST—Continued

30. The House of Representatives impeached Andrew Johnson in 1868 because he

    (A) supported civil rights legislation for African Americans
    (B) extended the Freedmen's Bureau, despite congressional opposition
    (C) violated the Tenure of Office Act
    (D) vetoed the Wade-Davis Bill
    (E) appointed a conservative justice to the Supreme Court

31. "For myself, Sir, I do not admit the competency of South Carolina, or any other State, to prescribe my constitutional duty; or to settle, between me and the people, the validity of laws of Congress for which I have voted. I decline her umpirage. I have not sworn to support the Constitution according to her construction of its clauses. I have not stipulated, by my oath of office or otherwise, to come under any responsibility, except to the people, and those whom appointed to pass upon the question, whether laws, supported by my votes, conform to the Constitution of the country. And, Sir, if we look to the general nature of the case, could any thing have been more preposterous, than to make a government for the whole Union, and yet leave its powers subject, not to one interpretation, but to thirteen or twenty-four interpretations?"

    In his response to Robert Hayne in the Senate, Daniel Webster was specifically addressing

    (A) slavery
    (B) voting rights
    (C) the electoral college
    (D) nullification
    (E) the War of 1812

32. The goal of the Manhattan Project was to

    (A) resolve problems in urban sectors after World War II
    (B) research racial segregation in public education
    (C) establish an interstate highway system
    (D) eliminate machine politics and governmental corruption
    (E) develop an atomic bomb

33. Ida Tarbell's "History of the Standard Oil Company" was an example of

    (A) muckraking
    (B) "new economic" history
    (C) pro-monopoly propaganda
    (D) populism
    (E) New Deal liberalism

34. All of the following are true of the presidential impeachment process EXCEPT

    (A) the grounds for impeachment are treason, bribery, or high crimes and misdemeanors
    (B) the House of Representatives has sole authority to impeach a president
    (C) only a unanimous vote by the Senate can remove a sitting president
    (D) the Chief Justice of the Supreme Court presides over the president's trial in the Senate
    (E) once convicted and removed from office, the president can still be brought to trial in criminal or civil court for his actions

35. In exchange for support of his plan to have the federal government assume state debts acquired during the Revolution, Alexander Hamilton offered the southern states

    (A) protection against the abolition of slavery
    (B) the repeal of a high protective tariff
    (C) the dissolution of the national bank
    (D) the placement of the national capital between Virginia and Maryland
    (E) increased power for state governments

36. In 1954, Joseph McCarthy lost his political power and was censured by the Senate after he

    (A) became a communist
    (B) switched to the Democratic party
    (C) accused the U.S. Army of harboring communists
    (D) advocated nuclear war with the Soviet Union
    (E) fell into disfavor with President Eisenhower

GO ON TO THE NEXT PAGE

37. The religious revivalism that swept across the American colonies in the 1730s was known as

   (A) the Enlightenment
   (B) the Glorious Revolution
   (C) Antinomianism
   (D) Bacon's Rebellion
   (E) the Great Awakening

38. Horrified at the prospect that land acquired during the Mexican War might promote the expansion of slavery, Henry David Thoreau refused to pay taxes that would support the war. He described his method of protest in a pamphlet entitled

   (A) *Democracy in America*
   (B) *Walden*
   (C) *On Civil Disobedience*
   (D) *The Promise of American Life*
   (E) *On Self-reliance*

39. During World War I, the Zimmerman Telegram revealed Germany's desire to ally with

   (A) Canada
   (B) Mexico
   (C) Russia
   (D) Cuba
   (E) Spain

40. The cartoon above suggests which of the following about Theodore Roosevelt's approach to monopolies?

    (A) He adopted a laissez-faire attitude toward all trusts.
    (B) He busted all trusts for being in restraint of trade and commerce.
    (C) He busted only bad trusts that refused to be regulated by the federal government.
    (D) He restored free competition to the marketplace.
    (E) He gave the Supreme Court the authority to tackle the issue of monopolies.

UNITED STATES HISTORY TEST—Continued

41. Horace Mann contributed which of the following ideas to American educational theory?

    (A) Students should be enrolled in elective courses to sharpen their skills.
    (B) Schools should be co-educational.
    (C) Teachers must be professionally trained.
    (D) Mathematics was an unnecessary part of higher education.
    (E) Analytical inquiry was an essential skill to be taught in secondary education.

42. Booker T. Washington's stance on race relations in the south comprised all of the following arguments EXCEPT

    (A) African Americans deserved immediate social and political equality
    (B) social and political equality would come gradually and should not be forced
    (C) African Americans should remain in the south, where the best opportunities existed for progress
    (D) African Americans should make themselves economically useful to the rebuilding of the south
    (E) higher education was not as valuable for the majority of African Americans as vocational training was

43. The Salem witchcraft trials, which occurred in 1692, were significant because they

    (A) purged Salem of nonbelievers who were corrupting the purity of the community
    (B) demonstrated that the community was vigilant and had the ability to deal effectively with a crisis
    (C) exemplified how hysteria could overcome rational thought during a time of instability
    (D) led to a series of other witchcraft trials in neighboring colonies
    (E) solidified the position of nonbelievers in the Puritan community

44. Which of the following people suggested that the best way to address the causes of the Depression was to increase government spending and run a deficit?

    (A) William Graham Sumner
    (B) John Maynard Keynes
    (C) Henry George
    (D) Andrew Mellon
    (E) Henry Stimson

45. The last years of the nineteenth century were referred to as the Gilded Age because

    (A) organized labor grew in power and significance
    (B) the federal government committed itself to massive infrastructure construction
    (C) industrial elites engaged in stewardship
    (D) technological innovations revolutionized domestic life for all Americans
    (E) industrialists spent their money lavishly on mansions, yachts, and other overt displays of their wealth

46. In his novel *Invisible Man*, Ralph Ellison depicts which of the following?

    (A) Discrimination against Native Americans in the nineteenth and twentieth centuries
    (B) An average man's conformity to the conservative ideals of the 1950s
    (C) The plight of the forgotten poor in the 1980s
    (D) An African-American man's struggle against a predominantly white American society
    (E) The attempt by a veteran of the Vietnam War to reintegrate into American society

47. Harriet Beecher Stowe's 1852 novel *Uncle Tom's Cabin* exacerbated sectional tensions over slavery because it

    (A) attacked the views of abolitionists
    (B) depicted the brutality and inhumanity of slavery
    (C) revealed that slaves were satisfied with their lives
    (D) supported a strong fugitive slave law
    (E) advocated violent slave rebellions

48. Woodrow Wilson's victory in the 1912 presidential election can best be attributed to

    (A) his liberal stance on civil rights and his interest in desegregation
    (B) the fact that he was the only Progressive candidate running for president
    (C) his pledge to allow trusts to expand without fear of government intervention
    (D) a split in the Republican Party between the traditional and progressive wings
    (E) his promise to keep the United States out of World War I

GO ON TO THE NEXT PAGE

49. Which of the following people was most responsible for applying social Darwinian thought to American society in the late nineteenth century?

    (A) Charles Darwin
    (B) Herbert Spencer
    (C) Charles Sumner
    (D) William Graham Sumner
    (E) Lester Frank Ward

50. Dwight Eisenhower won the presidential elections of 1952 and 1956 because

    (A) he was a popular war hero, credited with defeating Germany
    (B) his economic policies were more viable than his opponent's
    (C) he promised to abolish the federal income tax
    (D) his Republican Party proposed the best approach to ending the Cold War
    (E) he was the first presidential candidate to advocate African-American civil rights

51. "We accuse Sir William Berkeley as guilty of each and every one of the same, and as one who hath traiterously attempted, violated, and Injured his Majesties interest here, by a loss of a greate part of this his Colony and many of his faithfull loyall subjects, by him betrayed and in a barbarous and shamefull manner exposed to the Incursions and murther of the heathen."

    This excerpt from Nathaniel Bacon's grievances against Governor Berkeley of Virginia suggests that Bacon's Rebellion stemmed from

    (A) the high taxes imposed on western farmers by the Tidewater government
    (B) the lack of government protection against Native American attacks in the Piedmont
    (C) the continuation of indentured servitude past the normal seven-year period
    (D) the governor's practice of selling land to nonresidents
    (E) involuntary conscription into the state militia

52. Section 7A of the National Recovery Act was replaced by

    (A) the Soil Conservation and Domestic Allotment Act
    (B) the Wagner Labor Relations Act
    (C) the Public Works Administration
    (D) the Glass-Steagall Act
    (E) the Resettlement Administration

53. Which of the following was a utopian vision of an American society in which socialism replaced private ownership and disparities in wealth?

    (A) Henry George's *Progress and Poverty*
    (B) Russell Conwell's "Acres of Diamonds"
    (C) Horatio Alger's "rags to riches" novels
    (D) William Dean Howells's *The Rise of Silas Lapham*
    (E) Edward Bellamy's *Looking Backward*

54. All of the following were part of Franklin D. Roosevelt's "arsenal of democracy" EXCEPT

    (A) the Lend-Lease Act
    (B) the stationing of American troops in Greenland
    (C) the Atlantic Charter
    (D) the Manhattan Project
    (E) the patrolling of sea lanes in the Atlantic Ocean by American destroyers

55. The utopian community at Oneida defied American society by overtly advocating

    (A) communism
    (B) atheism
    (C) communal marriage
    (D) women's rights
    (E) drug use

56. "The Congress shall have power . . . to make all laws which shall be necessary and proper for carrying into execution the foregoing powers, and all other powers vested by this Constitution in the government of the United States, or in any department or officer thereof."

    This passage from the Constitution addresses the powers of the legislative branch of government, and it is known as

    (A) the Supreme Law of the Land clause
    (B) judicial review
    (C) the reserved powers clause
    (D) the takings clause
    (E) the elastic clause

UNITED STATES HISTORY TEST—Continued

57. Southerners defended the expansion of slavery into the western territories by arguing that

    (A) the Missouri Compromise borderline was not intended to be permanent
    (B) the Supreme Court had specifically approved slavery's expansion
    (C) the Constitution guaranteed a citizen's right to take his property into the territories
    (D) since abolition had not become law, slavery was permissible anywhere in the Union
    (E) slavery had been permitted in those territories under Mexican rule, thus setting a legal precedent for slavery in those lands

58. John F. Kennedy's policy of containment advocated

    (A) massive retaliation
    (B) flexible response
    (C) peaceful coexistence
    (D) measured intervention
    (E) shuttle diplomacy

59. The Continental Congress committee that edited the Declaration of Independence persuaded Thomas Jefferson to remove his attack on the institution of slavery because

    (A) southern colonies would have refused to sign the Declaration if it contained an attack on slavery
    (B) the issue was not relevant to the Revolution
    (C) the committee's members were all slaveholders
    (D) the abolition of slavery would have ruined the colonial economy
    (E) Britain had already ended the practice of slavery

60. Throughout the second half of the nineteenth century, the federal government

    (A) fiercely opposed big business
    (B) adopted a laissez-faire approach to trusts
    (C) exercised little regulatory authority over industry
    (D) exercised strict regulatory authority over industry, thus limiting excessive exploitation by big business
    (E) was divided, with Congress and the Supreme Court opposed to big business, and the executive branch in favor of trusts

61. The Truman Doctrine addressed the fears of the American public concerning the issue of

    (A) unemployment
    (B) labor unrest
    (C) communist expansion
    (D) Republican Party dominance
    (E) civil rights

62. The Fourteenth Amendment, ratified in 1868, was significant because it

    (A) defined citizenship rights and defended American citizens against discrimination from the states
    (B) formally ended the Reconstruction process and returned the former confederate states to the Union
    (C) abolished slavery and mandated that former slaves receive land and education in the South
    (D) prohibited secession as a political weapon and mandated that future conflicts over states rights be adjudicated by the Supreme Court
    (E) empowered Congress to control the Reconstruction process and to determine when the military occupation of the South would conclude

63. The purpose of the Navigation Acts was to

    (A) prohibit the colonies from breaking away from England
    (B) ensure a favorable balance of trade for England
    (C) reduce France's ability to employ its navy on the high seas
    (D) destroy the Spanish Empire
    (E) help the American colonies become self-governing

64. In an effort to regulate railroads in the late nineteenth century, Congress created the

    (A) Federal Trade Commission
    (B) Interstate Commerce Commission
    (C) Federal Reserve System
    (D) Pendleton Act
    (E) Sherman Antitrust Act

GO ON TO THE NEXT PAGE

UNITED STATES HISTORY TEST—Continued

65. Prior to the attack on Pearl Harbor, American interest in negotiating a durable peace with Japan was best illustrated by

   (A) its reference to the Atlantic Charter
   (B) its support for the Washington Naval Conference treaty
   (C) the passage of the Neutrality Acts
   (D) the continuation of diplomatic talks with Japanese representatives until very shortly before Pearl Harbor was attacked
   (E) its instructions to Russia and Britain to leave Japan alone

66. When slaves recited folktales, such as the Brer Rabbit stories, they were primarily

   (A) imagining what life would be like if they were free
   (B) feigning illness to avoid work
   (C) practicing religious rituals that had their roots in Africa
   (D) learning to read and teaching their children
   (E) ridiculing their masters through the use of children's stories

67. George Grenville's decision to levy taxes on the colonies was motivated by

   (A) his belief that the colonies were growing too independent and needed to be disciplined
   (B) a need to defray the large debt Britain incurred after the French and Indian War
   (C) Parliament's desire to wrest control of taxation policy from the Crown
   (D) an internal battle for control within the office of the Chancellor of the Exchequer
   (E) specific instructions from Robert Walpole to terminate the practice of salutary neglect

68. All of the following are true concerning the Nat Turner Insurrection in Virginia in 1831 EXCEPT

   (A) southerners blamed the rebellion on William Lloyd Garrison
   (B) Virginia subsequently debated the abolition of slavery
   (C) the "positive good" justification for slavery became more popular
   (D) the neighboring states of Maryland and North Carolina abolished slavery
   (E) southern states tightened their restrictions on slaves' mobility

69. The Supreme Court ruling in *Munn v. Illinois*, 1877, was a major victory for the Granger Movement because it

   (A) determined that businesses which affected the public interest could be regulated by the government
   (B) forced the federal government to subsidize farmers and establish parity pricing
   (C) upheld the constitutionality of antitrust legislation passed in Illinois
   (D) removed price controls that had hampered farmers' profits
   (E) placed substantial tariffs on imported European agricultural products

70. The practice of salutary neglect represented the colonial governing style of

   (A) Edmund Andros
   (B) Robert Walpole
   (C) Jonathan Edwards
   (D) Jonathan Winthrop
   (E) William Bradford

71. The March on Washington in 1963 was the brainchild of

   (A) Martin Luther King, Jr.
   (B) Malcolm X
   (C) A. Philip Randolph
   (D) James Farmer
   (E) Ella Baker

72. The emergence of a slave-based labor system using Africans occurred in the mid to late 1600s for all of the following reasons EXCEPT

   (A) indentured servitude was not a profitable or efficient system
   (B) recently freed indentured servants wanted a greater distinction made between themselves and African laborers
   (C) white planters required a stable labor force that could expand to meet their growing needs
   (D) Native Americans proved to be unwilling laborers and frequently escaped when forced to work
   (E) African slaves were relatively expensive purchases, making them a good long-term investment

GO ON TO THE NEXT PAGE

UNITED STATES HISTORY TEST—Continued

73. Attempts at establishing an effective Reconstruction policy after the Civil War

    (A) ran into formidable financial problems because of the Union war debt
    (B) revealed a power struggle between the legislative and executive branches of government
    (C) were impeded by the continuation of slavery in the South
    (D) were largely invalidated by the Supreme Court in a series of landmark decisions
    (E) proceeded smoothly, with little disagreement or political opposition

74. "We conclude that, in the field of public education, the doctrine of 'separate but equal' has no place. Separate educational facilities are inherently unequal. Therefore, we hold that the plaintiffs and others similarly situated for whom the actions have been brought are, by reason of the segregation complained of, deprived of the equal protection of the laws guaranteed by the Fourteenth Amendment."

    This Supreme Court ruling was known as

    (A) *Plessy v. Ferguson*
    (B) *Boynton v. Virginia*
    (C) *Brown v. Board of Education*
    (D) *Miranda v. Arizona*
    (E) the Civil Rights Cases

75. Woodrow Wilson's initial desire to keep the United States out of World War I was motivated largely by

    (A) his isolationist tendencies in foreign affairs and preference for domestic reforms
    (B) his Progressive inclination to avoid war
    (C) congressional opposition to intervention
    (D) disagreement among his advisors over the best strategy for intervention
    (E) his intention to mediate a peaceful and quick end to the war

76. Internal improvements became a central issue of the Jacksonian presidency, when Andrew Jackson

    (A) authorized extensive congressional spending on all requests for internal improvements
    (B) requested a bipartisan bill to increase improvements made in the southern states
    (C) refused to fund improvements in any state that permitted slavery
    (D) vetoed the funding for a road in Kentucky
    (E) rewarded Georgia for removing the Cherokees by promising the state extensive internal improvements

77. The slogan "Fifty-Four Forty or Fight" pertained to

    (A) the Missouri Compromise line
    (B) Texas' admission to the Union
    (C) the Oregon question
    (D) the Compromise of 1850
    (E) the Ostend Manifesto

78. The 1964 Civil Rights Act did all of the following EXCEPT

    (A) secure federal protection for African Americans who registered to vote in the South
    (B) prohibit segregation in public accommodations
    (C) give the federal government the power to pursue school integration
    (D) bar discrimination in employment
    (E) fulfill some of the goals Martin Luther King Jr. outlined when he began his civil rights protests in Birmingham, Alabama

79. The use of writs of assistance by British revenue officers in the American colonies angered colonists because the writs

    (A) were issued without the permission of the Crown
    (B) violated what the colonists considered to be traditional English civil liberties
    (C) required that officials show probable cause for suspicion in order to search or seize property, but colonists believed that probable cause was insufficient justification
    (D) were funded by taxpayers
    (E) were used to impress American colonists into the British Navy

GO ON TO THE NEXT PAGE

UNITED STATES HISTORY TEST—Continued

80. The Agricultural Adjustment Act attempted to do all of the following EXCEPT

    (A) encourage farmers to increase supplies to meet food shortages in the east
    (B) pay farmers to take land out of production
    (C) establish parity pricing
    (D) pay farmers to destroy crops and kill livestock to decrease supply
    (E) raise prices in the farm sector by responding to the imbalance of supply and demand

81. In the late nineteenth century, corporations were created to

    (A) reduce reliance on the federal government, since corporations were not federally regulated
    (B) protect businesses from labor unrest, since corporations welcomed labor unions into their factories
    (C) diffuse individual risk should a business fail, since many stockholders had invested in the industry
    (D) eliminate competition by buying out small businesses engaged in similar types of production
    (E) avoid taxation issues, since corporations, unlike private businesses, were not subject to income taxes

82. All of the following pushed the United States into war with Spain in 1898 EXCEPT

    (A) the Yellow Press
    (B) the Panama Canal Crisis
    (C) the sinking of the USS *Maine*
    (D) Spain's treatment of Cuba
    (E) growing American imperialism

83. "The questions before our country are problems of progress to higher standards; they are not the problems of degeneration. They demand thought and they serve to quicken the conscience and enlist our sense of responsibility for their settlement. And that responsibility rests upon you, my countrymen, as much as upon those of us who have been selected for office. Ours is a land rich in resources; stimulating in its glorious beauty; filled with millions of happy homes; blessed with comfort and opportunity. In no nation are the institutions of progress more advanced. In no nation are the fruits of accomplishment more secure. In no nation is the government more worthy of respect. No country is more loved by its people. I have an abiding faith in their capacity, integrity and high purpose. I have no fears for the future of our country. It is bright with hope."

    The optimism of Herbert Hoover's 1929 inaugural address masked the country's dire problems, which led to the

    (A) Teapot Dome Scandal
    (B) Scopes Trial
    (C) Great Depression
    (D) Immigration Restriction Acts
    (E) execution of Sacco and Vanzetti

84. The Battle of Saratoga in 1777 was a particularly significant military victory for the Americans during the Revolutionary War because it

    (A) ended the war
    (B) convinced France to ally with the colonists
    (C) decimated the British Navy
    (D) led to the signing of the Declaration of Independence
    (E) forced the abdication of King George

85. Theodore Roosevelt's New Nationalism promoted all of the following reforms EXCEPT

    (A) women's suffrage
    (B) recall, initiative, and referendum
    (C) the abolition of child labor
    (D) national presidential primary laws
    (E) desegregation and antilynching legislation

GO ON TO THE NEXT PAGE

UNITED STATES HISTORY TEST—Continued

86. The Pilgrims who settled Plymouth Plantation in 1620 were also known as

    (A) Puritans
    (B) Quakers
    (C) Lutherans
    (D) Separatists
    (E) Antinomians

87. As a result of the 1890 tariff he passed in Congress, William McKinley won the support of

    (A) the Populist Party
    (B) southern farmers
    (C) northern intellectuals
    (D) big business
    (E) social Darwinists

88. Spiro Agnew called Americans who supported the Nixon Administration's handling of the Vietnam War

    (A) loyal Republicans
    (B) the silent majority
    (C) patriotic hawks
    (D) strident anti-communists
    (E) the Christian Coalition

89. In the agricultural sector, the major problem confronting farmers in the 1950s was

    (A) a shortage of supply
    (B) infestation by the boll weevil
    (C) severe drought
    (D) legislation banning pesticides
    (E) falling prices due to overproduction

90. The settlers arriving at Plymouth colony signed the Mayflower Compact primarily because

    (A) their intention in coming to the New World was to create a democratic way of life
    (B) they settled outside the land given them by their charter and needed to create order before they left the *Mayflower*
    (C) they were required by English law to create a viable form of government in the New World that would mirror the government in England
    (D) they could not agree on which person should lead them
    (E) they hoped to abandon the charter that had authorized their voyage and needed a legal document to separate themselves officially from their mother country

S T O P

IF YOU FINISH BEFORE TIME IS CALLED, YOU MAY CHECK YOUR WORK ON THIS TEST ONLY.
DO NOT TURN TO ANY OTHER TEST IN THIS BOOK.

SAT II U.S. History Practice Test 2 Explanations

Calculating Your Score

Question Number	Correct Answer	Right	Wrong	Question Number	Correct Answer	Right	Wrong	Question Number	Correct Answer	Right	Wrong
1.	D			31.	D			61.	C		
2.	C			32.	E			62.	A		
3.	C			33.	A			63.	B		
4.	D			34.	C			64.	B		
5.	B			35.	D			65.	D		
6.	A			36.	C			66.	E		
7.	E			37.	E			67.	B		
8.	D			38.	C			68.	D		
9.	B			39.	B			69.	A		
10.	A			40.	C			70.	B		
11.	B			41.	C			71.	C		
12.	E			42.	A			72.	E		
13.	D			43.	C			73.	B		
14.	D			44.	B			74.	C		
15.	A			45.	E			75.	E		
16.	C			46.	D			76.	D		
17.	A			47.	B			77.	C		
18.	D			48.	D			78.	A		
19.	B			49.	D			79.	B		
20.	C			50.	A			80.	A		
21.	A			51.	B			81.	C		
22.	E			52.	B			82.	B		
23.	C			53.	E			83.	C		
24.	C			54.	D			84.	B		
25.	E			55.	C			85.	E		
26.	C			56.	E			86.	D		
27.	A			57.	C			87.	D		
28.	C			58.	B			88.	B		
29.	D			59.	A			89.	E		
30.	C			60.	C			90.	B		

Your raw score for the SAT II U.S. History test is calculated from the number of questions you answer correctly and incorrectly. Once you have determined your composite score, use the conversion table on page 19 of this book to calculate your scaled score. To calculate your raw score, count the number of questions you answered correctly: _____
$$A$$

Count the number of questions you answered incorrectly, and multiply that number by $\frac{1}{4}$:

$$\underline{}_{B} \times \frac{1}{4} = \underline{}_{C}$$

Subtract the value in field C from value in field A: _____
$$D$$

Round the number in field D to the nearest whole number. This is your raw score: _____
$$E$$

1. **(D)** Industrial Revolution *Trend Question*

Until 1885, American companies paid for the passage of immigrants to the United States, provided that these immigrants work for those companies upon arrival. The Foran Act of 1885 outlawed this practice.

2. **(C)** The 1960s *Trend Question*

The 1960s counterculture was made up of young people who felt alienated by middle-class American society and of antiwar activists who protested American involvement in Vietnam. Antiwar rallies, drug use, rock music, and free love were all prominent aspects of the youth counterculture in the 1960s.

3. **(C)** A New Nation *Fact Question*

The embargo injured the American economy by keeping American ships in port and by stopping all trade with England. The embargo was so detrimental to America's economic interests that Congress repealed it in 1808.

4. **(D)** Civil War & Reconstruction *Quotation Question*

In the Gettysburg Address, Lincoln stated his vision for the rebirth of the country after the Civil War. He believed that American democracy would emerge strengthened from the war.

5. **(B)** World War II *Fact Question*

The Taft-Hartley Act sought to curtail the power of unions by banning certain union practices. Although Congress overrode his veto, Truman's veto of the act won him the support of organized labor during the presidential election of 1948.

6. **(A)** Revolution & Constitution *Fact Question*

The authors of the Constitution thought that the Articles of Confederation, adopted in 1777, gave insufficient power to the federal government. The Constitution, which replaced the Articles in 1789, significantly strengthened the national government and diminished the amount of power given to individual states under the Articles.

7. **(E)** Cultural Trends *Except Question*

Open discussions of abolition were not a prominent aspect of slave life on southern plantations. Such conversations would probably have occurred in private, where they could not be overheard by slaveowners or other whites.

8. **(D)** The Roaring Twenties *Trend Question*

The Scopes Monkey Trial, also known as the "monkey trial," centered on a Tennessee statute that banned the teaching of evolution in public schools. The trial reflected the clash between traditional, fundamentalist beliefs based on the Bible and modern, scientific ways of understanding life and the universe.

9. **(B)** A New Nation *Trend Question*

In the last days of his presidency, Adams hastily appointed a number of Federalists, later called the "midnight judges," to judicial positions in an effort to retain power for the Federalists during the upcoming Republican rule. Adams feared that the next president, Thomas Jefferson, would fill court vacancies with members of his own Republican Party.

10. **(A)** The Great Depression & New Deal *Cartoon Question*

The National Recovery Administration created the Blue Eagle Codes, which dictated prices, working hours, wages, and product standards for American industry. Corporations or companies that agreed to abide by the codes proudly displayed the Blue Eagle poster, demonstrating that they were "doing their part" to assist in economic recovery.

11. **(B)** Industrial Revolution *Cartoon Question*

The Exclusion Act of 1882 prohibited the Chinese from immigrating to America. The act was the first congressional attempt to restrict a particular group from entering the United States

12. **(E)** The 1950s *Fact Question*

From its inception in 1909, the National Association for the Advancement of Colored People (NAACP) vowed to challenge racial segregation. In the 1930s, the NAACP started to bring test cases to the Supreme Court. These cases questioned the validity of the "separate but equal" law in higher education. By the early 1950s, the NAACP had amassed enough evidence to challenge the constitutionality of segregation before the Court, which in the end struck down segregation in public schools in *Brown v. Board of Education*.

13. **(D)** The Age of Jackson *Fact Question*

Jacksonian Democrats united in the wake of what they called "the corrupt bargain of 1824." Jackson won the popular vote in the presidential election of 1824, but he didn't receive a majority of the votes, so the election was thrown into the House of Representatives. Henry Clay, the Speaker of the House, backed John Quincy Adams, who emerged as president. When Adams subsequently made Clay the secretary of state, Jackson's supporters denounced the election as the result of a "corrupt bargain" and decided to split from the Republican Party.

14. **(D)** The Roaring Twenties *Fact Question*

The Harlem Renaissance refers to African-American cultural production during the 1920s. The Renaissance was a predominantly urban phenomenon in which African-American writers, painters, artists, and intellectuals produced new forms of cultural expression that reflected the African-American experience.

15. **(A)** Cultural Trends *Trend Question*

By the middle of the nineteenth century, a sharp distinction arose between the workplace and the home. Women, particularly of the middle class, were increasingly excluded from the paid labor force and expected to stay at home to oversee the domestic sphere.

16. **(C)** Revolution & Constitution *Fact Question*

Two-thirds of each house of Congress or two-thirds of state legislatures must vote to propose a new amendment to the Constitution. Ratification of a proposed amendment requires approval of three-quarters of the state legislatures or three-quarters of the states.

17. **(A)** Westward Expansion & Sectional Strife *Trend Question*

Abraham Lincoln, a Republican, did not campaign for president on an abolitionist platform, but citizens of South Carolina believed that the Republican president posed a threat to the institution of slavery. As a result of this perceived threat, South Carolina seceded from the Union.

18. **(D)** A New Nation *Fact Question*

Until the 1820s, custom duties were the the federal government's major source of revenue.

19. **(B)** The Great Depression & New Deal *Trend Question*

The Congress of Industrial Organizations (CIO) was created to organize all laborers, both skilled and unskilled, within a particular industry. Unlike the American Federation of Labor, which generally opposed the unionization of African Americans and women, the CIO attempted to create broad-based labor unions in various industries. The United Mine Workers, the United Automobile Workers, and the International Ladies Garment Workers Unions were the most prominent early members under the CIO umbrella.

20. **(C)** The Colonial Period *Fact Question*

The French and Indian War was the last of the colonial wars. More American colonies were involved in that conflict than in any of the other wars.

21. **(A)** 1970s–2000 *Fact Question*

In August 1990, Iraq invaded Kuwait. George Bush called for a counterattack to force out the invading Iraqis. In January 1991 the United States started the Gulf War by launching air assaults on Iraqi troops, military bases, and supply lines. Many people believe that the United States got involved in the war to protect American oil interests in Kuwait and Saudi Arabia.

22. **(E)** World War I *Cartoon Question*

Although his former allies paid attention to Wilson out of respect for the United States contribution to World War I, each allied country had its own agenda which conflicted with Wilson's peace plan. The cartoon depicts each nation holding a secret gun that reflects its intentions and prevents "everlasting peace."

23. **(C)** Cultural Trends *Fact Question*

Immigration between 1840 and 1860 significantly increased the populations of major eastern cities such as New York, Boston, and Philadelphia. Other major cities, such as Chicago and St. Louis, also saw their populations rise due to immigration.

24. **(C)** Industrial Revolution *Except Question*

The American Federation of Labor downplayed political involvement and sought harmony between employers and laborers.

25. **(E)** The 1950s *Fact Question*

The Kitchen Debates occurred in 1959, when Vice President Richard Nixon visited Moscow. During the visit, he engaged Russian Premier Nikita Khrushchev in a debate over the relative merits of U.S. and Soviet technology. The debate got its name because it was set against a display of a typical American kitchen.

26. **(C)** A New Nation *Except Question*

Jay's Treaty said nothing about impressment, angering the Anti-federalists. They criticized the Federalists for ratifying a treaty that benefited only American merchants and didn't address the concerns of common sailors who were directly affected by impressment.

27. **(A)** World War I *Trend Question*

During World War I, drinking alcohol was seen as an unpatriotic act. Enjoying alcohol while American soldiers fought in Europe seemed immoral to Americans at home. In addition, the grain saved from not distilling alcohol could be shipped to Europe to feed American soldiers. These moral and practical objections to alcohol during the war helped speed ratification of the Prohibition Amendment.

28. **(C)** The 1960s *Trend Question*

As the Vietnam War escalated between 1965 and 1968, Congress allocated an ever growing amount of money to the war effort, significantly curtailing funding for Johnson's domestic Great Society programs.

29. **(D)** The Great Depression & New Deal *Trend Question*

Hoover articulated his belief in rugged individualism during his 1928 presidential campaign. He argued that Americans possessed the determination to succeed without help from the government. Hoover maintained that providing direct relief to Americans would diminish their ability to survive on their own.

30. **(C)** Civil War & Reconstruction *Fact Question*

Johnson violated the Tenure of Office Act by firing the secretary of war, Edwin Stanton, without Senate approval. Despite the technicality that Abraham Lincoln, not Johnson, had appointed Stanton, the House impeached Johnson for this violation.

31. **(D)** The Age of Jackson *Quotation Question*

Outraged by South Carolina's determination to nullify the Tariff of 1832, Webster lectured Hayne on the problematic nature of nullification. Webster stated that the Union could not exist if each state decided which laws it would adhere to and which it would reject.

32. **(E)** World War II *Fact Question*

In 1939, Albert Einstein informed FDR that nuclear fission could be used to create a bomb. Fearful that Germany was trying to build a similar weapon, FDR secretly authorized J. Robert Oppenheimer to begin work on the Manhattan Project, which ultimately produced an atomic bomb in the summer of 1945.

33. **(A)** The Progressive Era *Fact Question*

Tarbell's exposé on Rockefeller's Standard Oil Trust is a good example of muckraking literature. Tarbell brought to light the corrupt business practices of Rockefeller's monopoly.

34. **(C)** Revolution & Constitution *Except Question*

Impeachment of a president requires a two-thirds vote in the Senate—not a unanimous Senate vote. If less than two-thirds of the Senate votes to impeach, the president remains in office, even if he was successfully impeached by the House.

35. **(D)** A New Nation *Trend Question*

Since the southern states had already paid off their debts, while northern states had not, Hamilton had to offer the south an incentive to accept his assumption plan, under which southern states would essentially pay taxes to help eliminate the debts of northern states. In return for their acceptance of his plan, Hamilton promised the southern states that the permanent site of the nation's capital would be located in the middle of the country, between Virginia and Maryland.

36. **(C)** The 1950s *Trend Question*

In 1954, McCarthy and his chief counsel, Roy Cohn, sought to obtain preferential treatment for Cohn's friend, G. David Shine, who had been drafted into the Army. When he was unsuccessful, McCarthy accused the Army of being infiltrated with communists. The charge and counter-charge led to the nationally televised Army-McCarthy hearings of 1954, which exposed McCarthy's tactics and viciousness to the American public. After the hearings concluded, it became apparent that McCarthy had no viable information about communists in government and that he was merely using the issue to gain political power. He was censured by the Senate in December 1954.

37. **(E)** The Colonial Period   *Fact Question*

The Great Awakening was a revivalist crusade aimed at ridding religion of material distractions and at renewing the individual's bond with God. Jonathan Edwards was one of the leading orators of the Awakening. He frightened his audiences by claiming the unfaithful would suffer eternal damnation and by urging people to repent their sins immediately.

38. **(C)** Westward Expansion & Sectional Strife   *Fact Question*

Thoreau's protest marked the beginning of a new protest tradition in the United States: passive resistance. His tract *On Civil Disobedience* subsequently inspired both Gandhi and Martin Luther King Jr.

39. **(B)** World War I   *Fact Question*

The Zimmerman Telegram was a German attempt to create an alliance with Mexico against the United States. Germany promised to help Mexico recover the land it lost during the Mexican War, as long as the United States was defeated in World War I.

40. **(C)** The Progressive Era   *Cartoon Question*

As the cartoon suggests, Roosevelt hunted down bad trusts and destroyed them, while he placed good trusts under governmental regulation. He believed that all corporations should be regulated by the federal government in order to prevent corrupt business practices, and he dissolved only those monopolies that refused federal regulation.

41. **(C)** Cultural Trends   *Trend Question*

Mann was a great proponent of public school reform. He believed that teachers needed professional training in order to do their jobs well.

42. **(A)** Industrial Revolution   *Except Question*

Washington did not publicly advocate immediate social and political rights for African Americans. Instead, he preached patience and gradualism. He believed that once African Americans proved themselves to be economically vital to the South, political and social equality would follow.

43. **(C)** The Colonial Period   *Trend Question*

In 1691, the loss of the charter for the Massachusetts Bay colony indirectly resulted in the Salem witch trials. Puritans believed the charter's loss occurred because someone in the community had sinned. This belief quickly led to hysteria as the Puritans decided to weed out the "witches," who were a threat to the Puritans' salvation. The witchcraft trials illustrated how rational beliefs could give way to hysteria during a time of instability.

44. **(B)** The Great Depression & New Deal   *Fact Question*

Keynesian economics addressed the imbalance of supply and demand by proposing that the government increase spending and abandon its traditional commitment to a balanced budget. Keynes suggested that massive public works spending would increase purchasing power without increasing supply. This economic theory was proven correct when American preparation for World War II created massive government spending that lifted the country out of depression.

45. **(E)** Industrial Revolution   *Trend Question*

Lavish spending by the wealthy created the image of a Gilded Age in the last years of the nineteenth century.

46. (D) The 1950s — *Except Question*

In *Invisible Man*, Ralph Ellison deals with race relations in America, as he depicts the struggle of a nameless African-American man against a hostile white society. Published in 1952, the novel was critically acclaimed for depicting the African-American experience, and it established Ellison's literary reputation.

47. (B) Westward Expansion & Sectional Strife — *Trend Question*

Stowe's depiction of slavery as a brutal institution, replete with violent masters and oppressed slaves, provided additional propaganda for the abolitionist cause. The book contributed to the increasing sectional tensions of the antebellum era.

48. (D) The Progressive Era — *Trend Question*

In the 1912 election, the Democrat Wilson ran against two Republican candidates: William Howard Taft, the incumbent, ran as a traditional candidate backed by the Republican Party, and Theodore Roosevelt ran as the nominee of the Progressive "Bull Moose" Party. Taft and Roosevelt divided the Republican vote, assisting Wilson's victory.

49. (D) Industrial Revolution — *Fact Question*

William Graham Sumner justified American business practices and laissez-faire government policy by arguing that only the fittest would survive in the natural state of competition. The government, he believed, should not assist businesses or individuals who could not survive on their own, since their extinction was a natural outcome of competition.

50. (A) The 1950s — *Trend Question*

Eisenhower was a hero of World War II—the architect of the D-Day invasion and the general in charge of the European Theater of Operations in World War II. He won both the 1952 and 1956 elections because his military successes made him a popular public figure.

51. (B) The Colonial Period — *Quotation Question*

Bacon organized his rebellion in response to frequent Native-American attacks on farmers in the Piedmont region and to Governor Berkeley's failure to protect the poor farmers there. Bacon accused Berkeley of purposely ignoring the plight of these farmers in order to maintain a profitable commercial relationship with the Native Americans.

52. (B) The Great Depression & New Deal — *Fact Question*

Section 7A of the National Recovery Act (NRA) ensured labor's right to collective bargaining with employers. When the NRA was declared unconstitutional, Congress passed the Wagner Act to reinstate labor's collective bargaining rights. The Wagner Act also established the National Labor Relations Board to mediate future labor disputes.

53. (E) Industrial Revolution — *Fact Question*

Bellamy envisioned a utopian future in which socialism would replace the misery he associated with capitalism and industrialization. Bellamy dreamed of a society free of inequities and class divisions, and hoped that all citizens would work for the common good.

54. **(D)** World War II   *Except Question*

In 1941, FDR continued to be cautious about U.S. intervention in World War II. Recognizing the seriousness of the situation in Europe and the likelihood that public opinion would soon favor U.S. involvement, he created the Lend-Lease plan (A), which lent $54 billion to Britain and Russia. He also ordered U.S. troops to Greenland (B) and American ships to Atlantic sea lanes in order to warn Britain of German submarines (E). The Atlantic Charter (C), with its emphasis on the self-determination of nations, the freedom of the seas, and a postwar security apparatus, expressed the democratic ideals of the arsenal of democracy. The Manhattan Project (D) was not part of FDR's arsenal of democracy.

55. **(C)** Cultural Trends   *Fact Question*

The Oneida community practiced communal marriage based on the philosophy that free love was both pleasurable and necessary for everyone's mental health.

56. **(E)** Revolution & Constitution   *Quotation Question*

Known as the elastic clause because of the flexibility it gives Congress, this passage was a major point of contention at the time it was created. For those who supported a strong federal government, the elastic clause gave Congress the power to do whatever was in the best interests of the nation. For those who supported state rights over federal rights, it represented a dangerous expansion of federal authority.

57. **(C)** Westward Expansion & Sectional Strife   *Trend Question*

John Calhoun argued that the Constitution guaranteed U.S. citizens occupying territories the same rights they had possessed in their former states. Accordingly, he argued, since southerners were allowed to own slaves in their states, the Constitution permitted them to keep their slave property when they relocated to new territories.

58. **(B)** The 1960s   *Fact Question*

Kennedy practiced flexible response because he understood that the United States could not react to every instance of communist aggression. Under flexible response, Kennedy responded only to the events that posed the greatest threats to American interests, such as the Cuban Missile Crisis of 1962. He created an elite fighting force, the Green Berets, which could be deployed anywhere around the world to combat communism.

59. **(A)** Revolution & Constitution   *Trend Question*

The committee successfully argued that Jefferson should delete his attack on slavery from the Declaration in order to preserve unity among the colonies. Jefferson acquiesced, although this incident marked the beginning of his ambivalence about slavery's existence and morality.

60. **(C)** Industrial Revolution   *Trend Question*

Pro-business sentiment dominated Congress during the second half of the nineteenth century. Most legislation passed by Congress tended to be in favor of industry, although Congress did pass some regulatory laws, such as the Interstate Commerce Act of 1887 and the Sherman Antitrust Act of 1890—but these acts were largely ineffective.

61. **(C)** World War II   *Trend Question*

The Truman Doctrine of 1947 initiated the policy of containment, which was designed to counter the spread of Soviet communism beyond boundaries established by the Allies at Yalta. Truman first announced his "doctrine" in an address to Congress in March 1947, when he requested funds to bolster the democratic governments of Greece and Turkey against Soviet influence.

62. (A) Civil War & Reconstruction — *Trend Question*

The Fourteenth Amendment defined U.S. citizens as individuals born or naturalized in the United States. It protected citizens from any attempt by a state to "abridge the privileges or immunities of citizens" and guaranteed all citizens "due process of law" and "equal protection of the laws."

63. (B) The Colonial Period — *Trend Question*

England established the Navigation Acts in order to profit from colonial trade. The Navigation Acts specified what goods could be shipped in and out of the colonies; taxed all imports to the colonies; and restricted trade with English and English colonial ports to English or English colonial ships.

64. (B) Industrial Revolution — *Fact Question*

In 1887, Congress created the Interstate Commerce Commission to regulate the railroads. Although the commission was largely ineffective in its early years because of pro-business sentiment among its members, it became a major regulatory force in the twentieth century.

65. (D) World War II — *Trend Question*

American diplomats continued to negotiate with Japan throughout 1941, up until the attack on Pearl Harbor. The Japanese government demanded recognition as the major economic power in Asia, but the United States stated that such recognition violated the Open Door Policy. The talks continued, despite Secretary of State Cordell Hull's warning that hostilities might break out at any time.

66. (E) Cultural Trends — *Trend Question*

Folktales allowed slaves to talk openly about their plight and to tell stories in which the weak and oppressed eventually overcome their masters. They told these stories as children's tales to hide the fact that they were mocking the plantation owners.

67. (B) Revolution & Constitution — *Trend Question*

The French and Indian War drained the resources of the English treasury. Grenville was desperate to raise revenue for England, so he levied additional taxes on the colonies, arguing they had not done their fair share to finance the war.

68. (D) Westward Expansion & Sectional Strife — *Except Question*

Neither Maryland nor North Carolina abolished slavery as a result of Turner's insurrection, although Virginia did debate the abolition of slavery after the revolt.

69. (A) Industrial Revolution — *Trend Question*

After gaining control of the Illinois legislature, the Grangers passed legislation designed to control the railroads. The *Munn* ruling validated their legislation because it declared that any business affecting the public could be regulated by government.

70. (B) The Colonial Period — *Fact Question*

Robert Walpole, the prime minister of England from 1721 to 1742, instituted a policy of salutary neglect, allowing the American colonies to trade without subjection to the Navigation Acts. Walpole had two main motives for implementing this policy: one, the American colonies made substantial profits for England; two, Walpole wanted to win the colonists' support for England in case France challenged England for control of North America.

71. **(C)** The 1960s *Fact Question*

A. Philip Randolph had threatened to march on Washington, D.C., several times during the 1940s. His first threat forced FDR to desegregate the defense industries, and his second threat prodded Harry Truman to integrate the armed forces. In 1963, Randolph finally acted on his threat: approximately 250,000 people marched on the capital to support the Civil Rights Act proposed by JFK and to demand jobs and economic opportunity. Martin Luther King Jr. (A) delivered his stirring "I Have a Dream" speech at the march.

72. **(E)** The Colonial Period *Except Question*

The cost of purchasing African slaves was low throughout the seventeenth century. The low cost was one of the reasons why planters formalized the slave-based labor system in the mid-1600s.

73. **(B)** Civil War & Reconstruction *Trend Question*

At the conclusion of the Civil War, Congress was determined to redress the balance of power between itself (the legislative branch) and the president (the executive branch). Congress struggled with Lincoln to gain control of Reconstruction policy, with members of Congress accusing Lincoln of being too lenient on the former Confederate states.

74. **(C)** The 1950s *Quotation Question*

This excerpt is from the Supreme Court's ruling in *Brown v. Board of Education*, 1954. *Brown* was the landmark case that overturned *Plessy v. Ferguson*, 1896, and integrated public schools in the United States.

75. **(E)** World War I *Trend Question*

Wilson viewed the outbreak of World War I as a tragic mistake and wanted the United States to remain neutral. In January 1917, Wilson proposed his "peace without victory" plan, hoping to negotiate a peaceful, diplomatic resolution to the war.

76. **(D)** The Age of Jackson *Trend Question*

Arguing that the Constitution limited his powers, Jackson vetoed federal funding for the Maysville Road in Kentucky. In his veto message, he suggested that if Congress wanted him to approve such funding, it would first need to amend the Constitution to give him the power to do so. Jackson's veto was partially motivated by his hatred of Henry Clay, who stood to benefit from the completion of the road in his home state.

77. **(C)** Westward Expansion & Sectional Strife *Fact Question*

The slogan expressed Americans' determination to acquire the Oregon territory, up to the 54°40' north latitude line, as part of James K. Polk's plans for westward expansion.

78. **(A)** The 1960s *Except Question*

The 1964 Civil Rights Act did not specifically address the voting rights of African Americans. Both Martin Luther King Jr. and Lyndon Johnson devoted the following year to resolving that issue. The 1964 bill did eliminate segregation nationally in all public places (B), while it also took firm stands against employment discrimination (D) and school integration (C). Taken as a whole, it opened up American society to blacks, fulfilling some of the goals King had outlined in Birmingham in 1963 (E).

79. **(B)** The Colonial Period *Trend Question*

The British Parliament legalized the use of writs of assistance during the French and Indian War. These writs were general search warrants that allowed British officials to search colonial buildings and ships believed to contain smuggled goods. The officials were not required to show probable cause for suspicion before conducting their searches. The use of writs angered the colonists, who believed the writs infringed upon their civil liberties.

80. **(A)** The Great Depression & New Deal *Except Question*

Despite widespread hunger in the northeast, the Agricultural Adjustment Act did not recommend that farmers increase levels of production. Although this policy was perceived as inhumane at the time, it would have run counter to the agency's attempt to balance supply and demand in the farm sector.

81. **(C)** Industrial Revolution *Trend Question*

Corporations allowed industrialists to accumulate vast amounts of capital through sales of stock while avoiding individual financial liability in case the corporations failed.

82. **(B)** The Age of Imperialism *Except Question*

The Panama Canal was built in the early twentieth century, after the conclusion of the 1898 Spanish-American War (which lasted for only two months). The crisis over the canal occurred in 1903 and resulted in Panama's independence from Columbia.

83. **(C)** The Roaring Twenties *Quotation Question*

Less than a year after Hoover's inaugural address, in which he proudly proclaimed the economic health of the country, the stock market crashed, and the country entered an extended period of economic depression. Despite his optimism, Hoover was blamed for the financial chaos.

84. **(B)** Revolution & Constitution *Trend Question*

The victory over the British at Saratoga convinced the French that the colonists could defeat the British and win their independence. In February 1778, France entered into an alliance with America, and five months later France declared war on England.

85. **(E)** The Progressive Era *Except Question*

Despite his progressive tendencies, Theodore Roosevelt was not a civil rights champion. He never took a strong position on African-American equality. Desegregation and antilynching laws were not an aspect of his New Nationalist platform.

86. **(D)** The Colonial Period *Fact Question*

The Pilgrims belonged to a religious sect known as Separatists. After they settled in Massachusetts, they were called "pilgrims" because they believed they had made the spiritual and physical journey to salvation.

87. **(D)** Industrial Revolution *Trend Question*

The protective McKinley Tariff of 1890 raised the price of imports by almost fifty percent. McKinley won the support of business interests after he negotiated the passage of this tariff. The large contributions he received from John D. Rockefeller and J. P. Morgan helped him win the 1896 presidential election.

88. **(B)** 1970s–2000 *Fact Question*

Agnew called supporters of Nixon's Vietnam policy the silent majority in order to contrast them with what he deemed the vocal minority of antiwar protesters. He wanted to persuade Americans that most people continued to support U.S. involvement in Vietnam during the early 1970s.

89. **(E)** The 1950s *Trend Question*

During the 1950s, farmers saw crop prices drop due to overproduction. This trend severely impeded farmers' ability to profit from crop production, and the government was forced to renew farm subsidies in 1956.

90. **(B)** The Colonial Period *Trend Question*

Misnavigation and bad weather forced the *Mayflower* off course. When the Pilgrims landed outside of the area designated by their royal charter, they feared they did not have the authority to settle the land. In order to prevent chaos during the early years of settlement, they drafted the Mayflower Compact, which laid claim to the land and established a rudimentary form of government.

SAT II U.S. History Practice Test 3

UNITED STATES HISTORY TEST 3 ANSWER SHEET

1. Ⓐ Ⓑ Ⓒ Ⓓ Ⓔ	31. Ⓐ Ⓑ Ⓒ Ⓓ Ⓔ	61. Ⓐ Ⓑ Ⓒ Ⓓ Ⓔ
2. Ⓐ Ⓑ Ⓒ Ⓓ Ⓔ	32. Ⓐ Ⓑ Ⓒ Ⓓ Ⓔ	62. Ⓐ Ⓑ Ⓒ Ⓓ Ⓔ
3. Ⓐ Ⓑ Ⓒ Ⓓ Ⓔ	33. Ⓐ Ⓑ Ⓒ Ⓓ Ⓔ	63. Ⓐ Ⓑ Ⓒ Ⓓ Ⓔ
4. Ⓐ Ⓑ Ⓒ Ⓓ Ⓔ	34. Ⓐ Ⓑ Ⓒ Ⓓ Ⓔ	64. Ⓐ Ⓑ Ⓒ Ⓓ Ⓔ
5. Ⓐ Ⓑ Ⓒ Ⓓ Ⓔ	35. Ⓐ Ⓑ Ⓒ Ⓓ Ⓔ	65. Ⓐ Ⓑ Ⓒ Ⓓ Ⓔ
6. Ⓐ Ⓑ Ⓒ Ⓓ Ⓔ	36. Ⓐ Ⓑ Ⓒ Ⓓ Ⓔ	66. Ⓐ Ⓑ Ⓒ Ⓓ Ⓔ
7. Ⓐ Ⓑ Ⓒ Ⓓ Ⓔ	37. Ⓐ Ⓑ Ⓒ Ⓓ Ⓔ	67. Ⓐ Ⓑ Ⓒ Ⓓ Ⓔ
8. Ⓐ Ⓑ Ⓒ Ⓓ Ⓔ	38. Ⓐ Ⓑ Ⓒ Ⓓ Ⓔ	68. Ⓐ Ⓑ Ⓒ Ⓓ Ⓔ
9. Ⓐ Ⓑ Ⓒ Ⓓ Ⓔ	39. Ⓐ Ⓑ Ⓒ Ⓓ Ⓔ	69. Ⓐ Ⓑ Ⓒ Ⓓ Ⓔ
10. Ⓐ Ⓑ Ⓒ Ⓓ Ⓔ	40. Ⓐ Ⓑ Ⓒ Ⓓ Ⓔ	70. Ⓐ Ⓑ Ⓒ Ⓓ Ⓔ
11. Ⓐ Ⓑ Ⓒ Ⓓ Ⓔ	41. Ⓐ Ⓑ Ⓒ Ⓓ Ⓔ	71. Ⓐ Ⓑ Ⓒ Ⓓ Ⓔ
12. Ⓐ Ⓑ Ⓒ Ⓓ Ⓔ	42. Ⓐ Ⓑ Ⓒ Ⓓ Ⓔ	72. Ⓐ Ⓑ Ⓒ Ⓓ Ⓔ
13. Ⓐ Ⓑ Ⓒ Ⓓ Ⓔ	43. Ⓐ Ⓑ Ⓒ Ⓓ Ⓔ	73. Ⓐ Ⓑ Ⓒ Ⓓ Ⓔ
14. Ⓐ Ⓑ Ⓒ Ⓓ Ⓔ	44. Ⓐ Ⓑ Ⓒ Ⓓ Ⓔ	74. Ⓐ Ⓑ Ⓒ Ⓓ Ⓔ
15. Ⓐ Ⓑ Ⓒ Ⓓ Ⓔ	45. Ⓐ Ⓑ Ⓒ Ⓓ Ⓔ	75. Ⓐ Ⓑ Ⓒ Ⓓ Ⓔ
16. Ⓐ Ⓑ Ⓒ Ⓓ Ⓔ	46. Ⓐ Ⓑ Ⓒ Ⓓ Ⓔ	76. Ⓐ Ⓑ Ⓒ Ⓓ Ⓔ
17. Ⓐ Ⓑ Ⓒ Ⓓ Ⓔ	47. Ⓐ Ⓑ Ⓒ Ⓓ Ⓔ	77. Ⓐ Ⓑ Ⓒ Ⓓ Ⓔ
18. Ⓐ Ⓑ Ⓒ Ⓓ Ⓔ	48. Ⓐ Ⓑ Ⓒ Ⓓ Ⓔ	78. Ⓐ Ⓑ Ⓒ Ⓓ Ⓔ
19. Ⓐ Ⓑ Ⓒ Ⓓ Ⓔ	49. Ⓐ Ⓑ Ⓒ Ⓓ Ⓔ	79. Ⓐ Ⓑ Ⓒ Ⓓ Ⓔ
20. Ⓐ Ⓑ Ⓒ Ⓓ Ⓔ	50. Ⓐ Ⓑ Ⓒ Ⓓ Ⓔ	80. Ⓐ Ⓑ Ⓒ Ⓓ Ⓔ
21. Ⓐ Ⓑ Ⓒ Ⓓ Ⓔ	51. Ⓐ Ⓑ Ⓒ Ⓓ Ⓔ	81. Ⓐ Ⓑ Ⓒ Ⓓ Ⓔ
22. Ⓐ Ⓑ Ⓒ Ⓓ Ⓔ	52. Ⓐ Ⓑ Ⓒ Ⓓ Ⓔ	82. Ⓐ Ⓑ Ⓒ Ⓓ Ⓔ
23. Ⓐ Ⓑ Ⓒ Ⓓ Ⓔ	53. Ⓐ Ⓑ Ⓒ Ⓓ Ⓔ	83. Ⓐ Ⓑ Ⓒ Ⓓ Ⓔ
24. Ⓐ Ⓑ Ⓒ Ⓓ Ⓔ	54. Ⓐ Ⓑ Ⓒ Ⓓ Ⓔ	84. Ⓐ Ⓑ Ⓒ Ⓓ Ⓔ
25. Ⓐ Ⓑ Ⓒ Ⓓ Ⓔ	55. Ⓐ Ⓑ Ⓒ Ⓓ Ⓔ	85. Ⓐ Ⓑ Ⓒ Ⓓ Ⓔ
26. Ⓐ Ⓑ Ⓒ Ⓓ Ⓔ	56. Ⓐ Ⓑ Ⓒ Ⓓ Ⓔ	86. Ⓐ Ⓑ Ⓒ Ⓓ Ⓔ
27. Ⓐ Ⓑ Ⓒ Ⓓ Ⓔ	57. Ⓐ Ⓑ Ⓒ Ⓓ Ⓔ	87. Ⓐ Ⓑ Ⓒ Ⓓ Ⓔ
28. Ⓐ Ⓑ Ⓒ Ⓓ Ⓔ	58. Ⓐ Ⓑ Ⓒ Ⓓ Ⓔ	88. Ⓐ Ⓑ Ⓒ Ⓓ Ⓔ
29. Ⓐ Ⓑ Ⓒ Ⓓ Ⓔ	59. Ⓐ Ⓑ Ⓒ Ⓓ Ⓔ	89. Ⓐ Ⓑ Ⓒ Ⓓ Ⓔ
30. Ⓐ Ⓑ Ⓒ Ⓓ Ⓔ	60. Ⓐ Ⓑ Ⓒ Ⓓ Ⓔ	90. Ⓐ Ⓑ Ⓒ Ⓓ Ⓔ

UNITED STATES HISTORY TEST 3

Directions: Each of the questions or incomplete statements below is followed by five suggested answers or completions. Select the one that is best in each case and then fill in the corresponding oval on the answer sheet.

1. The disagreement between the Federalists and the Anti-federalists over the establishment of the First Bank of the United States centered on their

    (A) differing tax policies
    (B) opposite views on debt restructuring
    (C) sectional allegiances
    (D) interpretations of the Constitution
    (E) aspirations to run for president

2. In 1848, the Treaty of Guadalupe Hidalgo resulted in the

    (A) Cuban Missile Crisis
    (B) end of the Spanish-American War
    (C) annexation of Texas as a free state
    (D) acquisition by the United States of Texas, New Mexico, and California from Mexico
    (E) Mexican War

3. The 1894 Pullman strike was instigated by

    (A) Eugene Debs
    (B) Samuel Gompers
    (C) Edward Bellamy
    (D) W. E. B. Du Bois
    (E) the Grangers

4. The first African captives brought to the New World landed in 1619 at

    (A) Boston
    (B) Jamestown
    (C) Charleston
    (D) Plymouth
    (E) Newport

5. Attendees of the Seneca Falls Convention issued

    (A) the Declaration of Independence
    (B) the Fourteen Points
    (C) the Atlantic Charter
    (D) a report called *To Secure These Rights*
    (E) the Declaration of Sentiments

6. "But the character of every act depends upon the circumstances in which it is done. The most stringent protection of free speech would not protect a man in falsely shouting fire in a theatre and causing a panic. It does not even protect a man from an injunction against uttering words that may have all the effect of force. The question in every case is whether the words used are used in such circumstances and are of such a nature as to create clear and present danger that they will bring about the substantive evils that Congress has a right to prevent. It is a question of proximity and degree."

    In this decision, the Supreme Court ruled that

    (A) draft resistance was constitutionally permissible in times of war
    (B) socialism was a threat to the country and was unconstitutional
    (C) civil liberties could be restricted in times of national crisis
    (D) the right to free speech was inviolable
    (E) protests against American involvement in war were treasonous

7. In vetoing the recharter of the Second Bank of the United States, Andrew Jackson made all of the following arguments EXCEPT

    (A) the bank was an illegal monopoly
    (B) he had no power to support the recharter
    (C) the Constitution did not give Congress explicit power to create a bank
    (D) the bank benefited only wealthy citizens
    (E) the bank was an unconstitutional extension of the federal government

GO ON TO THE NEXT PAGE

UNITED STATES HISTORY TEST—*Continued*

8. In one of its first efforts to exert control over the colonies, Britain issued the Proclamation of 1763, which

    (A) levied a series of heavy internal taxes
    (B) prohibited the colonies from engaging in internal trade
    (C) took away all the corporate charters and replaced them with royal governors
    (D) drew a line at the Appalachian mountains beyond which only Native Americans could live
    (E) abolished slavery in New England

9. Which immigrant group was most prominently associated with building the first transcontinental railroad in the United States?

    (A) The Chinese
    (B) The Irish
    (C) The English
    (D) The Germans
    (E) The French

10. All of the following were border states during the Civil War EXCEPT

    (A) Delaware
    (B) Pennsylvania
    (C) Maryland
    (D) Kentucky
    (E) Missouri

11. The Mayflower Compact implied that

    (A) the British monarchy would never be overthrown
    (B) a class system would rapidly develop in Plymouth
    (C) England could not revoke the Pilgrims' charter
    (D) a government's authority emanates directly from the consent of the governed
    (E) only whites could be members of Plymouth society

12. Which of the following best characterizes mainstream American life in the 1950s?

    (A) Interest in societal change
    (B) Renewed participation in politics
    (C) Conformity and conservatism
    (D) Interest in reformist causes
    (E) The existence of dual income families

13. In 1906, the Interstate Commerce Commission was given the power to

    (A) desegregate interstate public transportation
    (B) integrate the railroad industry into a government monopoly
    (C) set maximum railroad rates
    (D) seize any private land for new railway tracks
    (E) oversee intrastate transportation

14. American colonists opposed the 1764 Sugar Act, arguing that

    (A) the act benefited England at the expense of the colonies
    (B) the act failed to stop the smuggling of foreign sugar
    (C) enforcement of the act would be nearly impossible
    (D) the act deprived the colonies of self-government
    (E) the passage of the act was illegal, since the colonies did not have a representative in Parliament

15. The Compromise of 1850 included all of the following provisions EXCEPT

    (A) a strengthened fugitive slave law
    (B) California's admission to the Union as a free state
    (C) the federal government's assumption of Texas's debt
    (D) New Mexico's admission to the Union as a slave state
    (E) the outlaw of the slave trade in Washington, D.C.

16. John D. Rockefeller created the Standard Oil Company of Ohio in order to control the process of oil refining in the United States. By controlling one aspect of the oil business, he was practicing

    (A) social Darwinism
    (B) horizontal integration
    (C) corporate consistency
    (D) debt restructuring
    (E) rugged individualism

GO ON TO THE NEXT PAGE

UNITED STATES HISTORY TEST—Continued

17. The three principal types of colonies created in America were

   I. self-governing
   II. autonomous
   III. royal
   IV. participatory
   V. proprietary

   (A) I and V only
   (B) I, II, and V
   (C) II, III, and V
   (D) I, III, and V
   (E) I, III, and IV

18. One of the United States' primary motivations for fighting in the Korean War was to

   (A) demonstrate American military power to the Soviet Union
   (B) assist the Chinese government, which the United States supported
   (C) prove to Joseph McCarthy that there were no communists in the U.S. Armed Forces
   (D) increase public morale after the Vietnam War
   (E) contain the spread of communism from North Korea to South Korea

19. Between 1860 and 1890, the majority of newly arrived immigrants in the West were

   (A) eastern Europeans
   (B) northern and western Europeans
   (C) Chinese
   (D) Jews
   (E) Africans

20. The willingness of the United States to sign the Kellogg-Briand Pact of 1928 indicated

   (A) the prevailing mood of isolationism in the country
   (B) a desire to work closely with the League of Nations
   (C) Republican intentions to remain actively involved in European affairs
   (D) a determination to reengage the Open Door policy in China
   (E) a commitment to begin colonization on the African continent

21. The Yalta Agreements contained all of the following EXCEPT

   (A) a Soviet promise to enter the war against Japan
   (B) a Soviet pledge to let Britain and America govern Germany after the war
   (C) a recognition of Soviet claims in eastern Europe and Asia
   (D) free elections in Poland
   (E) a plan for the establishment of the United Nations

UNITED STATES HISTORY TEST—Continued

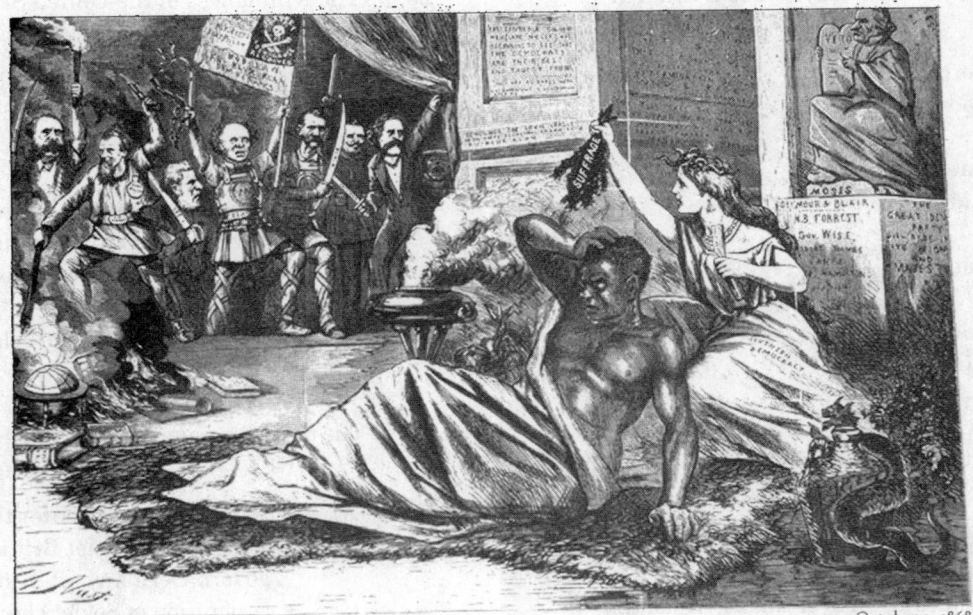

October 3, 1868

22. To which aspect of Reconstruction does the cartoon above refer?

   (A) The emphasis on education for African Americans
   (B) The return to white supremacy
   (C) The renewal of the Freedmen's Bureau
   (D) The beginning of sharecropping
   (E) The birth of the Ku Klux Klan

UNITED STATES HISTORY TEST—Continued

23. "We meet in the midst of a nation brought to the verge of moral, political and material ruin. Corruption dominates the ballot-box.... The people are demoralized ... public opinion silenced ... homes covered with mortgages, labor impoverished, and the land concentrating in the hands of capitalists. The fruits of the toils of millions are boldly stolen to build up colossal fortunes for a few, unprecedented in the history of mankind.... From the same prolific womb of governmental injustice we breed the two great classes—tramps and millionaires."

    This preamble best represents the political philosophy of the

    (A) Anti-federalists
    (B) Progressives
    (C) Populists
    (D) New Deal coalition
    (E) mugwumps

24. The native population in Spanish America was decimated by

    (A) wars with Spain over the conquest of land
    (B) starvation
    (C) climatic changes
    (D) diseases brought from Europe
    (E) enslavement and relocation in Europe

25. Up until the War of 1812, the United States and England clashed over the issue of

    (A) impressment
    (B) tariff policy
    (C) debt restructuring
    (D) determining the Canadian-American border
    (E) navigating of the Mississippi River

26. The "positive good" justification for the continuation of slavery in the United States held that

    (A) the American economy was expanding tremendously due to slavery and that the north and west would soon use slaves as their main source of labor
    (B) slavery was superior to free labor in terms of sheer profits
    (C) slavery afforded whites the leisure time befitting their elite status and was thus central to southern culture
    (D) the total absence of slave rebellions indicated that the system was the best possible way to maintain a labor force
    (E) slavery served an important function in civilizing "inferior" people who could not survive in American society on their own

27. The Open Door policy in China

    (A) gave the United States exclusive trading rights with the Chinese
    (B) was greeted with enthusiasm by European imperial powers
    (C) gave China "most favored nation" trading status
    (D) allowed the United States to combat Chinese communism
    (E) tried to open the Chinese markets to American business

28. The American public generally believed governmental assurances that the United States was winning the Vietnam war until the

    (A) bombing of Cambodia
    (B) Tet Offensive
    (C) My Lai incident
    (D) Battle of Dienbienphu
    (E) Tonkin Gulf incident

29. Which of the following novels captured the Depression's impact on farmers who lost their land and headed west in search of employment?

    (A) *The Grapes of Wrath*
    (B) *On The Road*
    (C) *The Sun Also Rises*
    (D) *Invisible Man*
    (E) *The Promise of American Life*

GO ON TO THE NEXT PAGE

UNITED STATES HISTORY TEST—Continued

30. The Ostend Manifesto found widespread southern support because it

    (A) proposed that the United States acquire Cuba and make it a slave state
    (B) prohibited abolitionist propaganda from being distributed in the slaveholding states
    (C) opposed California's admission to the Union as a free state
    (D) proposed the expansion of slavery to northern states
    (E) strengthened the Fugitive Slave Law of 1850

31. The Tenure of Office Act of 1867

    (A) restricted a sitting president from serving more than two consecutive terms
    (B) limited the power Supreme Court justices who had been censured by the Senate
    (C) gave Senators and Congressmen immunity from prosecution when engaged in debates over controversial issues
    (D) prohibited a president from removing any government official who had been confirmed by the Senate without first getting Senate approval
    (E) extended the length of a Senator's term from four years to six

32. W. E. B. Du Bois argued that African Americans

    (A) deserved the same educational opportunities as whites
    (B) would use their vocational training to secure economic independence from the white community
    (C) should try to integrate gradually into American society
    (D) should serve in segregated units of the Armed Forces
    (E) should return to Africa and create an independent nation there

33. As he wrote the Declaration of Independence, Thomas Jefferson was heavily influenced by which of the following thinkers?

    (A) Georg Hegel
    (B) Immanuel Kant
    (C) Jean Jacques Rousseau
    (D) John Locke
    (E) Thomas Hobbes

34. All of the following were prominent literary works of the mid-nineteenth century EXCEPT

    (A) *Moby-Dick*
    (B) *Walden*
    (C) *The Deerslayer*
    (D) *Leaves of Grass*
    (E) *The Jungle*

35. Although farmers won a substantial victory over the railroads when the Supreme Court ruled that state governments could regulate businesses that affected the public interest, they were subsequently disappointed when

    (A) railroads ignored the regulating legislation and continued to exploit them
    (B) politicians in the employ of the railroads subverted the legislation's language
    (C) Republican presidents vetoed legislation intended to curb the railroads' excesses
    (D) the Supreme Court modified its ruling, restoring Congress' power to oversee interstate commerce
    (E) railroads ceased operating in those areas where regulation was prohibiting them from operating freely

36. The Boston Tea Party resulted directly in the

    (A) repeal of the Tea Act
    (B) Boston Massacre
    (C) signing of the Declaration of Independence
    (D) Coercive Acts
    (E) Declaratory Act

37. Harry Truman's veto of the Taft-Hartley Act won him the allegiance of

    (A) African Americans
    (B) women
    (C) southerners
    (D) businessmen
    (E) organized labor

GO ON TO THE NEXT PAGE

38. J. P. Morgan decided to reorganize the railroad industry in the 1890s based on all of the following beliefs EXCEPT

    (A) wasteful competition had impeded profits
    (B) consolidation would streamline management decisions
    (C) consolidation would result in lower freight rates
    (D) the acquisition of personal power was not a factor in business decisions
    (E) investment banks were more effective in supplying capital than the federal government was

39. The expression "last to be hired, first to be fired" refers to which group of Americans during the Depression?

    (A) Women
    (B) Irish
    (C) African Americans
    (D) Catholics
    (E) Jews

40. The northern colonies did not develop a reliance on African slavery to the same degree that southern colonies did because

    (A) racism did not permeate New England society
    (B) the terrain in the north was not conducive to large-scale plantation agriculture
    (C) northerners found the slave trade to be inhumane and uncivilized
    (D) Africans could not survive the cold temperatures of New England winters
    (E) antislavery activists prevented the importation of slaves in the north by forcing colonial governments to pass laws prohibiting slavery

41. A major difference between Theodore Roosevelt and Woodrow Wilson was that

    (A) Roosevelt was a trust buster, while Wilson appreciated the monopolies' contribution to the American economy
    (B) Roosevelt believed some trusts were vital to the economy, while Wilson wanted to dissolve all of them to restore free competition to the economy
    (C) Roosevelt rejected women's suffrage, while Wilson supported it
    (D) Roosevelt sought to overhaul the banking system, while Wilson advocated keeping it intact
    (E) Roosevelt advocated price supports for farmers, while Wilson wanted the marketplace to dictate prices

42. The Know-Nothings advocated

    (A) educational reform
    (B) religious evangelicalism
    (C) labor unrest
    (D) American missionary volunteerism
    (E) American nativism

43. The number of slaves in the south rose significantly after 1790 as a result of

    (A) greater demand for tobacco in Europe
    (B) the invention of the cotton gin
    (C) the closing of the Atlantic slave trade
    (D) the repeal of the tax on slaves
    (E) the abolition of slavery in the northern states

44. The investigation into the Alger Hiss case led to Hiss's

    (A) defection to the Soviet Union
    (B) acquittal on all charges
    (C) conviction for perjury
    (D) election to the New York legislature
    (E) deportation to the Soviet Union

45. By 1700, all of the following colonies were considered part of New England EXCEPT

    (A) New Hampshire
    (B) New York
    (C) Massachusetts
    (D) Connecticut
    (E) Rhode Island

46. The Works Progress Administration did all of the following EXCEPT

    (A) increase the purchasing power of some people receiving government relief
    (B) grant workers the right to join unions and to engage in collective bargaining
    (C) help lower unemployment levels between 1935 and 1937
    (D) employ people on federal building projects
    (E) commission works of art

47. Which of the following groups would be most sympathetic to this depiction of Andrew Jackson's presidency?

   (A) Republicans
   (B) Federalists
   (C) Southern Democrats
   (D) Masons
   (E) Whigs

48. In the late nineteenth century, advocates of the Social Gospel argued that

   (A) a return to evangelical religion was necessary to cure the immorality that resulted from industrialization
   (B) Christians, through their churches, were obligated to help the poor
   (C) the wealthy deserved their success and should not be condemned for it
   (D) industrialists had an obligation to provide educational opportunities for other Americans
   (E) hard work, honesty, and some luck could make anyone wealthy and successful

49. Herbert Hoover's response to the economic depression was characterized by

   (A) an unwavering belief in the resilience of free markets
   (B) a focus on giving assistance to individual Americans
   (C) the establishment of public works programs
   (D) denial of the depression
   (E) an emphasis on business recovery over public relief

50. The Intolerable Acts of 1774 mandated all of the following EXCEPT

   (A) the restructuring of the Massachusetts government with more power given to the Crown
   (B) the closing of the port of Boston
   (C) the authorization of the housing (quartering) of British troops in the homes of private citizens
   (D) the transfer of the trials of British soldiers accused of murder to England
   (E) the seizure of the Massachusetts charter

51. The executions of Sacco and Vanzetti in 1927 signified that

   (A) the fear of anarchy permeated the United States in the 1920s
   (B) draft resistance had become a capital offense
   (C) the Ku Klux Klan had far-reaching political influence
   (D) the United States would not tolerate espionage during times of war
   (E) illegal immigration would be stopped at all costs

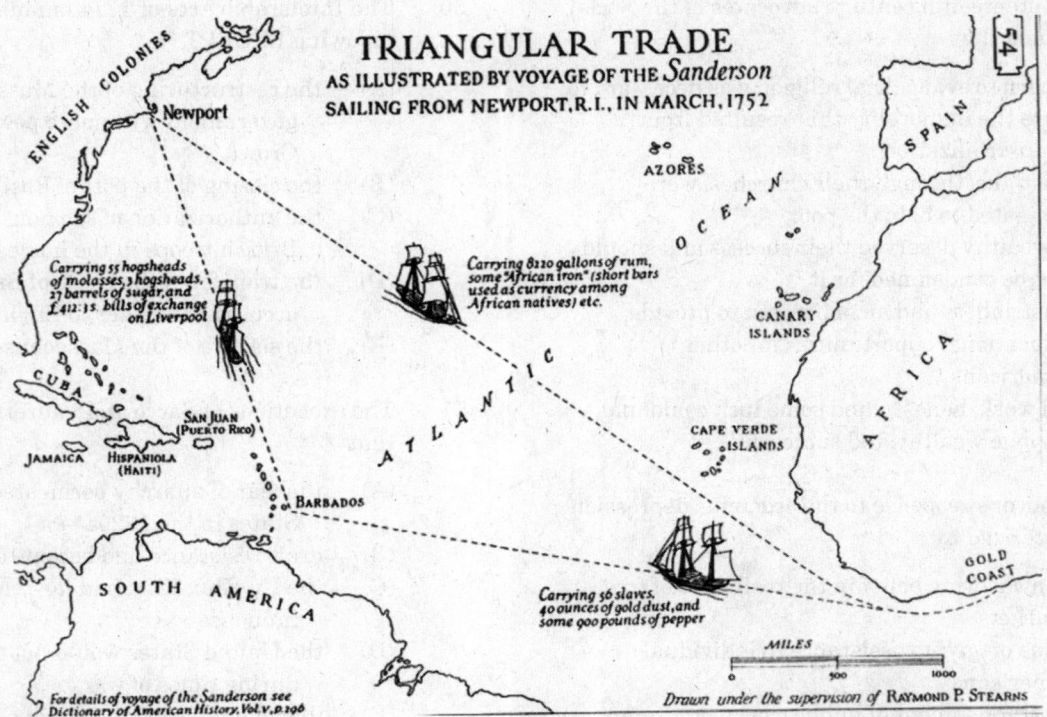

52. The map pictured above illustrates the economic policy known as

   (A) supply-side economics
   (B) free trade
   (C) export focused economics
   (D) mercantilism
   (E) protective tariffs

53. The Agricultural Adjustment Act tried to raise farm prices by

    (A) limiting agricultural production by paying subsidies to farmers
    (B) removing farmers from worn-out land to new farms
    (C) electrifying farmland
    (D) levying a national tax
    (E) shipping crops to Europe at reduced prices

54. In order to prevent northern antislavery propaganda from causing turmoil in the South and from threatening the institution of slavery, southern congressmen proposed

    (A) the Ostend Manifesto
    (B) the Compromise of 1850
    (C) a gag rule
    (D) the Wilmot Proviso
    (E) nullification

55. After the signing of the Declaration of Independence, a sharp division arose between Whigs and Tories in the colonies over

    (A) the status of slavery in the new nation
    (B) whether to grant citizenship to Native Americans
    (C) the national language of the United States
    (D) interpretations of the Constitution
    (E) whether to seek independence from Britain

56. Immediately following the Civil War, many southern states established Black Codes, which

    (A) abolished slavery entirely and created a free labor force
    (B) granted former slaves all citizenship rights that had been denied them previously
    (C) provided former slaves with education, health care, and small land grants
    (D) defined African Americans as second-class citizens and restricted their economic opportunities
    (E) facilitated African Americans' transition from slavery to freedom by creating local political offices specifically designed for them

57. All of the following were candidates in the presidential election of 1968 EXCEPT

    (A) Joseph McCarthy
    (B) George Wallace
    (C) Eugene McCarthy
    (D) Robert F. Kennedy
    (E) Hubert Humphrey

58. Anne Hutchinson was banished from Massachusetts Bay colony for all of the following reasons EXCEPT

    (A) she conducted discussion groups at her home on religious topics raised in church sermons
    (B) she was a woman who was involved in Puritan theology
    (C) she advanced the doctrine of antinomianism
    (D) she practiced witchcraft
    (E) she advocated the separation of church and state

59. All of the following are true of Shays's Rebellion in 1786 EXCEPT

    (A) it was instigated by poor farmers who wanted to prevent foreclosure on their farms
    (B) it resulted from settlers' defiance of the Northwest Ordinance
    (C) it took place during a time of economic depression
    (D) it demonstrated the new government's inability to maintain law and order
    (E) it challenged the viability of the Articles of Confederation

UNITED STATES HISTORY TEST—Continued

Greene, in New York (N. Y.) Telegram

A WOMAN'S WORK IS NEVER DONE

60. The cartoon illustrated above suggests that

(A) women should not be allowed to vote
(B) the Democratic Party supported progressive ideals
(C) women played a prominent part in progressive era politics
(D) suffrage should be deferred until other political matters were settled
(E) women, in general, should not become involved in politics

GO ON TO THE NEXT PAGE

UNITED STATES HISTORY TEST—Continued

61. The Haymarket riot of 1886 increased Americans' fears of

    (A) civil rights demonstrations
    (B) anarchists preaching revolution
    (C) police brutality
    (D) corporate suppression of unions
    (E) alcohol abuse

62. When the Republican Party was created in 1854, it focused primarily on

    (A) abolishing slavery
    (B) repealing the Fugitive Slave Law
    (C) counteracting the congressional gag law
    (D) smoothing over sectional differences
    (E) repealing the Kansas-Nebraska Act

63. "The money changers have fled from their high seats in the temple of our civilization. We may now restore that temple to the ancient truths. The measure of the restoration lies in the extent to which we apply social values more noble than mere monetary profit."

    Franklin D. Roosevelt's 1933 inaugural address suggested that the Great Depression was

    (A) caused by the greed of corporations
    (B) easy to solve through economic reforms
    (C) not as a critical as the potential war in Europe
    (D) the fault of the Republican party
    (E) exacerbated by Herbert Hoover's commitment to "rugged individualism"

64. In reaching its landmark *Brown v. Board of Education* ruling in 1954, the Supreme Court rejected the earlier precedent concerning racial segregation established in

    (A) *Schenck v. The United States*
    (B) *Plessy v. Ferguson*
    (C) *Roe v. Wade*
    (D) *Miranda v. Arizona*
    (E) *The United States v. E.C. Knight Company*

65. African-American critics of Booker T. Washington argued that his 1895 Atlanta Exposition Address was a compromise because

    (A) he did not demand immediate civil rights for African Americans
    (B) he dismissed the necessity of education for African Americans
    (C) he understood that the Supreme Court would use his views to legalize segregation
    (D) he offered African-American intellectuals an opportunity to teach at the Tuskegee Institute only if they renounced the effectiveness of higher education for African Americans
    (E) in return for giving the address, he was given a prominent role in Atlanta politics

66. In protesting "the Tariff of Abominations," John Calhoun argued that

    (A) Congress did not possess the constitutional authority to pass tariff legislation
    (B) Andrew Jackson had violated his campaign promise to keep tariffs low
    (C) states were sovereign and thus could nullify federal law
    (D) Congress could not reconsider the tariff because the Supreme Court had already declared it unconstitutional
    (E) tariffs needed to be developed scientifically by economists

67. The United States bought the Louisiana territory from the

    (A) English
    (B) Dutch
    (C) Spanish
    (D) Cajuns
    (E) French

68. The outbreak of World War I in Europe occurred after

    (A) Germany invaded France
    (B) the Russian Revolution
    (C) China formally ended the Open Door policy
    (D) the assassination of Archduke Ferdinand
    (E) Austria annexed Italy

GO ON TO THE NEXT PAGE

UNITED STATES HISTORY TEST—*Continued*

69. During the 1700s, which region accounted for the largest number of new immigrants in the American colonies?

    (A) England
    (B) France
    (C) Africa
    (D) Ireland
    (E) the West Indies

70. Settlement houses, such as Jane Addams's Hull House in Chicago, were designed to

    (A) offer religious services to the homeless
    (B) help immigrants adjust to urban life
    (C) provide mortgages for the purchase of new homes
    (D) rehabilitate alcoholics and drug users
    (E) clean up the political corruption of municipal government

71. Progressivism was characterized by all of the following EXCEPT

    (A) a desire to counter the detrimental effects of industrialization
    (B) reformist impulses
    (C) anti-immigration sentiment
    (D) a lack of business regulation
    (E) a sense of moral and social duty

72. Which of the following best characterizes Malcolm X's contribution to the civil rights movement?

    (A) He urged African Americans to take pride in their heritage, and he extolled the virtues of self-defense and community action.
    (B) Throughout his life, he maintained a virulent racist attitude toward whites and advocated violent rebellion.
    (C) He supported the major civil rights organizations and their campaign to integrate African Americans fully into American society.
    (D) He was a prominent speaker at the March on Washington and advocated the passage of the 1964 Civil Rights Act.
    (E) He was the architect of the voting rights drive in Alabama, which the Student Non-violent Coordinating Committee undertook in the early 1960s.

73. King William's and Queen Anne's wars can best be described as

    (A) major occurrences in the colonies that totally disrupted normal life
    (B) serious conflicts that forced colonists to choose sides
    (C) economic dislocations that interrupted colonial trade and threatened the stability of the colonies
    (D) conflicts with much more significance in Europe than in the colonies
    (E) minor skirmishes that ended quickly

74. The Dawes Severalty Act of 1887 included all of the following provisions EXCEPT

    (A) the Americanization of Native Americans
    (B) the destruction of Native American tribes
    (C) the return of eastern lands to Native Americans
    (D) the parceling out of former reservation lands to individual Native American families
    (E) the abolition of the reservation system

75. Richard Nixon's strategy for ending American involvement in the Vietnam war entailed

    (A) immediate withdrawal of all American combat troops and a formal surrender
    (B) turning the war over to the South Vietnamese army after an appropriate period of military training
    (C) involving the United Nations in a peacekeeping role before American withdrawal from the region
    (D) using nuclear weapons to weaken the North Vietnamese prior to American withdrawal
    (E) giving the North American Treaty Organization primary responsibility for continuing the war against the communists in the North

GO ON TO THE NEXT PAGE

76. George Kennan's policy of containment was based on

    (A) a belief that the communists would win the Chinese civil war
    (B) an understanding with Britain regarding the post–World War II German government
    (C) a belief that the Soviet Union would try to expand the reach of communism
    (D) a need to decrease government spending in an effort to halt inflation
    (E) a desire to keep the Republicans from regaining the White House in the 1948 election

77. Slaveholders in the south opposed high protective tariffs because these tariffs

    (A) made the price of slaves more expensive
    (B) increased the cost of manufactured goods
    (C) affected the cost of tobacco
    (D) impeded rice and indigo sales in Europe
    (E) represented the political platform of the Free Soil Party

78. "The soul is the perceiver and revealer of truth. We know truth when we see it, let skeptic and scoffer say what they choose. Foolish people ask you, when you have spoken what they do not wish to hear, 'How do you know it is truth, and not an error of your own?' We know truth when we see it, from opinion, as we know when we are awake that we are awake."

    This discussion of knowledge and truth is characteristic of which intellectual movement?

    (A) The Enlightenment
    (B) The Great Awakening
    (C) Deism
    (D) Transcendentalism
    (E) Antinomianism

79. F. Scott Fitzgerald captured the culture, lifestyle, and excessive materialism that characterized the 1920s in his novel

    (A) *The Sun Also Rises*
    (B) *The Great Gatsby*
    (C) *The Iceman Cometh*
    (D) *Look Homeward, Angel*
    (E) *The Sound and the Fury*

80. Under the Articles of Confederation, Congress could do all of the following EXCEPT

    (A) wage war
    (B) coin and print money
    (C) tax and regulate trade
    (D) maintain an army and navy
    (E) conduct foreign affairs

81. In the 1860 election, the Democratic Party's presidential nomination

    (A) was a moderate pro-slavery candidate
    (B) was reluctant to discuss the expansion of slavery
    (C) supported high protective tariffs to protect southern agriculture
    (D) was split between two candidates along northern and southern lines
    (E) offered to compromise on the issue of popular sovereignty

82. The Cuban Missile Crisis of 1962 resulted in

    (A) the Bay of Pigs invasion
    (B) the Soviet Union's agreement to remove its missiles from Cuba
    (C) the beginning of strategic arms limitations talks between Khruschev and Kennedy
    (D) the building of nuclear missiles aimed at Cuba
    (E) Fidel Castro's alliance with the United States

83. The Montgomery Bus Boycott, which began in 1955, was significant for all of the following reasons EXCEPT

    (A) it marked the emergence of Martin Luther King Jr. as a civil rights leader
    (B) it led the Interstate Commerce Commission to enact a law banning segregation on interstate transportation
    (C) it proved that an economic boycott could be used as a civil rights strategy
    (D) it forced the Montgomery Bus Company to integrate its buses
    (E) it led to the establishment of the Southern Christian Leadership Conference

GO ON TO THE NEXT PAGE

UNITED STATES HISTORY TEST—Continued

84. Which of the following was one of the earliest examples of industrial corruption in nineteenth-century America?

    (A) Credit Mobilier
    (B) The XYZ affair
    (C) Patronage
    (D) The spoils system
    (E) Joint-stock companies

85. The Missouri Compromise of 1820 did everything EXCEPT

    (A) prohibit slavery north of Missouri's southern border
    (B) allow Maine to enter the Union as a free state
    (C) legitimize the doctrine of popular sovereignty
    (D) establish the congressional precedent of admitting states in pairs of one free and one slave state
    (E) admit Missouri to the Union as a slave state

86. The Albany Plan of 1754

    (A) had the support of British officials
    (B) called for the creation of a unified colonial government
    (C) was supported by the majority of the colonies
    (D) was proposed to counter threats from the Spanish
    (E) rejected the use of writs of assistance by British revenue officers

GO ON TO THE NEXT PAGE

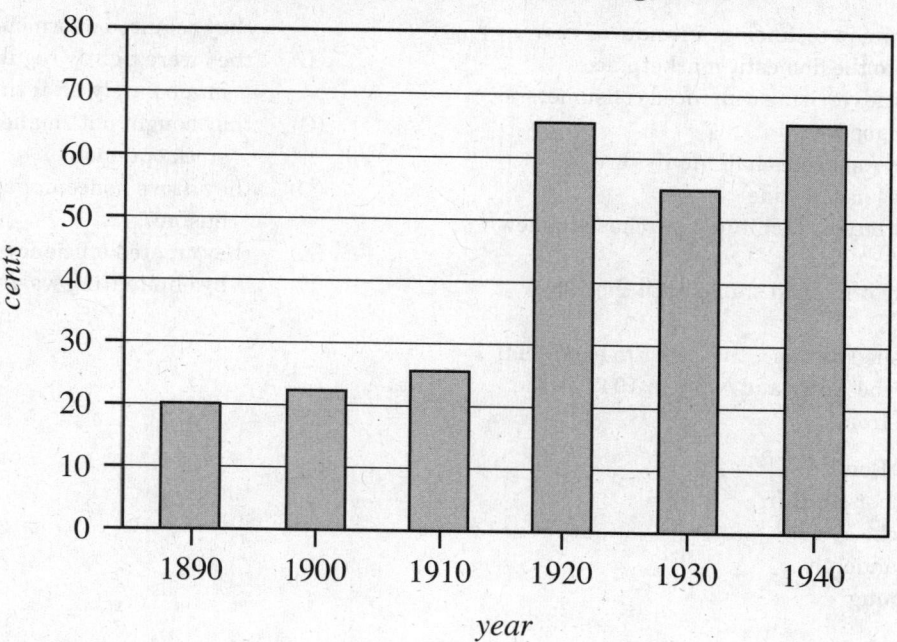

Hourly Wage in Manufacturing, 1890-1940

87. Which of the following reasons could account for the change in hourly wage between 1910 and 1920?

    (A) During World War I, the United States experienced an economic boom and enjoyed a favorable balance of trade.
    (B) The influenza epidemic of 1916 reduced the labor force, raising demand and wages for unskilled laborers.
    (C) The federal government succesfully prevented workers' strikes by invoking the Sherman Antitrust Act.
    (D) During the 1910s, the American economy was marked by overproduction and underconsumption.
    (E) Because Woodrow Wilson's Progressive reforms resulted in inflation, factory owners were forced to increase wages so that workers could afford to live.

88. All of the following accurately describe the consumer culture of the 1920s EXCEPT

    (A) advancements in technology introduced new products to the domestic marketplace
    (B) a growth in advertising convinced consumers to buy more goods
    (C) chain stores replaced small family-owned businesses nationwide
    (D) installment buying facilitated purchases of new products
    (E) the economy remained stable until the 1930s

89. Harry Truman issued an executive order to end racial discrimination in the Army and Navy in 1947 as the result of pressure from

    (A) W. E. B. Du Bois
    (B) Martin Luther King Jr.
    (C) Ralph Bunche
    (D) A. Philip Randolph
    (E) Whitney Young

90. All of the following are true of the development of trusts in the nineteenth century EXCEPT

    (A) they required enormous sums of capital
    (B) they were tightly regulated by Congress immediately after the Civil War
    (C) they bought out smaller competitors by offering stock options
    (D) they drove noncompliant companies out of business
    (E) they created efficiency in individual industries by eliminating wasteful competition

S T O P

IF YOU FINISH BEFORE TIME IS CALLED, YOU MAY CHECK YOUR WORK ON THIS TEST ONLY.
DO NOT TURN TO ANY OTHER TEST IN THIS BOOK.

SAT II U.S. History Practice Test 3 Explanations

Calculating Your Score

Question Number	Correct Answer	Right	Wrong	Question Number	Correct Answer	Right	Wrong	Question Number	Correct Answer	Right	Wrong
1.	D			31.	D			61.	B		
2.	D			32.	A			62.	E		
3.	A			33.	D			63.	A		
4.	B			34.	E			64.	B		
5.	E			35.	D			65.	A		
6.	C			36.	D			66.	C		
7.	B			37.	E			67.	E		
8.	D			38.	D			68.	D		
9.	A			39.	C			69.	C		
10.	B			40.	B			70.	B		
11.	D			41.	B			71.	D		
12.	C			42.	E			72.	A		
13.	C			43.	B			73.	D		
14.	A			44.	C			74.	C		
15.	D			45.	B			75.	B		
16.	B			46.	B			76.	C		
17.	D			47.	E			77.	B		
18.	E			48.	B			78.	D		
19.	C			49.	C			79.	B		
20.	A			50.	E			80.	C		
21.	B			51.	A			81.	D		
22.	B			52.	D			82.	B		
23.	C			53.	A			83.	B		
24.	D			54.	C			84.	A		
25.	A			55.	E			85.	C		
26.	E			56.	D			86.	B		
27.	E			57.	A			87.	E		
28.	B			58.	D			88.	E		
29.	A			59.	B			89.	D		
30.	A			60.	C			90.	B		

Your raw score for the SAT II U.S. History test is calculated from the number of questions you answer correctly and incorrectly. Once you have determined your composite score, use the conversion table on page 19 of this book to calculate your scaled score. To calculate your raw score, count the number of questions you answered correctly: _____
                                                                                                                A

Count the number of questions you answered incorrectly, and multiply that number by $\frac{1}{4}$:

$$\underline{}_{B} \times \frac{1}{4} = \underline{}_{C}$$

Subtract the value in field C from value in field A: _____
                                                       D

Round the number in field D to the nearest whole number. This is your raw score: _____
                                                                                   E

1. **(D) A New Nation** *Trend Question*

The Federalists argued that the Constitution gave Congress the power to create a national bank. According to this argument, the creation of the bank was a "necessary and proper" use of the law, since the bank would strengthen the American economy. The Anti-federalists rejected the Federalists' interpretation of the Constitution, arguing instead that all powers not specifically given to Congress by the Constitution belonged to the states and to the American people. The Anti-federalists believed that the bank was unconstitutional because the Constitution did not specifically state that Congress could create it.

2. **(D) Westward Expansion & Sectional Strife** *Fact Question*

The Treaty of Guadalupe Hidalgo ended the Mexican War and gave the United States the territories of Texas, New Mexico, and California. In exchange, the United States paid Mexico $15 million and assumed the monetary claims of U.S. citizens against the Mexican government.

3. **(A) Industrial Revolution** *Fact Question*

Eugene Debs instigated the Pullman strike, leading thousands of workers in a strike against the Pullman Palace Car Company. Debs was arrested, and federal troops were brought in to disband the strikers. The strikers clashed with the troops; as a result of the violence, thirteen workers died and fifty-three were injured.

4. **(B) The Colonial Period** *Fact Question*

The Dutch brought approximately twenty Africans to Jamestown in 1619. This incident marked the beginning of the importation of Africans into the colonies for use as laborers.

5. **(E) Cultural Trends** *Fact Question*

The Seneca Falls Convention met in 1848 to support women's rights. The convention issued the Declaration of Sentiments, which stated that men and women are created equal. The declaration was modeled after the Declaration of Independence.

6. **(C) World War I** *Quotation Question*

In the *Schenck* decision, the Supreme Court ruled that the U.S. government could suspend Americans' civil liberties during times of war or "clear and present danger." This ruling placed limits on the protections granted to citizens by the Bill of Rights.

7. **(B) The Age of Jackson** *Except Question*

Jackson never questioned his power to accept the Bank recharter. He vetoed the recharter for the reasons given in the other answer choices. His veto was also motivated by his dislike of Henry Clay, who was Jackson's political adversary as well as a supporter of the recharter.

8. **(D) Revolution & Constitution** *Fact Question*

The Proclamation of 1763 was part of England's policy on Native Americans. The proclamation was made in the wake of Pontiac's Rebellion, which demonstrated that Native Americans on the frontier posed a significant danger to English settlers. England hoped to prevent further bloodshed by drawing a line separating English lands from the Native-American lands.

9. **(A) Industrial Revolution** *Fact Question*

Chinese workers built the Central Pacific Railway in the west and joined that line to the Union Pacific Railway at Promontory Point, Utah, in 1869, thus creating the first transcontinental railroad.

10. **(B)** Civil War & Reconstruction *Except Question*

Pennsylvania was a free state; it fought with the Union during the Civil War.

11. **(D)** The Colonial Period *Trend Question*

The Mayflower Compact created a "civil body politick," which established laws and organized society. The government created by the compact derived its authority from the people who established it and who voted to elect its officials.

12. **(C)** The 1950s *Trend Question*

In the 1950s, in the wake of the Great Depression and World War II, many Americans turned to traditional values and became politically conservative. They wanted to conform to middle-class values, which placed great importance on the family, and to the ideal of a suburban middle-class life.

13. **(C)** The Progressive Era *Fact Question*

In 1906 Theodore Roosevelt negotiated the passage of the Hepburn Act. The act empowered the Interstate Commerce Commission to set maximum railroad rates and inspect the financial records of railroad companies.

14. **(A)** Revolution & Constitution *Trend Question*

The Sugar Act established a British monopoly on the American sugar trade. Unlike previous regulatory acts, which were designed to profit the entire British Empire, the Sugar Act specifically benefited England at the expense of the American colonies, raising the ire of the colonists.

15. **(D)** Westward Expansion & Sectional Strife *Except Question*

New Mexico did not become a slave state as part of the Compromise of 1850. According to the compromise, all lands acquired from Mexico, except for California, would be settled without reference to the issue of slavery.

16. **(B)** Industrial Revolution *Trend Question*

Monopolizing the process of oil refining allowed Rockefeller to play a pivotal role in the oil industry. Because Standard Oil came to control over ninety percent of oil-refining plants in the country, Rockefeller essentially dominated the industry, setting his own prices and avoiding destructive competition. This process of monopolization is known as horizontal integration.

17. **(D)** The Colonial Period *Fact Question*

The three principal types of American colonies were self-governing, royal, and proprietary. Self-governing colonies were created by a commercial charter, in which investors held their own charter and created their own form of government. Royal colonies were those established and controlled by the Crown. Proprietary colonies were controlled by a wealthy proprietor, who was given the land by the Crown and allowed to settle it at his own discretion.

18. **(E)** The 1950s *Trend Question*

After World War II, the United States spent much energy and money on containing the spread of communism in Asia. In 1950, the Soviet-backed North Koreans invaded South Korea. In response, Harry Truman sent U.S. troops to Korea as part of a United Nations "police force." The U.S. troops constituted the majority of this police force and waged a war against the communist North Koreans.

19. **(C)** Industrial Revolution *Fact Question*

In the second half of the nineteenth century, most newly-arrived immigrants in the West came from China. Although the influx of European immigrants to the West increased in that period, the Chinese constituted the majority of new immigrants in western states. They worked on the expanding westward railroad system, and many of them settled in California.

20. **(A)** The Roaring Twenties *Trend Question*

Throughout the 1920s, the U.S. government advocated isolationism—in other words, a United States retreat from global affairs. In keeping with this isolationist spirit, the United States signed the Kellogg-Briand Pact, which outlawed war, hoping to keep the country out of another international conflict. Although the pact had over sixty signatories, it ultimately proved ineffective.

21. **(B)** World War II *Except Question*

One of the major points of contention during the Yalta talks was how to deal with Germany after the war. In the end, Germany was divided into "zones of occupation," each controlled by an Allied power. Britain and the U.S. controlled West Germany, while the Soviets controlled East Germany until the collapse of the Soviet Union and the destruction of the Berlin Wall.

22. **(B)** Civil War & Reconstruction *Cartoon Question*

In this cartoon, Southern Democracy cuts the hair, which represents suffrage, off an African-American man. The cartoon's message is that white supremacy will soon rise in the South, disenfranchising African Americans and depriving them of their civil rights. The biblical reference to Samson and Delilah suggests that suffrage is the source of African Americans' strength and power. Without the vote, African Americans in the South are left powerless.

23. **(C)** Industrial Revolution *Quotation Question*

This quotation is from the preamble to the Populist Party platform of 1892. The Populists distrusted big business and the wealthy. Their platform called for the nationalization of the railroads, secret ballot box laws, and regulation of industry.

24. **(D)** The Pre-Columbian Period *Trend Question*

Europeans brought new diseases to the Americas. Because Native Americans had never built up immunity to these diseases, they succumbed quickly to illness. In the end, these imported diseases decimated the native population in Spanish America.

25. **(A)** A New Nation *Fact Question*

In the early 1800s, the British frequently boarded American ships in search of British naval deserters, whom they would force back into the Royal Navy. The British would periodically seize native-born and naturalized Americans and impress them into service as well. This practice, known as impressment, outraged Americans, and it became a major point of contention between the two countries. Eventually, the issue helped spark the War of 1812.

26. **(E)** Cultural Trends *Trend Question*

After the Nat Turner insurrection of 1831, southerners changed their defense of slavery from the "necessary evil" justification to the "positive good" justification. According to the "positive good" justification, the institution of slavery functioned like a school, caring for and educating slaves. This justification implied that slaves were inferior people who depended on whites for survival.

27. **(E)** The Age of Imperialism *Fact Question*

Secretary of State John Hay designed the Open Door policy to open the Chinese markets to American business. By securing exclusive trading rights in key Chinese ports, European and Japanese spheres of influence threatened to squeeze the United States out of Chinese markets. In response, Hay proclaimed the Open Door policy, which would get rid of favoritism at Chinese ports. Although the European powers refused to endorse this policy, Hay continued to press for U.S. interests in China.

28. **(B)** The 1960s *Trend Question*

The American public first learned that the United States was not winning the war when the North Vietnamese launched the Tet Offensive, expanding the conflict into South Vietnam and attacking major southern cities like Saigon. Despite government reports of U.S. victories, the Tet Offensive demonstrated to the public that U.S. forces were not in control of the war. After the month-long offensive, many Americans believed that a U.S. victory in Vietnam was unattainable, adding momentum to the growing anti-war movement.

29. **(A)** The Great Depression & New Deal *Fact Question*

John Steinbeck's *The Grapes of Wrath* portrayed the effects of the Great Depression on the Joad family in Oklahoma. After losing their home, the Joads join the mass migration of "Okies" to California in search of jobs.

30. **(A)** Westward Expansion & Sectional Strife *Trend Question*

The Ostend Manifesto suggested that the United States take Cuba from Spain by force if Spain refused to sell the island. Southerners supported the manifesto because the acquisition of Cuba would protect slavery by both increasing the slaveholding forces in Congress and widening slavery's geographical range.

31. **(D)** Civil War & Reconstruction *Fact Question*

Hoping to redress the expanding powers of the executive after the Civil War, radical Republicans in Congress passed the Tenure of Office Act, which limited presidential powers. The act prohibited the president from dismissing a government official who had been confirmed by the Senate without first obtaining Senate approval. The act was a direct challenge to President Andrew Johnson, who had fallen into disfavor with Republicans in Congress. In 1868, Congress impeached Johnson for violating the act.

32. **(A)** Progressive Era *Trend Question*

Du Bois fought for the equal treatment of African Americans and whites. He emphasized that African Americans deserved immediate access to all the educational opportunities white Americans had—not just to vocational training.

33. **(D)** Revolution & Constitution *Fact Question*

Jefferson borrowed many of his ideas for the Declaration of Independence from Locke's *Treatises on Civil Government*. Among these were the notions that governments derive authority from the consent of the governed and that all men are created equal.

34. **(E)** Cultural Trends *Except Question*

The Jungle, written by Upton Sinclair, was not published until 1906. The works named in the other answer choices were famous literary works published in the mid-nineteenth century.

35. (D) Industrial Revolution *Trend Question*

In the *Wabash* ruling of 1886, the Supreme Court modified its earlier ruling, which permitted the state regulation of businesses that affected the public interest. In *Wabash*, the Court ruled that the authority to regulate interstate business belonged to Congress, not to the state governments. However, since congressional sentiment was overwhelmingly pro-business in the late nineteenth century, congressional regulation had little effect on interstate business.

36. (D) Revolution & Constitution *Fact Question*

As a result of the Tea Party, Parliament punished the colonists in Boston by issuing a set of rules known as the Coercive Acts of 1774. To indicate how repugnant they found the acts, the colonists referred to them as the Intolerable Acts.

37. (E) World War II *Trend Question*

The Taft-Hartley Act stripped organized labor of the power it had accumulated under the New Deal. The act banned certain union practices; upheld a worker's right not to join a union; and allowed the president to delay strikes. Although Congress overrode Truman's veto, his action won him the support of organized labor during the 1948 election.

38. (D) Industrial Revolution *Except Question*

Morgan thrived on the power he amassed through his business ventures.

39. (C) The Great Depression & New Deal *Trend Question*

African Americans experienced employment discrimination throughout the 1930s. They struggled to obtain jobs, and when the Depression began, they were the first people to be fired.

40. (B) The Colonial Period *Trend Question*

With its rocky, infertile terrain, the north was inhospitable to large cash crops. Since northerners didn't need a large labor force to work plantation land, slavery never developed to the same degree in the north as it did in the south. Although slavery did exist for a time in the north, the northerners did not depend on slavery for their livelihoods as the southerners did.

41. (B) The Progressive Era *Trend Question*

Roosevelt believed that trusts could play a pivotal role in the expansion of the U.S. economy as long as they refrained from corrupt practices. Wilson opposed all trusts and wanted them dissolved in order to restore free competition to the marketplace. Wilson's advocacy of the Clayton Antitrust Act of 1914 highlights the difference in their stances on trusts.

42. (E) Cultural Trends *Fact Question*

The Know-Nothings developed in the 1840s and fell apart in the late 1850s. Know-Nothings were members of secret orders opposed to Irish immigration and to Catholicism. In response to increasing immigration, the Know-Nothings fervently supported nativism, encouraging the election of native-born Americans and trying to combat "foreign" influence. The Know-Nothings also agitated for temperance and the abolition of slavery.

43. **(B)** A New Nation *Trend Question*
The cotton gin increased the efficiency of cotton production in the south. Using the cotton gin, plantation owners could produce cotton more rapidly than before, allowing them to send large supplies to England and earning them increased profits from cotton sales. In order to take full advantage of the cotton gin's efficiency, plantation owners increased their slave populations.

44. **(C)** The 1950s *Fact Question*
Although Nixon believed that Hiss had been involved in sending classified State Department documents to the Soviet Union, he was unable to prove that charge in court. During the trial, Hiss perjured himself, and the court ultimately convicted him of perjury.

45. **(B)** The Colonial Period *Except Question*
New York was never part of New England. Established as New Netherland by the Dutch, it was renamed New York in 1664, when the English captured the colony from the Dutch.

46. **(B)** The Great Depression & New Deal *Except Question*
Part of FDR's Second New Deal, the Works Progress Administration (WPA) pumped $11 million into the U.S. economy over eight years of operation. The WPA hired unemployed people of all backgrounds—from unskilled laborers to engineers to artists—to work on federal projects such as construction, murals, and state guides. The WPA was not concerned with unions or collective bargaining.

47. **(E)** The Age of Jackson *Cartoon Question*
Formed in opposition to Jackson, the Whig Party perceived him to be power hungry. His frequent use of the veto, especially regarding the Second Bank of the United States, became the critical issue of the 1836 presidential election, which Jackson won easily.

48. **(B)** Industrial Revolution *Trend Question*
The Social Gospel preached the idea that Christians had a moral duty to assist the poor. Poverty, they believed, was the result of unbridled capitalism. Those individuals neglected by the process deserved help from others more fortunate.

49. **(C)** The Great Depression & New Deal *Trend Question*
Initially, Hoover expressed optimism about the market's ability to rebound on its own, but as the depression continued, he was forced to intervene. He spent $2 billion on the creation of the Reconstruction Finance Corporation (RFC) in 1932. The purpose of the RFC was to lend money to banks, railway companies, insurance firms, and other large institutions in need of assistance. Hoover opposed the use of federal funds for public relief and concentrated his efforts on rebuilding industry and the business sector.

50. **(E)** Revolution & Constitution *Except Question*
The Massachusetts Charter was revoked in 1691—well before the implementation of the Intolerable Acts in 1774.

51. **(A)** The Roaring Twenties *Trend Question*
In 1920, Sacco and Vanzetti, anarchists and Italian immigrants, were sentenced to death for murder and armed robbery. At the time, the country was in the grip of the Red Scare, and the prevailing suspicion of anarchists and foreigners influenced the jury's guilty verdict.

52. (D)   The Colonial Period   *Map Question*

Copying Britain's successful practice of mercantilism, the American colonies used triangular trade routes to increase their profits and create a favorable balance of trade. This cartoon illustrates the triangular trade between the United States, Africa, and the West Indies. New England rum was shipped to Africa, where it was traded for slaves. Then the slaves were shipped to the West Indies, and they were traded for sugar and molasses. The sugar and molasses were brought back to New England, where they were traded for rum. This cycle continued, bringing in substantial profits, particularly for New England tradesmen.

53. (A)   The Great Depression & New Deal   *Trend Question*

The Agricultural Adjustment Act, part of FDR's New Deal, created the Agricultural Adjustment Administration (AAA), which distributed federal aid to farmers and controlled agricultural production. The AAA provided subsidies to farmers who agreed to produce below production quotas. The purpose of this exchange was to raise the price of farm produce by cutting overall agricultural production in the United States. According to the laws of supply and demand, a decrease in a product's supply results in an increase in its price.

54. (C)   Westward Expansion & Sectional Strife   *Fact Question*

In 1836, southerners introduced the gag rule into Congress. The gag rule prohibited all debates on slavery in Congress. Southerners hoped this ban would gradually decrease tensions over slavery, since these tensions were weakening the pro-slavery cause. In 1844, the gag rule was repealed.

55. (E)   Revolution & Constitution   *Trend Question*

The Whigs and Tories disagreed over the issue of independence. The Whigs supported the Revolution, while the Tories were British loyalists.

56. (D)   Civil War & Reconstruction   *Trend Question*

Fearful that African Americans would seek revenge for slavery or that they would migrate north, leaving the South no source of cheap labor, southern states passed the Black Codes in order to restrict the movements of African Americans. These codes effectively made former slaves into second-class citizens.

57. (A)   The 1960s   *Except Question*

Joseph McCarthy was the Republican senator from Wisconsin who orchestrated the communist witch hunts of the early 1950s. He died in 1956—long before the 1968 presidential election. The men named in the other answer choices did run in the presidential election. Robert Kennedy (A) was assassinated in June 1968, after winning the California Democratic Primary. George Wallace (B), an ardent segregationist, ran as a third party candidate. Eugene McCarthy (C) was the candidate of the antiwar movement. Hubert Humphrey (E) was the Democratic nominee for the presidency; he lost to Richard Nixon in the November election.

58. (D)   The Colonial Period   *Except Question*

Hutchinson never practiced witchcraft, nor was she accused of doing so. She did, however, anger the Puritans in Massachusetts Bay with her public discussion groups (A), her belief that no one could name saints in the community (C), and her support for the separation of church and state (E). The male-dominated colony also resented that Hutchinson was a woman taking on a public role (B).

59. **(B)** Revolution & Constitution — *Except Question*

In 1786, Daniel Shays organized a rebellion of about 2,000 men who were angry that high taxes and mounting debts would result in the foreclosure of their farms. The men closed the courts in three western Massachusetts counties to prevent the foreclosures. The rebellion demonstrated the government's inability to maintain law and order, particularly during a time of economic depression. It also heightened the colonists' dislike of the centralized authority created by the Articles of Confederation. The Northwest Ordinance of 1787 also challenged the Articles of Confederation, but it had nothing to do with Shays's Rebellion.

60. **(C)** The Progressive Era — *Cartoon Question*

The message of this 1918 cartoon is that women played an important role in progressive change in the United States and that they deserved the right to vote. Several progressive concerns, including health insurance and child labor laws, are prominently featured on the laundry line, and they are placed there by a woman hard at work.

61. **(B)** Industrial Revolution — *Fact Question*

The Knights of Labor organized a rally to protest police brutality against striking workers, but the rally quickly became violent when someone threw a bomb, killing seven police officers. The public was indignant after the riot and blamed the incident on anarchists exploiting the labor strike. Chicago authorities arrested eight alleged anarchists, four of whom were subsequently convicted and executed, despite scanty evidence.

62. **(E)** Westward Expansion & Sectional Strife — *Fact Question*

The Republican Party began as an antislavery party, formed in opposition to the Kansas-Nebraska Act, which nullfied the prohibition of slavery above the 36°30'-latitude. Although the party's platform expanded over time, at its inception, the party was concerned primarily with repeal of the Kansas-Nebraska provisions. In 1860, the Republican Abraham Lincoln became president, and the Republicans dominated politics throughout the Civil War and early stages of reconstruction.

63. **(A)** The Great Depression & New Deal — *Quotation Question*

Roosevelt believed the corporate greed and corrupt business practices had been major causes of the depression. In offering people hope during his inaugural address, he made clear his intention to reform business practices as one way of solving the financial crisis they all faced.

64. **(B)** The 1950s — *Fact Question*

In *Plessy v. Ferguson*, 1896, the Supreme Court ruled that segregation laws were constitutional as long as segregated facilities adhered to the "separate but equal" provision. The Court argued that segregation did not imply inferiority. Nearly fifty years later, in *Brown v. Board of Education*, the Court overturned its previous ruling, arguing that segregation was discriminatory and unconstitutional and that it forced African Americans into a second-class position in American society.

65. **(A)** Industrial Revolution — *Trend Question*

Critics accused Washington of compromising on the issue of civil rights and equality for African Americans. Washington argued that African Americans should focus on acquiring technical skills and economic independence from whites. He believed that interaction and equality between African Americans and whites was not essential for the immediate future of African Americans in the United States. He publicly downplayed interaction between the races in all things "social and political."

66. (C) The Age of Jackson — *Trend Question*

The 1828 tariff, known as the "Tariff of Abominations," outraged South Carolina, which argued that Congress had no right to levy the tariff, since the tariff protected regional rather than national interests. In the South Carolina Exposition and Protest, Calhoun argued for the sovereignty of states, saying that states had entered the Union voluntarily so they had the right to nullify federal laws with which they disagreed.

67. (E) A New Nation — *Fact Question*

In April 1803, Napoleon sold the entire Louisiana territory to the United States for $15 million. Although Napoleon initially intended to create a French empire in and around the Gulf of Mexico, a slave rebellion in Haiti severely depleted his troops in the region, ruining his colonial plans. The sale of the territory to the United States was known as the Louisiana Purchase.

68. (D) World War I — *Fact Question*

The assassination of Archduke Franz Ferdinand by a Serbian nationalist triggered a series of alliances that began the Great War in Europe. Austria-Hungary allied with Germany against Serbia in retaliation for the killing. Serbia, in turn, allied with Russia. By August 1914, most of Europe was involved in the conflict.

69. (C) The Colonial Period — *Fact Question*

Although their immigration was not voluntary, more Africans came to the colonies than any other group in the eighteenth century.

70. (B) Industrial Revolution — *Trend Question*

In the late nineteenth century, settlement houses tried to help recently arrived immigrants cope with unfamiliar and often hostile urban surroundings. They provided education, childcare, and room and board.

71. (D) The Progressive Era — *Except Question*

Progressivism was a reform movement promoting social justice, morality, and democracy. Many Progressives, associating social problems with the poor immigrant communities, lobbied for an end to immigration, but immigration restriction was on the extreme end of Progressive reforms. Progressives focused primarily on "cleaning up" American society through moral and business reform. The regulation of business was a key element of the Progressive platform.

72. (A) The 1960s — *Trend Question*

Malcolm X urged African Americans to take pride in their heritage and history, and to look to Africa as their ancestral home. He stressed the necessity of self-defense and called for the African-American community to unite. Although he was frequently depicted as a violent racist, he never advocated violence. Near the end of his life, he came to understand that racism, in any form, grew out of ignorance.

73. (D) The Colonial Period — *Trend Question*

Both wars were fought primarily in Europe. Although each involved some fighting in the colonies, the conflict did not disrupt colonial life. Most American colonies were not directly affected by either war.

74. **(C)** Industrial Revolution *Except Question*

The Dawes Severalty Act did not return any land in the east to Native Americans. The act deliberately addressed Native Americans as individuals rather than as tribes (B), and tried to address Native American needs on a family-by-family basis. The act broke up the reservation system (E) and offered reservation land to individual Native American families (D). The government hoped that Native Americans, after receiving these lands, would adopt the American concept of land ownership. Although the act intended to integrate Native Americans into white society (A), it further isolated them by increasing homelessness and poverty in the Native American population.

75. **(B)** 1970s–2000 *Trend Question*

Nixon wanted to withdraw U.S. troops from Vietnam and let the South Vietnamese take over the fighting. Although Nixon announced this exit strategy soon after his election to the presidency in 1968, U.S. troops stayed in Vietnam until 1973.

76. **(C)** World War II *Trend Question*

Kennan, an expert on Soviet affairs, believed that the Soviet Union would attempt to expand its boundaries and spread communism. In 1946, he urged the United States to implement a policy of containment. According to Kennan's argument, the Soviets would back down from acquiring new territory if the United States challenged them.

77. **(B)** Westward Expansion & Sectional Strife *Trend Question*

High protective tariffs increased the price of manufactured goods. Southern plantation owners relied heavily on manufactured goods from abroad to cultivate their crops. They opposed high tariffs because these tariffs increased their expenditures.

78. **(D)** Cultural Trends *Quotation Question*

This quotation from Ralph Waldo Emerson is characteristic of transcendentalism. In the 1830s, a period marked by growing consumption, transcendentalists like Emerson preached self-reliance and self-knowledge. They believed that people could acquire knowledge through emotional openness, intuition, and the senses.

79. **(B)** The Roaring Twenties *Fact Question*

In *The Great Gatsby,* Fitzgerald depicted the lavish lifestyles of the wealthy during the 1920s. The novel mocked the excesses and the superficiality of the decade.

80. **(C)** Revolution & Constitution *Except Question*

The Articles of Confederation did not allow Congress to raise money through taxation. Realizing that the taxation policies of Parliament led to the Revolution, the authors of the Articles deliberately denied Congress the power to tax.

81. **(D)** Westward Expansion & Sectional Strife *Trend Question*

In the 1860 election, the Democratic Party split in support of two candidates. Northern Democrats supported Stephen Douglas, who believed in the doctrine of popular sovereignty. Southern Democrats opposed popular sovereignty, pushing instead for the expansion of slavery to all American territories. The southern Democrats nominated John Breckinridge for president, splitting the Democratic vote and ultimately handing the election to the Republicans.

82. **(B)** The 1960s *Fact Question*

When the United States discovered Soviet missile bases on Cuba, Kennedy threatened to quarantine Cuba with a naval blockade and to dismantle the bases by force. For several days, the United States and the USSR seemed on the brink of nuclear war, but finally Soviet Premier Krushchev sent a proposal to Kennedy: the Soviets would dismantle the bases if the Americans promised never to invade Cuba. Kennedy agreed, and the USSR removed its missiles from Cuba.

83. **(B)** The 1950s *Except Question*

The bus boycott had no effect on the Interstate Commerce Commission (ICC) or on interstate transportation. The protest concerned transportation within the city limits of Montgomery, Alabama. The ICC did not desegregate transportation carriers and facilities until 1962.

84. **(A)** Industrial Revolution *Fact Question*

Directors of the Union Pacific Railroad Company created a fake company called Credit Mobilier. The railroad was charged substantial amounts for work allegedly completed by this company. The directors kept the money and paid members of the Grant administration to ignore the entire matter.

85. **(C)** A New Nation *Except Question*

The Missouri Compromise did not propose popular sovereignty as a solution to the slavery question. The doctrine of popular sovereignty did not develop until the 1850s.

86. **(B)** The Colonial Period *Fact Question*

In 1754, colonial delegates met in Albany, New York, to discuss the threats from French and Native American attacks. Benjamin Franklin proposed the Albany Plan, which called for the creation of a unified colonial government to deal with these attacks. Although the plan won the support of the delegates, the colonies rejected the plan. British officials also opposed the plan because they feared it would create a strong colonial government that would challenge British rule.

87. **(A)** *Chart Question*

According to this chart, the hourly wage for workers in manufacturing rose from 26 cents per hour in 1910 to 66 cents per hour in 1920. Of the reasons given in the answer choices, the booming economy during World War I, choice (A), is the best explanation for this rise in wages. During the war, factory output increased, and the United States experienced a favorable balance of trade, exporting more goods to other nations than it imported. The economic boom continued even after the war ended, since American products were in high demand in war-torn European countries.

88. **(E)** The Roaring Twenties *Except Question*

The U.S. economy was not very stable during the 1920s; after an initial postwar recession, the economy boomed for the rest of the decade. Americans enjoyed unprecedented prosperity, and new consumer products flooded the market. The enormous growth, the speculative investments, and the spending of the 1920s finally overwhelmed the economy in 1929, leading to the stock market crash on October 24.

89. **(D)** World War II *Fact Question*

A. Philip Randolph threatened to march on Washington, D.C., in 1947 unless Truman desegregated the armed forces. Truman, unwilling to show any U.S. weakness during the early years of the Cold War, issued the order to desegregate in 1947. Actual integration proceeded slowly.

90. **(B)** Industrial Revolution *Except Question*

Trusts were largely unregulated in America until Congress passed antitrust legislation in 1890. Even after the Sherman Antitrust Act passed, government regulation of trusts remained slight until the twentieth century.

SAT II U.S. History Practice Test 4

UNITED STATES HISTORY TEST 4 ANSWER SHEET

1. Ⓐ Ⓑ Ⓒ Ⓓ Ⓔ	31. Ⓐ Ⓑ Ⓒ Ⓓ Ⓔ	61. Ⓐ Ⓑ Ⓒ Ⓓ Ⓔ
2. Ⓐ Ⓑ Ⓒ Ⓓ Ⓔ	32. Ⓐ Ⓑ Ⓒ Ⓓ Ⓔ	62. Ⓐ Ⓑ Ⓒ Ⓓ Ⓔ
3. Ⓐ Ⓑ Ⓒ Ⓓ Ⓔ	33. Ⓐ Ⓑ Ⓒ Ⓓ Ⓔ	63. Ⓐ Ⓑ Ⓒ Ⓓ Ⓔ
4. Ⓐ Ⓑ Ⓒ Ⓓ Ⓔ	34. Ⓐ Ⓑ Ⓒ Ⓓ Ⓔ	64. Ⓐ Ⓑ Ⓒ Ⓓ Ⓔ
5. Ⓐ Ⓑ Ⓒ Ⓓ Ⓔ	35. Ⓐ Ⓑ Ⓒ Ⓓ Ⓔ	65. Ⓐ Ⓑ Ⓒ Ⓓ Ⓔ
6. Ⓐ Ⓑ Ⓒ Ⓓ Ⓔ	36. Ⓐ Ⓑ Ⓒ Ⓓ Ⓔ	66. Ⓐ Ⓑ Ⓒ Ⓓ Ⓔ
7. Ⓐ Ⓑ Ⓒ Ⓓ Ⓔ	37. Ⓐ Ⓑ Ⓒ Ⓓ Ⓔ	67. Ⓐ Ⓑ Ⓒ Ⓓ Ⓔ
8. Ⓐ Ⓑ Ⓒ Ⓓ Ⓔ	38. Ⓐ Ⓑ Ⓒ Ⓓ Ⓔ	68. Ⓐ Ⓑ Ⓒ Ⓓ Ⓔ
9. Ⓐ Ⓑ Ⓒ Ⓓ Ⓔ	39. Ⓐ Ⓑ Ⓒ Ⓓ Ⓔ	69. Ⓐ Ⓑ Ⓒ Ⓓ Ⓔ
10. Ⓐ Ⓑ Ⓒ Ⓓ Ⓔ	40. Ⓐ Ⓑ Ⓒ Ⓓ Ⓔ	70. Ⓐ Ⓑ Ⓒ Ⓓ Ⓔ
11. Ⓐ Ⓑ Ⓒ Ⓓ Ⓔ	41. Ⓐ Ⓑ Ⓒ Ⓓ Ⓔ	71. Ⓐ Ⓑ Ⓒ Ⓓ Ⓔ
12. Ⓐ Ⓑ Ⓒ Ⓓ Ⓔ	42. Ⓐ Ⓑ Ⓒ Ⓓ Ⓔ	72. Ⓐ Ⓑ Ⓒ Ⓓ Ⓔ
13. Ⓐ Ⓑ Ⓒ Ⓓ Ⓔ	43. Ⓐ Ⓑ Ⓒ Ⓓ Ⓔ	73. Ⓐ Ⓑ Ⓒ Ⓓ Ⓔ
14. Ⓐ Ⓑ Ⓒ Ⓓ Ⓔ	44. Ⓐ Ⓑ Ⓒ Ⓓ Ⓔ	74. Ⓐ Ⓑ Ⓒ Ⓓ Ⓔ
15. Ⓐ Ⓑ Ⓒ Ⓓ Ⓔ	45. Ⓐ Ⓑ Ⓒ Ⓓ Ⓔ	75. Ⓐ Ⓑ Ⓒ Ⓓ Ⓔ
16. Ⓐ Ⓑ Ⓒ Ⓓ Ⓔ	46. Ⓐ Ⓑ Ⓒ Ⓓ Ⓔ	76. Ⓐ Ⓑ Ⓒ Ⓓ Ⓔ
17. Ⓐ Ⓑ Ⓒ Ⓓ Ⓔ	47. Ⓐ Ⓑ Ⓒ Ⓓ Ⓔ	77. Ⓐ Ⓑ Ⓒ Ⓓ Ⓔ
18. Ⓐ Ⓑ Ⓒ Ⓓ Ⓔ	48. Ⓐ Ⓑ Ⓒ Ⓓ Ⓔ	78. Ⓐ Ⓑ Ⓒ Ⓓ Ⓔ
19. Ⓐ Ⓑ Ⓒ Ⓓ Ⓔ	49. Ⓐ Ⓑ Ⓒ Ⓓ Ⓔ	79. Ⓐ Ⓑ Ⓒ Ⓓ Ⓔ
20. Ⓐ Ⓑ Ⓒ Ⓓ Ⓔ	50. Ⓐ Ⓑ Ⓒ Ⓓ Ⓔ	80. Ⓐ Ⓑ Ⓒ Ⓓ Ⓔ
21. Ⓐ Ⓑ Ⓒ Ⓓ Ⓔ	51. Ⓐ Ⓑ Ⓒ Ⓓ Ⓔ	81. Ⓐ Ⓑ Ⓒ Ⓓ Ⓔ
22. Ⓐ Ⓑ Ⓒ Ⓓ Ⓔ	52. Ⓐ Ⓑ Ⓒ Ⓓ Ⓔ	82. Ⓐ Ⓑ Ⓒ Ⓓ Ⓔ
23. Ⓐ Ⓑ Ⓒ Ⓓ Ⓔ	53. Ⓐ Ⓑ Ⓒ Ⓓ Ⓔ	83. Ⓐ Ⓑ Ⓒ Ⓓ Ⓔ
24. Ⓐ Ⓑ Ⓒ Ⓓ Ⓔ	54. Ⓐ Ⓑ Ⓒ Ⓓ Ⓔ	84. Ⓐ Ⓑ Ⓒ Ⓓ Ⓔ
25. Ⓐ Ⓑ Ⓒ Ⓓ Ⓔ	55. Ⓐ Ⓑ Ⓒ Ⓓ Ⓔ	85. Ⓐ Ⓑ Ⓒ Ⓓ Ⓔ
26. Ⓐ Ⓑ Ⓒ Ⓓ Ⓔ	56. Ⓐ Ⓑ Ⓒ Ⓓ Ⓔ	86. Ⓐ Ⓑ Ⓒ Ⓓ Ⓔ
27. Ⓐ Ⓑ Ⓒ Ⓓ Ⓔ	57. Ⓐ Ⓑ Ⓒ Ⓓ Ⓔ	87. Ⓐ Ⓑ Ⓒ Ⓓ Ⓔ
28. Ⓐ Ⓑ Ⓒ Ⓓ Ⓔ	58. Ⓐ Ⓑ Ⓒ Ⓓ Ⓔ	88. Ⓐ Ⓑ Ⓒ Ⓓ Ⓔ
29. Ⓐ Ⓑ Ⓒ Ⓓ Ⓔ	59. Ⓐ Ⓑ Ⓒ Ⓓ Ⓔ	89. Ⓐ Ⓑ Ⓒ Ⓓ Ⓔ
30. Ⓐ Ⓑ Ⓒ Ⓓ Ⓔ	60. Ⓐ Ⓑ Ⓒ Ⓓ Ⓔ	90. Ⓐ Ⓑ Ⓒ Ⓓ Ⓔ

UNITED STATES HISTORY TEST 4

Directions: Each of the questions or incomplete statements below is followed by five suggested answers or completions. Select the one that is best in each case and then fill in the corresponding oval on the answer sheet.

1. The Federal Reserve Act of 1913 contained all of the following provisions EXCEPT

    (A) only the Federal Reserve can lend money to individuals
    (B) the Federal Reserve banks are authorized to distribute currency
    (C) the Federal Reserve consists of twelve regional Federal Reserve banks
    (D) private bankers own the Federal Reserve System banks
    (E) the Federal Reserve controls the discount rate

2. The Stamp Act of 1765 was primarily intended to

    (A) punish the colonies for protesting the Sugar Act
    (B) suppress the distribution of propaganda pamphlets
    (C) shut down colonial newspapers critical of the Crown
    (D) increase British revenues to offset Britain's mounting debt after the French and Indian War
    (E) thwart the colonial mercantile practice of triangular trade

3. Stephen Douglas proposed the Kansas-Nebraska Act in order to

    (A) bring the issue of slavery to a final resolution
    (B) facilitate the building of a transcontinental railroad
    (C) ensure that slavery would be excluded in the territories
    (D) sabotage the Free Soilers
    (E) increase the value of his land holdings in the West

4. Population growth in the 1950s was due to

    (A) Populism
    (B) the sexual revolution
    (C) the baby boom
    (D) European immigration
    (E) Chinese immigration

5. The New Deal resulted in all of the following EXCEPT

    (A) the institution of collective bargaining
    (B) insurance for Americans' savings accounts
    (C) a constitutional amendment requiring a balanced budget
    (D) government involvement in public utilities
    (E) an expansion in the size and power of the federal government

6. All of the following were factors leading to the industrialization of the United States in the second half of the nineteenth century EXCEPT

    (A) available capital
    (B) a large labor force
    (C) foreign investment
    (D) abundant natural resources
    (E) government subsidies for industry

GO ON TO THE NEXT PAGE

UNITED STATES HISTORY TEST—Continued

7. The cartoon above criticizes American involvement in the League of Nations on the grounds that involvement would result in

   (A) the exploitation of American military power by other nations
   (B) damage to the American economy
   (C) a reduction in protective tariffs
   (D) American obligation to participate in wars under the collective security clause
   (E) further hostilities with Germany

GO ON TO THE NEXT PAGE

UNITED STATES HISTORY TEST—*Continued*

8. Which of the following was an advantage that the Confederacy had over the Union during the Civil War?

    (A) More heavy industry
    (B) Stronger military tradition
    (C) Larger military forces
    (D) Greater wealth
    (E) More abundant food crops

9. The outcome of the Whiskey Rebellion pleased Alexander Hamilton because

    (A) the rebels were successful in evading the Whiskey tax
    (B) Anti-federalists lost the backing of the rebels, who then became supporters of the Federalists
    (C) the defeat of the rebels demonstrated the power of the federal government
    (D) he profited financially from the revolt
    (E) the rebels' victory weakened Thomas Jefferson's political support

10. During the colonial period, Native American culture changed most when the Spanish introduced which of the following into North America?

    (A) Tobacco
    (B) Cotton
    (C) Compasses
    (D) Christianity
    (E) Horses

11. The only immigrants to face governmental immigration restriction in the United States prior to the twentieth century were the

    (A) Chinese
    (B) Irish
    (C) Jews
    (D) Russians
    (E) Germans

12. All of the following groups were part of the Democratic coalition that supported Franklin D. Roosevelt in the 1936 presidential election EXCEPT

    (A) African Americans
    (B) Farmers
    (C) Bankers and financiers
    (D) Women
    (E) Organized labor

13. The Atlantic Charter, co-written by Franklin D. Roosevelt and Winston Churchill, contained all the following provisions EXCEPT

    (A) the unconditional surrender by the Axis powers as a prerequisite for peace
    (B) freedom of the seas
    (C) the establishment of an institution for collective world security after the war
    (D) a division of labor for the British, Russian, and American armies
    (E) the self-determination of nations after the war

14. The book that had the greatest impact on the passage of the Pure Food and Drug Act of 1906 was

    (A) *The Octopus*
    (B) *The Jungle*
    (C) *The Rise of Silas Lapham*
    (D) *The Promise of American Life*
    (E) *The Age of Innocence*

15. "Now finding I had arrived to man's estate, and was a slave, and these revelations being made known to me, I began to direct my attention to this great object, to fulfill the purpose for which, by this time, I felt assured I was intended. Knowing the influence I had obtained over the minds of my fellow servants ... I now began to prepare them for my purpose, by telling them something was about to happen that would terminate in fulfilling the great promise that had been made to me."

    The subject of Nat Turner's discussion is

    (A) his role in the abolition movement
    (B) the coming of the Civil War
    (C) a slave insurrection
    (D) the Emancipation Proclamation
    (E) the cotton gin

16. Part of the New Deal, the Public Works Administration was established in order to

    (A) stabilize the banking industry
    (B) ensure that all legislation was approved by public referendum
    (C) guarantee labor's collective bargaining rights
    (D) create jobs for unemployed citizens
    (E) integrate African Americans into American industries

GO ON TO THE NEXT PAGE

UNITED STATES HISTORY TEST—*Continued*

17. The first human inhabitants of North America came from

    (A) Asia
    (B) South America
    (C) Africa
    (D) Europe
    (E) Australia

18. Under the Marshall Plan, the United States pledged to

    (A) place limits on immigration to the United States
    (B) establish homeless shelters in major urban centers
    (C) provide government jobs for unemployed workers during the Great Depression
    (D) join the Allied powers in World War II
    (E) provide financial assistance to European nations

19. In the *McCulloch v. Maryland* decision of 1819, the Supreme Court ruled

    (A) that federal power had supremacy over the power of the states
    (B) that the Bank of the United States was unconstitutional
    (C) to overturn congressional authorization for internal improvements
    (D) to renounce the doctrine of judicial review
    (E) to affirm the states' right to tax federal property

20. Although John F. Kennedy won the Democratic presidential nomination in 1960, many political analysts believed that he would not be elected because he

    (A) was an aggressive anti-communist
    (B) was opposed to civil rights
    (C) was a Roman Catholic
    (D) was fiscally liberal
    (E) chose Lyndon B. Johnson as his running mate

21. Abraham Lincoln's Reconstruction plan was designed to

    (A) facilitate the quick return of the southern states to the Union
    (B) punish the southern states for secession and impose harsh economic penalties on them
    (C) give African Americans complete civil and political equality
    (D) provide former slaves with "forty acres and a mule"
    (E) subvert the Democrats in Congress and keep the Republicans in power

22. Local politics during the Industrial Revolution were dominated by

    (A) political machines
    (B) James Garfield
    (C) the Populists
    (D) the Knights of Labor
    (E) supporters of anti-immigration laws

23. During World War I, Americans increasingly viewed Germany as inhumane because of all of the following EXCEPT the

    (A) sinking of the *Lusitania*
    (B) Zimmerman Telegram
    (C) invasion of Belgium
    (D) construction of concentration camps
    (E) use of submarine warfare

24. Within the context of American reform in the nineteenth century, Dorothea Dix was primarily associated with

    (A) prisons
    (B) temperance
    (C) mental institutions
    (D) abolition
    (E) institutes for the blind

25. The Republican Party political platform of 1856 included all of the following EXCEPT

    (A) the Homestead Act
    (B) a central route for the transcontinental railroad
    (C) the expansion of slavery into the territories
    (D) high protective tariffs
    (E) liberal immigration policies

GO ON TO THE NEXT PAGE

UNITED STATES HISTORY TEST—*Continued*

26. Lyndon B. Johnson was given unlimited authority to protect American interests in Vietnam under

    (A) the War Powers Act
    (B) Article II of the U.S. Constitution
    (C) the collective security agreement reached by NATO
    (D) the Gulf of Tonkin Resolution
    (E) a peacekeeping resolution passed in the United Nations Security Council

27. "We shall not realize our objectives, however, unless we are willing to help free peoples to maintain their free institutions and their national integrity against aggressive movements that seek to impose upon them totalitarian regimes. This is no more than a frank recognition that totalitarian regimes imposed on free peoples, by direct or indirect aggression, undermine the foundations of international peace and hence the security of the United States."

    When Harry Truman read this statement, as part of his "Truman Doctrine" address to Congress, he was promoting a policy of

    (A) NATO-sponsored collective security
    (B) containment
    (C) deference to the United Nations
    (D) isolationism
    (E) massive retaliation

28. The enforcement of the Navigation Acts in the late eighteenth century marked the end of Britain's policy of

    (A) triangular trade
    (B) mercantilism
    (C) salutary neglect
    (D) taxing tea entering England
    (E) virtual representation

29. The American Liberty League criticized the New Deal for

    (A) reducing government spending
    (B) promoting the ideals of rugged individualism
    (C) restricting individuals' rights to save money and acquire property
    (D) neglecting to provide for the poor
    (E) failing to address industrial recovery

30. All of the following contributed to the end of Reconstruction in the South EXCEPT

    (A) factions within the Democratic Party
    (B) corruption in the Ulysses S. Grant administration
    (C) the rise of the Liberal Republicans
    (D) a stock market crash
    (E) the waning influence of Radical Republicans in Congress

31. The War Hawks supported the War of 1812 for all of the following reasons EXCEPT

    (A) they thought that peace with Britain would result in the disgrace of the United States
    (B) they wanted to end the recession in the southern and western regions of the United States
    (C) they advocated the continuation of impressment
    (D) they wanted to annex Canada
    (E) they feared the British alliance with Native Americans

32. Students at Kent State University in Ohio were killed by the national guard in May 1974 because they were

    (A) protesting Richard Nixon's Cambodian incursion
    (B) attempting to desegregate the university's dormitories
    (C) protesting against an increase in tuition
    (D) attempting to close an army recruiting office located on campus
    (E) looting stores following a victory by a sports team

33. In keeping with his stance on big business, Woodrow Wilson supported

    (A) measures that would strip organized labor of power
    (B) the complete privatization of the banking system
    (C) raising protective steel tariffs
    (D) the principles of laissez-faire economics
    (E) federal regulation of interstate trade and business monopolies

GO ON TO THE NEXT PAGE

UNITED STATES HISTORY TEST—Continued

34. Which political party did John Calhoun and Henry Clay establish in opposition to the Jacksonian Democrats?

    (A) The Republicans
    (B) The Whigs
    (C) The Federalists
    (D) The Populists
    (E) The Nationalists

35. Congress's override of Harry Truman's veto of the Taft-Hartley Act is an example of

    (A) America's respect for organized labor
    (B) the system of checks and balances
    (C) socialism's presence in American democracy
    (D) executive privilege
    (E) judicial review

36. All of the following were causes of the stock market crash in 1929 EXCEPT

    (A) the expansion of credit and installment buying
    (B) overproduction by American industries
    (C) the lack of purchasing power among American consumers
    (D) farm production falling beneath government quotas
    (E) banks speculating on stocks

37. The Puritans left England for the New World primarily because they

    (A) lost their land and homes in England
    (B) intended to purify the Anglican Church of its Catholic rituals
    (C) were opposed to England's involvement in the African slave trade
    (D) believed the taxes they were required to pay were unjust
    (E) adhered to the concept of the separation of church and state

38. "Our greatest danger is that in the great leap from slavery to freedom we may overlook the fact that the masses of us are to live by the productions of our hands, and fail to keep in mind that we shall prosper in proportion as we learn to dignify and glorify common labour and put brains and skill into the common occupations of life;... No race can prosper till it learns that there is as much dignity in tilling a field as in writing a poem. It is at the bottom of life we must begin, and not at the top."

    This statement reflects the philosophy of

    (A) Frederick Douglass
    (B) Booker T. Washington
    (C) W.E.B. Du Bois
    (D) Marcus Garvey
    (E) A. Philip Randolph

39. The Spanish Empire was primarily interested in the Americas as a

    (A) source of raw materials
    (B) marketplace for finished products
    (C) mechanism to ease overcrowding
    (D) source of gold and silver
    (E) penal colony for convicted criminals

40. All of the following are true of the Hartford Convention EXCEPT that

    (A) the New England Federalists threatened to secede from the Union
    (B) the delegates argued that states possessed the right to nullify federal law
    (C) the resolutions of the Convention included a call for the end of the War of 1812
    (D) the Convention significantly weakened the Federalist party by making it appear unpatriotic
    (E) Republicans agreed wholeheartedly with the resolutions offered by the Convention

41. In 1767, John Dickinson published *Letters from a Pennsylvania Farmer* in response to the

    (A) Stamp Act
    (B) Declaratory Act
    (C) Townshend Duties
    (D) Tea Act
    (E) Intolerable Acts

GO ON TO THE NEXT PAGE

42. All of the following were established as utopian communities in the nineteenth century EXCEPT

    (A) New Harmony
    (B) Oneida
    (C) Fruitlands
    (D) Shaker villages
    (E) Walden Pond

43. Lyndon B. Johnson's Great Society plan was undermined in Congress by

    (A) a Republican filibuster
    (B) the failure of Johnson's "war on poverty" to gain the support of Democratic leaders
    (C) corporate lobbying against the proposed reform programs
    (D) the federal government's increasing focus on the war in Vietnam
    (E) the freedom rides, which turned prominent politicians against the civil rights movement

44. Roger Williams was banished from the Massachusetts Bay Colony for

    (A) being a Catholic
    (B) trying to establish a rival colony
    (C) marrying a Native American woman
    (D) advocating the separation of church and state
    (E) assisting Anne Hutchinson

45. The railroad industry gave out rebates

    (A) in order to avoid costly lawsuits from customers
    (B) because Congressional law mandated them in 1881
    (C) in order to increase its overall profit
    (D) in exchange for stock in other companies
    (E) as favors to its largest customers

46. Which of the following was ruled unconstitutional by the Supreme Court in the *Dred Scott v. Sandford* case?

    (A) The "separate but equal" doctrine
    (B) The denial of civil rights for African Americans
    (C) Slavery throughout the United States
    (D) The extension of slavery into the territories
    (E) Popular sovereignty

THE WORLD'S CONSTABLE

47. The image of the United States as "The World's Constable" (as portrayed above) refers specifically to

(A) the Open Door policy
(B) the Roosevelt corollary to the Monroe Doctrine
(C) the Panama Canal crisis
(D) dollar diplomacy
(E) the annexation of Hawaii

48. The Northwest Ordinance of 1787 called for the

    (A) deportation of Native Americans to the west of the Mississippi River
    (B) prohibition of slavery north of the Ohio River
    (C) expansion of slavery into the territories
    (D) regulation of commerce in the territories
    (E) the abolition of popular sovereignty

49. The Interstate Commerce Commission (1887) sought to regulate railroads by mandating all of the following EXCEPT the

    (A) publication of all railroad rates
    (B) consolidation of competing railroads into a single government-regulated industry
    (C) elimination of different rate structures depending on the level of competition
    (D) end of the practice of pooling of business by the railroads
    (E) abolition of rebates

50. The *Brown v. Board of Education* (1954) decision relied most heavily on which of the following in overturning the constitutionality of segregation in public schools?

    (A) The elastic clause
    (B) Habeas corpus
    (C) The First Amendment
    (D) The "Supreme Law of the Land" clause
    (E) The Fourteenth Amendment

51. The first president of the Confederate States of America was

    (A) John Calhoun
    (B) Stephen Douglas
    (C) Jefferson Davis
    (D) Robert E. Lee
    (E) James Buchanan

52. The National Origins Act of 1924 sought specifically to limit the number of immigrants arriving annually to the United States from

    (A) Ireland
    (B) western Europe
    (C) southern and eastern Europe
    (D) Latin America
    (E) Asia

53. Prior to the 1830s, the vast majority of southern slaveholders justified the institution of slavery by referring to it as a

    (A) charitable institution
    (B) civilizing agent
    (C) positive good
    (D) necessary evil
    (E) humane system

54. The mass production of war materials for use in World War II resulted domestically in

    (A) a decline in real wages
    (B) a series of strikes by organized labor
    (C) the end of the depression
    (D) renewed stock speculation and margin buying
    (E) the re-emergence of the Republican Party

UNITED STATES HISTORY TEST—*Continued*

55. The cartoon above satirizes the political contest in which

    (A) Henry Clay deprived Andrew Jackson of the presidency in 1824
    (B) Andrew Jackson destroyed the Second Bank of the United States
    (C) John Calhoun defied the 1828 tariff legislation
    (D) Andrew Jackson vetoed the Maysville Road bill passed by Congress
    (E) Peggy Eaton was humiliated by members of Jackson's cabinet

GO ON TO THE NEXT PAGE

UNITED STATES HISTORY TEST—Continued

56. The United States gained access to the land through which the Panama Canal was built by

    (A) purchasing it outright from Panama for $10 million
    (B) trading several battleships to Panama for the land
    (C) promoting the Panamanian Revolution against Columbia
    (D) defeating Spain in 1898
    (E) negotiating with the British Empire for the rights to the land

57. Shays's Rebellion worried some American political leaders, including George Washington, because

    (A) it demonstrated that the central government could not respond effectively to upheavals by the lower classes
    (B) they feared that their slaves would be emancipated should such a rebellion occur in Virginia
    (C) they suspected a similar uprising could overthrow the central government
    (D) no one was putting an end to Native American attacks in the West
    (E) the British supported the revolt and were seeking to reclaim the colonies

58. During Reconstruction, the Radical Republicans opposed President Andrew Johnson when they supported

    (A) Abraham Lincoln's "ten percent plan" for southern states' readmission to the Union
    (B) banning powerful plantation owners from participating in government
    (C) the ratification of the Thirteenth Amendment, which outlawed slavery in the United States
    (D) southern states' imposition of Black Codes, which placed restrictions on the actions of African Americans
    (E) the passage of the Fourteenth Amendment, which guaranteed citizenship to all people born or naturalized in the United States

59. In the 1890s, the federal government often used the Sherman Antitrust Act to

    (A) stop railroads from practicing price discrimination
    (B) prevent workers from striking
    (C) bust corrupt trusts, while regulating "good" ones
    (D) impose protective tariffs
    (E) raise the rate of inflation

60. A proprietary colony was a colony that was

    (A) controlled by a small corporation that received a charter from the Crown
    (B) established after settlers arrived in America and settled on previously unclaimed land
    (C) created when the king gave a huge land grant to a wealthy subject who controlled how the colony would be settled
    (D) developed according to precise religious tenets to ensure that tolerance would be practiced and that all religions would be welcome
    (E) prohibited from establishing slavery or any form of indentured servitude

61. The policy of brinkmanship refers to

    (A) an aggressive, threatening style of diplomacy toward the Soviet Union
    (B) a determination to stimulate the American economy through deficit spending
    (C) a willingness to provide welfare for America's poor
    (D) a commitment to exploring outer space
    (E) a willingness to support the women's rights movement

62. At the Constitutional Convention of 1787 in Philadelphia, the main issue of debate was the

    (A) method by which slaves would be counted in the U.S. population
    (B) location of the nation's capital in Washington, D.C.
    (C) establishment of two competing political parties
    (D) balance between the needs of large and small states
    (E) first presidential election and George Washington's candidacy

GO ON TO THE NEXT PAGE

UNITED STATES HISTORY TEST—Continued

63. Franklin D. Roosevelt's New Deal measures achieved all of the following EXCEPT

   (A) they raised spending by the federal government
   (B) they created Social Security
   (C) they won Democrats the support of African-American voters
   (D) they strengthened white southerners' support for the Democratic Party
   (E) they cast the Democratic Party as the political representative of the poor

64. In *Progress and Poverty* (1879), Henry George proposed his solution to the disparity of wealth created by industrialization when he advocated

   (A) the dissolution of all trusts and the restoration of free trade
   (B) socialist revolution to give workers control of the means of production
   (C) a popular referendum on the issue of antitrust legislation
   (D) that the government use tax income to fund social programs
   (E) enforcement of the Sherman Antitrust Act

65. Bacon's Rebellion resulted from

   (A) tensions between the rich and poor in the Virginia colony
   (B) a dispute over tariffs
   (C) the British policy of impressment
   (D) southern colonists' outrage at the triangular trade, which primarily benefited northern colonists
   (E) tensions between slaves and their owners on plantations around Jamestown

GO ON TO THE NEXT PAGE

UNITED STATES HISTORY TEST—Continued

66. The shaded countries illustrated on the map above represent the

   (A) Allied powers during World War II
   (B) members of the League of Nations
   (C) original members of NATO
   (D) members of the Warsaw Pact
   (E) partners in the Peace Corps

GO ON TO THE NEXT PAGE

UNITED STATES HISTORY TEST—Continued

67. At the end of World War I, Woodrow Wilson called on the leaders who met at Versailles to create "peace without victory" because

    (A) the United States stood to gain economically from helping to rebuild Europe
    (B) the imposition of a harsh settlement on Germany would create resentment
    (C) no country had actually won the war, and resumption of the status quo was the best remaining alternative to continued fighting
    (D) that policy would ensure freedom of the seas, about which Wilson was passionate
    (E) he wanted to return to his progressive reform agenda and not worry any longer about foreign affairs

68. Plantation owners in the antebellum south often required their slaves to attend Sunday church services because

    (A) the owners felt guilty for enslaving the slaves and sought atonement
    (B) the services taught obedience and urged slaves to be content with their fate
    (C) southern law required religious worship for all adults
    (D) the owners were attempting to deflect antislavery criticism
    (E) some slaves demanded that they be allowed to attend

69. The Reagan Doctrine influenced all of the following foreign policy ventures EXCEPT

    (A) the Marines' invasion of Grenada
    (B) American support for the contras in Nicaragua
    (C) the invasion of Cambodia
    (D) the deployment of Marines to Lebanon
    (E) the American bombing of Libya

70. All of the following are true of the Molasses Act of 1733 EXCEPT

    (A) it was enacted after complaints from British sugar planters in the West Indies
    (B) it resulted in much smuggling by American colonists, who intended to avoid the tax
    (C) British sugar planters were supportive of the act and were pleased that the government had listened to them
    (D) it was rigidly enforced and led to bitter feelings in the American colonies
    (E) it was an example of the policy of salutary neglect

71. Warren Harding's election to the presidency in 1920 reflected Americans'

    (A) interest in supply-side economic policies
    (B) willingness to be actively engaged in world affairs
    (C) desire for a return to normalcy
    (D) determination to fight communism after the Russian Revolution
    (E) support for women's right to vote

72. All of the following rights are included in the term "due process of law" EXCEPT

    (A) trial by a jury of one's peers
    (B) assistance from a lawyer
    (C) the ability to call witnesses
    (D) being informed of charges made against you
    (E) financial compensation if acquitted

73. "I stand for the square deal. But when I say that I am for the square deal, I mean not merely that I stand for fair play under the present rules of the games, but that I stand for having those rules changed so as to work for a more substantial equality of opportunity and of reward for equally good service . . . Now, this means that our government, national and state, must be freed from the sinister influence or control of special interests. We must drive the special interests out of politics. The citizens of the United States must effectively control the mighty commercial forces which they have themselves called into being."

    Theodore Roosevelt's progressive philosophy addressed the problem of corporate corruption and political interference by

    (A) seeking to bust all trusts and restore free competition to the economic marketplace
    (B) dissolving corrupt corporations and regulating the others
    (C) adopting a laissez-faire governmental approach based on corporate goodwill
    (D) mandating that the Supreme Court regulate the trusts
    (E) nationalizing all industry under full government control

GO ON TO THE NEXT PAGE

74. The *Narrative of the Life of Frederick Douglass* (1845) was an important part of the abolitionist movement for all of the following reasons EXCEPT that it

   (A) presented a picture of slavery as a harsh and oppressive system
   (B) motivated Nat Turner to rebel in Virginia
   (C) complemented the work being done by northern abolitionists
   (D) was written by an escaped slave who had become an abolitionist
   (E) called for complete political and economic equality

75. Which of the following men promoted the Gospel of Success?

   (A) Horatio Alger
   (B) Herbert Hoover
   (C) Ralph Waldo Emerson
   (D) Brigham Young
   (E) Horace Mann

76. Indentured servants were brought to the American colonies primarily in order to

   (A) replace expensive slave labor
   (B) decrease the size of the working class in England
   (C) secure an initial workforce for the colonies
   (D) increase the workforce in the South after regulations were placed on the slave trade
   (E) defend colonial settlements from Native American attacks

77. During his administration, Andrew Jackson came into direct conflict with the Supreme Court when he

   (A) vetoed the recharter of the Second Bank of the United States
   (B) refused to strike down the "Tariff of Abominations"
   (C) ordered the removal of Native Americans in order to clear land for American settlement
   (D) formed a "Kitchen Cabinet" composed of his supporters and political allies
   (E) signed the Force Bill, which authorized the use of the military to collect customs duties

78. The main issue debated during the Scopes Monkey Trial was

   (A) the teaching of evolution in Tennessee schools
   (B) scientific experimentation on animals
   (C) the legality of the Ku Klux Klan
   (D) the constitutionality of a Tennessee law banning the American Civil Liberties Union
   (E) the validity of creationism

UNITED STATES HISTORY TEST—Continued

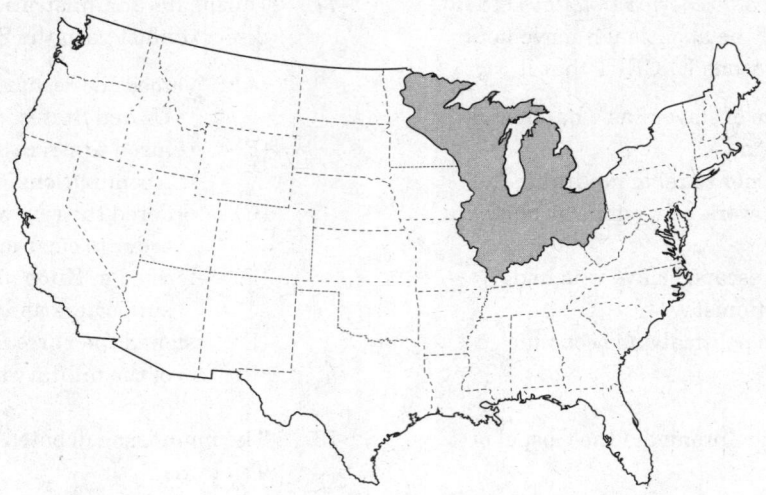

79. The shaded area on the map represents land that was

   (A) under French control after the American Revolution
   (B) part of the original thirteen colonies
   (C) governed by the Northwest Ordinances
   (D) sold to the United States as part of the Louisiana Purchase
   (E) set aside for the expansion of slavery

80. Andrew Carnegie believed in the idea of stewardship, which held that the

    (A) wealthy had an obligation to create opportunities to help the poor improve their situations
    (B) federal government should assist those in poverty and despair
    (C) wealthy should give money and food to the poor
    (D) poor deserved their fate and that the wealthy had no social obligation to assist them
    (E) industrial magnates should enter into collective bargaining agreements with organized labor

81. All of the following cities were large centers of trade and commerce in the American colonies EXCEPT

    (A) Philadelphia
    (B) New York
    (C) Boston
    (D) Chicago
    (E) Charleston

82. A small farmer from Texas in the 1890s would most likely have supported

    (A) a flat income tax
    (B) the free coinage of silver
    (C) the deregulation of the transportation industry
    (D) an end to immigration restrictions
    (E) loans made by the business sector to the federal government

83. The goal of labor strikes in the Age of Jackson was primarily to

    (A) force employers to recognize workers' collective bargaining rights
    (B) raise workers' wages
    (C) demand better working conditions in factories
    (D) petition Congress to restrict further immigration of Irish workers
    (E) advance the antislavery movement

UNITED STATES HISTORY TEST—*Continued*

Votes of Delegates to Connecticut, Pennsylvania, and New Hampshire Ratifying Conventions, by Occupation

	Federalist	Antifederalist
Merchants, manufacturers, doctors, lawyers, ministers, large landholders	84%	16%
Artisans, innkeepers, surveyors	64%	36%
Farmers	46%	54%

84. According to the chart above, which of the following people would most likely support a loose interpretation of the Constitution?

    (A) Lawyers
    (B) Farmers
    (C) Innkeepers
    (D) Politicians
    (E) Not enough information to tell

UNITED STATES HISTORY TEST—Continued

85. In 1948, Harry Truman invoked the Smith Act to prosecute

    (A) communists in the United States
    (B) Joseph McCarthy for his witch-hunting tactics
    (C) members of organized labor who engaged in violence
    (D) members of the Student Non-violent Coordinating Committee
    (E) war criminals from World War II

86. The Black Power movement advocated

    (A) the integration of African Americans into all aspects of American life
    (B) gradualism in African Americans' acquiring of basic civil rights
    (C) a decrease in interracial cooperation
    (D) economic opportunity instead of voting rights for African Americans
    (E) the creation of a civil rights act

87. The First Great Awakening can best be described as a movement that

    (A) advocated immediate repentance and rejection of material comforts
    (B) called for the separation of church and state
    (C) praised human reason and encouraged skepticisim
    (D) supported the abolition of slavery and the granting of citizenship rights to former slaves
    (E) encouraged introspection and a return to nature

88. The America First Committee

    (A) opposed American involvement in World War II prior to Pearl Harbor
    (B) favored American intervention in World War II prior to Pearl Harbor
    (C) sent relief aid to American troops overseas
    (D) supported Franklin D. Roosevelt's decision to make precautionary preparations for war in 1939
    (E) campaigned actively in support of the Lend-Lease Act

89. After emancipation, sharecropping in the south

    (A) revived the southern economy and helped rebuild its infrastructure
    (B) provided African Americans with the economic stake they needed to migrate north
    (C) mired African Americans in a cycle of debt and turned them into second-class citizens
    (D) was declared unconstitutional
    (E) was Booker T. Washington's method of making African Americans economically useful to the southern economy

90. Which of the following motivated the formal announcement of the Monroe Doctrine in 1823?

    (A) James Monroe's desire to build a political platform for re-election
    (B) John Quincy Adams's fears that Russia and Spain were interested in colonizing parts of North America
    (C) A general feeling in the United States that England would once again attempt to regain her former colonies
    (D) An economic need to stimulate trade with foreign countries
    (E) A Republican attempt to destroy the Federalist party

S T O P

IF YOU FINISH BEFORE TIME IS CALLED, YOU MAY CHECK YOUR WORK ON THIS TEST ONLY.
DO NOT TURN TO ANY OTHER TEST IN THIS BOOK.

SAT II U.S. History Practice Test 4 Explanations

Calculating Your Score

Question Number	Correct Answer	Right	Wrong	Question Number	Correct Answer	Right	Wrong	Question Number	Correct Answer	Right	Wrong
1.	A			31.	C			61.	A		
2.	D			32.	A			62.	D		
3.	B			33.	E			63.	D		
4.	C			34.	B			64.	D		
5.	C			35.	B			65.	A		
6.	E			36.	D			66.	C		
7.	D			37.	B			67.	B		
8.	B			38.	B			68.	B		
9.	C			39.	D			69.	C		
10.	E			40.	E			70.	D		
11.	A			41.	C			71.	C		
12.	C			42.	E			72.	E		
13.	D			43.	D			73.	B		
14.	B			44.	D			74.	B		
15.	C			45.	E			75.	A		
16.	D			46.	E			76.	C		
17.	A			47.	B			77.	C		
18.	E			48.	B			78.	A		
19.	A			49.	B			79.	C		
20.	C			50.	E			80.	A		
21.	A			51.	C			81.	D		
22.	A			52.	C			82.	B		
23.	D			53.	D			83.	B		
24.	C			54.	C			84.	A		
25.	C			55.	B			85.	A		
26.	D			56.	C			86.	C		
27.	B			57.	A			87.	A		
28.	C			58.	E			88.	A		
29.	C			59.	B			89.	C		
30.	A			60.	C			90.	B		

Your raw score for the SAT II U.S. History test is calculated from the number of questions you answer correctly and incorrectly. Once you have determined your composite score, use the conversion table on page 19 of this book to calculate your scaled score. To calculate your raw score, count the number of questions you answered correctly: _____
                                                                          A

Count the number of questions you answered incorrectly, and multiply that number by $\frac{1}{4}$:

$$\underline{}_{B} \times \frac{1}{4} = \underline{}_{C}$$

Subtract the value in field C from value in field A: _____
                                                    D

Round the number in field D to the nearest whole number. This is your raw score: _____
                                                                                  E

1. **(A)** The Progressive Era   *Except Question*

The Federal Reserve lends money to commercial banks in the United States. It does not deal directly with individuals.

2. **(D)** Revolution & Constitution   *Trend Question*

After mounting a large debt during the French and Indian War, Britain imposed the Stamp Act on the American colonies in order to raise revenue. The 1765 act required colonists to buy special watermarked paper for legal documents, newspapers, and playing cards.

3. **(B)** Westward Expansion & Sectional Strife   *Fact Question*

Douglas wanted the government to build a transcontinental railroad between Chicago and the Pacific coast. Douglas tried to facilitate the building of this railroad by settling Nebraska as a U.S. territory under the Kansas-Nebraska Act.

4. **(C)** The 1950s   *Trend Question*

During the 1950s, the birth rate skyrocketed in a phenomenon commonly known as the baby boom. Americans started their families earlier and had more children than they did in the past. The conservative views of that decade promoted the idea of the nuclear family and encouraged women to stay at home to raise their children.

5. **(C)** The Great Depression & New Deal   *Except Question*

A balanced budget was not part of the New Deal measures, which used deficit spending to relieve the depression. FDR hoped that federal spending would revive the U.S. economy by increasing individuals' purchasing power.

6. **(E)** Industrial Revolution   *Except Question*

Although the federal government grew increasingly supportive of industrialization during the nineteenth century, it never provided outright subsidies to industries. The government assisted industry by approving high tariffs that would protect industrial development and growth, by not prosecuting trusts under the Sherman Antitrust Act, and by preventing many labor strikes.

7. **(D)** The Roaring Twenties   *Cartoon Question*

The cartoon shows a helpless Uncle Sam (the United States) with his hands tied behind his back and tugged in different directions by foreign countries. The binds that attach the United States to the other countries are labeled "The League of Nations." The message of the cartoon is that membership in the League of Nations will bind the United States to the interests of other countries, and these binds will render the United States powerless. This suspicion of the League of Nations was shared by many senators at the time. Under the leadership of Henry Cabot Lodge, the Senate rejected membership in the League of Nations, fearing that a collective security measure would force Americans into future wars that did not necessarily involve the United States.

8. **(B)** Civil War & Reconstruction   *Fact Question*

From the outset of the Civil War, the Union held an advantage over the Confederacy in terms of resources, population, and wealth. One of the Confederacy's main advantages, though, was a strong military tradition. The Confederate military leaders tended to have more battle experience than their counterparts in the North, and the fact that fewer Confederate troops than Northern troops defected suggests that the Confederate troops had higher morale.

9. **(C)** A New Nation *Trend Question*

The federal government quickly raised an army and quelled the Whiskey Rebellion. Hamilton approved of the government's response, since it demonstrated the strength of the federal government and the new Constitution. The defeat of the rebels was especially important, since the government had come under fire for failing to respond effectively to Shays's Rebellion in Massachusetts.

10. **(E)** The Colonial Period *Fact Question*

The introduction of horses had profound effects on Native American life. It altered the way Native Americans conducted war and increased their success in hunting buffalo.

11. **(A)** Industrial Revolution *Fact Question*

The Chinese Exclusion Act of 1882 prohibited Chinese immigrants from entering the United States over the following ten-year period. The act was passed in response to rising anti-immigration sentiment in the United States.

12. **(C)** The Great Depression & New Deal *Except Question*

Bankers and financiers were not part of the New Deal coalition. The business sector was highly critical of FDR's policies and opposed the New Deal's relief measures.

13. **(D)** World War II *Except Question*

Using Woodrow Wilson's fourteen points as a model, Churchill and Roosevelt drafted the Atlantic Charter, which presented their vision of the ideal postwar world. This ideal included unconditional surrender by the Axis powers (A), freedom of the seas (B), the establishment of an international security institution (C), and self-determination for all nations (E). Although the United States had not yet entered the war in August 1941, when the Charter was created, these goals would become a major focus for the Allies throughout the war. The Charter did not propose the division of labor among armies.

14. **(B)** The Progressive Era *Trend Question*

In *The Jungle*, Upton Sinclair depicted the unhealthy conditions that prevailed in American meatpacking plants. In response to the novel's popularity and influence, the government passed the Pure Food and Drug Act and a meat inspection act in 1906.

15. **(C)** Westward Expansion & Sectional Strife *Quotation Question*

In his "confessions," Nat Turner explained how he prepared his fellow slaves for the rebellion in Southampton County, Virginia, in 1831. Believing that he had been divinely inspired, Turner gathered a small band of slaves to revolt against his owner and white neighbors.

16. **(D)** The Great Depression & New Deal *Fact Question*

The Public Works Administration gave jobs to unemployed Americans during the depression. In keeping with the New Deal's commitment to increasing purchasing power without increasing production, the PWA employed people on building schools, post offices, bridges, and other pieces of infrastructure. These construction jobs gave workers income without flooding the domestic market with new consumer goods.

17. **(A)** The Pre-Columbian Period *Fact Question*

The first humans arrived in the Americas from Asia, crossing over a land bridge that connected Siberia (in modern-day Russia) to Alaska.

18. **(E)** The 1950s   *Fact Question*

Created in 1948, the Marshall Plan pledged American financial assistance to European nations recovering from the war. The United States hoped that this financial aid would prevent communist expansion into Europe by eliminating political instability and economic insecurity. The Marshall Plan was the financial counterpart to the Truman Doctrine, which established the United States in the role of global policeman.

19. **(A)** A New Nation   *Fact Question*

In the *McCulloch* ruling, the Supreme Court prohibited the state of Maryland from taxing a local branch of the First Bank of the United States. This decision affirmed the supremacy of the federal government over the states and demonstrated that the Supreme Court would carefully monitor state laws in order to ensure their constitutionality.

20. **(C)** The 1960s   *Trend Question*

Until Kennedy, no American president had been Catholic. Anti-Catholicism was rampant in political and social arenas, and many people believed that Kennedy would not win the election because of his religion.

21. **(A)** Civil War & Reconstruction   *Trend Question*

Lincoln wanted to return the southern states to the Union as quickly as possible. His plan required ten percent of the voters in each state to take an oath of allegiance to the Union. Once a state obtained this ten percent, it could create a new government and elect representatives to send to Congress.

22. **(A)** Industrial Revolution   *Trend Question*

During the Industrial Revolution, the American political scene was dominated by "machines." Machine politics got its name because political parties, rather than individuals, held power. Machines were run by local officials who ensured voter loyalty by dispensing favors, such as jobs and government contracts.

23. **(D)** World War I   *Except Question*

Germany did not use concentration camps during World War I. At the time, anti-German sentiment in the United States resulted from Germany's aggressive tactics, such as the sinking of the *Lusitania* (A), the Zimmerman Telegram (B), the invasion of Belgium (C), and the use of submarine warfare (E).

24. **(C)** Cultural Trends   *Fact Question*

Dix's main concern was the treatment of the insane in American poorhouses and prisons. She worked diligently to reform the care given to the mentally ill and to improve their living conditions. Her efforts helped create mental institutions, where the mentally ill could receive humane treatment.

25. **(C)** Westward Expansion & Sectional Strife   *Except Question*

The Republicans formed between 1854 and 1855 as a northern-based party opposed to the extension of slavery into the territories. The party formed as a coalition of groups with disparate aims: some Republicans supported the complete abolition of slavery, while others believed that slavery should be allowed where it already existed. Despite these differences, the Republicans were united in their support of free-soil territories, and in the 1856 election, they were the main opposition to the pro-slavery Democrats.

26. **(D)** The 1960s   *Fact Question*

After North Vietnamese gunboats attacked American destroyers in the Tonkin Gulf, Johnson requested congressional authorization to use whatever power he deemed necessary to protect American interests in Vietnam. The Gulf of Tonkin Resolution gave Johnson the authority he needed to send ground troops to Vietnam in 1965.

27. **(B)** World War II *Quotation Question*

The Truman Doctrine advocated containment. Believing that the Soviet Union would continue to expand its influence, Truman asked Congress to give financial assistance to the democratic governments in Greece and Turkey in order to suppress "totalitarian regimes." The Truman Doctrine was a major aspect of American policy during the late 1940s.

28. **(C)** Revolution & Constitution *Trend Question*

The Navigation Acts, passed between 1651 and 1673, were designed to secure a favorable balance of trade for England at the expense of the colonies. The acts were not rigorously enforced, though, until the late eighteenth century. For most of the colonial period, England used a policy of salutary neglect toward the colonies. Under salutary neglect, England did not enforce trade laws, such as the Navigation Acts, that were detrimental to the colonial economy. By the late eighteenth century, England began to enforce the Navigation Acts because it needed to pay off its debts from the French and Indian War. This enforcement represented a shift in England's colonial policies, away from salutary neglect toward tighter regulation.

29. **(C)** The Great Depression & New Deal *Trend Question*

The conservative American Liberty League argued that the New Deal restricted democratically guaranteed freedoms, such as the the right to save money and to acquire property. Most of the members of the American Liberty League were wealthy business leaders who felt that capitalism could run properly only under small government.

30. **(A)** Civil War & Reconstruction *Except Question*

During Reconstruction, the Democratic Party was united in its efforts to return the South to Democratic control. A combination of other factors, including the ones stated in choices (B), (C), (D), and (E), contributed to the end of Reconstruction.

31. **(C)** A New Nation *Except Question*

The War Hawks, a group of westerners and southerners, pushed for a war against Britian in 1812, partially because they objected to Britain's policy of impressment. Under the leadership of John Calhoun and Henry Clay, they argued that a peace settlement with Britain would embarrass and weaken the new American government.

32. **(A)** 1970s–2000 *Trend Question*

During the Vietnam War, Nixon decided to expand the fighting into Cambodia in an effort to root out North Vietnamese soldiers who were hiding there. His decision prompted widespread antiwar protests on college campuses across the United States. At Kent State University, the confrontation turned violent, as national guardsmen fired on student demonstrators, killing four of them.

33. **(E)** The Progressive Era *Fact Question*

A Progressive, Woodrow Wilson pushed through an agenda of corporate reform. He supported lowering tariffs, creating a publicly-controlled centralized bank, workers' rights, and government regulation of trade and trusts. The Federal Trade Commision Act of 1914 created an agency that would investigate violations of interstate trade regulations, and the Clayton Antitrust Act of 1914 built on the vaguely worded Sherman Antitrust Act by defining illegal business practices.

34. (B) The Age of Jackson — *Fact Question*

John Calhoun and Henry Clay established the Whig Party in opposition to Jackson's Democrats. Calhoun and Clay objected to Jackson's policies and his frequent use of the veto. Taking their name from the British party that sought to reduce the power of the Crown, the Whigs first ran a candidate for president in 1836.

35. (B) World War II — *Trend Question*

Congress's override of Truman's veto demonstrated the system of checks and balances. Although the president supported the rights of labor in this case, more than two-thirds of Congress disagreed with his decision and thus voted against him, limiting his power to legislate.

36. (D) The Great Depression & New Deal — *Except Question*

The stock market crash resulted from a combination of overproduction and underconsumption. Underproduction on American farms was not a cause of the crash. In fact, one of FDR's New Deal measures was designed to encourage farmers to reduce production. The Agricultural Adjustment Administration provided subsidies to farmers who were willing to lower production levels; the AAA hoped that reduced production would result in increased prices for farm products.

37. (B) The Colonial Period — *Trend Question*

The Puritans left for Massachusetts Bay, hoping to purify the Anglican Church of its Catholic trappings. In 1630, under the leadership of John Winthrop, the Puritans settled in modern-day Boston, establishing a community they hoped would be a beacon of religious righteousness.

38. (B) Industrial Revolution — *Quotation Question*

This excerpt is from Booker T. Washington's Atlanta Exposition Address, in which Washington presented a blueprint for African-American advancement in the South. Washington emphasized vocational education and manual skills, which he claimed would make African Americans economically useful in the rebuilding of the South. Other civil rights leaders, such as W.E.B. Du Bois, criticized Washington for not demanding immediate political and social rights.

39. (D) The Colonial Period — *Fact Question*

The Spanish Empire was primarily interested in its American colonies as a source of gold and silver. Because Spain had no manufacturing or agricultural base, it relied on the acquisition of precious metals to buy needed products from other European countries.

40. (E) A New Nation — *Except Question*

At the 1814 Hartford Convention, Federalists gathered to complain about the policies of the ruling Republican Party. The New England-based Federalists accused the Republicans of neglecting the needs of New England commerce, which was hurt by the trade restrictions imposed during the War of 1812. The Republicans, of course, did not agree with the Federalists on this point.

41. (C) Revolution & Constitution — *Fact Question*

In *Letters from a Pennsylvania Farmer*, Dickinson argued against the legality of the Townshend Duties, which taxed glass, lead, paint, paper, and tea entering the colonies.

42. (E) Cultural Trends — *Except Question*

Walden Pond was, for a brief time, the experimental home of the transcendentalist Henry David Thoreau. There Thoreau escaped the materialism and technology of his society, but Walden Pond was not, as he himself acknowledged, a utopia.

43. (D) The 1960s — *Trend Question*

The Great Society's failure was primarily due to the government's shifting focus from domestic to foreign policy, as the situation in Vietnam worsened. The program's poor design and its enormous scope also contributed to its failure.

44. (D) The Colonial Period — *Fact Question*

Williams was banished from Massachusetts for advocating the complete separation of church and state. He argued that without complete separation, the state would eventually corrupt the church. In the colony of Rhode Island, which Williams established in 1647, the government broke from the Church of England and permitted religious freedom.

45. (E) Industrial Revolution — *Trend Question*

The railroad industry's largest customers, such as Rockefeller's Standard Oil, demanded rebates in return for doing exclusive business with railroad companies. Rockefeller reasoned that Standard Oil would give a railroad company so much business that he was entitled to a financial kickback.

46. (E) Westward Expansion & Sectional Strife — *Fact Question*

In the *Dred Scott* ruling, the Supreme Court declared that popular sovereignty was unconstitutional because it violated the Fifth Amendment, which stated that a citizen's property, including slaves, could not be taken away without due process. According to the Court's interpretation of the amendment, any attempt to prohibit slavery was unconstitutional. Popular sovereignty fell into this category, since it could potentially result in the prohibition of slavery in the territories. The Court also ruled that no African American, even if free, could become a citizen of the United States.

47. (B) The Age of Imperialism — *Cartoon Question*

The cartoon shows Theodore Roosevelt as a policeman, swinging a "big stick" labeled "The New Diplomacy." The Roosevelt corollary to the Monroe Doctrine stated that the United States had the right to monitor and intervene in the affairs of Latin America. The corollary did not express any expansionist desires, but it did help create the image of the United States as the world's policeman.

48. (B) Revolution & Constitution — *Fact Question*

The 1787 Northwest Ordinance prohibited slavery north of the Ohio River. The ordinance also created a settler's bill of rights and established the process through which territories became states.

49. (B) Industrial Revolution — *Except Question*

The main function of the Interstate Commerce Commission was to stop railroad companies from practicing price discrimination. The ICC did not consolidate the railroad companies into a single industry regulated by the government.

50. (E) The 1950s — *Trend Question*

In the *Brown* case, the Supreme Court ruled that segregation deprived African Americans of their rights under the Fourteenth Amendment, which guaranteed citizenship rights to all people born or naturalized in the United States. By ruling in this manner, the Court created an important precedent of using the Fourteenth Amendment to attack racial discrimination.

51. (C) Westward Expansion & Sectional Strife — *Fact Question*

The first—and only—president of the Confederate States of America was Jefferson Davis.

52. (C) The Roaring Twenties — *Fact Question*

The National Origins Act restricted the number of immigrants from southern and eastern Europe during the 1920s. At the time, southern and eastern Europeans were considered "inferior races," and they were also suspected of holding radical political views that threatened American stability.

53. (D) Cultural Trends — *Trend Question*

Arguing that their livelihoods depended on slave labor, slave owners called the institution of slavery a "necessary evil."

54. (C) World War II — *Trend Question*

When the United States began production of war materials, many formerly unemployed citizens were hired to work in the defense industry. Since the goods produced were shipped to Europe, the United States saw a rise in consumer purchasing power without the burden of additional supply. The United States emerged from the economic depression as demand rose while supply remained constant.

55. (B) The Age of Jackson — *Cartoon Question*

After vetoing the recharter of the Second Bank of the United States, Andrew Jackson began removing government funds from that bank and placing them in state banks. As the cartoon suggests, Jackson's actions effectively destroyed the Second Bank and its directors, who are seen running from the bank's ruins.

56. (C) The Age of Imperialism — *Trend Question*

After negotiations between Theodore Roosevelt and Columbia stalled, the United States fomented a revolution that resulted in Panamanian independence. Panama then signed a treaty that gave the United States perpetual use of what became the Canal Zone.

57. (A) Revolution & Constitution — *Trend Question*

During Shays's Rebellion, western Massachusetts farmers violently revolted against three county courthouses to prevent the foreclosure of their farms. Politicians believed the rebellion was an expression of lower class discontent and worried that the newly formed government was too weak to control such outbreaks.

58. (E) Civil War & Reconstruction — *Fact Question*

In 1864, Johnson, a Southern Democrat, became president after Lincoln's assassination. Although he pushed through a slightly modified version of Lincoln's Reconstruction plan, he was quite lenient, particularly in the opinion of the Radical Republicans, on the former Confederate states. He pardoned many powerful pro-slavery southerners and allowed southern governments to be dominated by pro-slavery groups. After gaining control of Congress in 1866, the Radical Republicans began to implement their own Reconstruction plans, which Johnson opposed but was unable to stop. The Fourteenth Amendment, which gave citizenship rights to all people born or naturalized in the United States, was one of the measures the Radical Republicans passed despite Johnson's opposition.

59. (B) Industrial Revolution — *Trend Question*

Although the Sherman Antitrust Act was intended to outlaw trusts, which prohibited free trade, the pro-business government of the 1890s frequently used the act to stop workers from striking, claiming that strikes were "in restraint of trade." In the early 1900s, the Progressive government, under Theodore Roosevelt, began using the act to bust corrupt trusts and to regulate other ones.

60. (C) The Colonial Period — *Fact Question*

Proprietary colonies were large land grants given by the British government to wealthy individuals who governed the land and reported directly to the king. The largest proprietary colonies in North America were Pennsylvania, Maryland, and Delaware.

61. (A) The 1950s — *Fact Question*

During the Eisenhower administration, Secretary of State John Foster Dulles practiced brinkmanship in his dealings with the Soviet Union. Criticizing earlier containment policies as passive, Dulles wanted to force Russia to the "brink" of war without actually getting the United States involved in armed conflict. By forcing the Soviets to back down from these confrontations, Dulles believed that he could humiliate them, giving the United States the upper hand during the Cold War.

62. (D) Revolution & Constitution — *Fact Question*

Delegates at the Constitutional Convention debated how to balance the competing needs of large and small states. Small states secured protection in the Senate, where each state was equally represented by two senators. In the House of Representatives, the number of representatives from each state was in proportion to the state's population.

63. (D) The Great Depression & New Deal — *Except Question*

The New Deal measures redefined the Democratic and Republican parties. African Americans, who consistently voted Republican ("the party of Lincoln") until the 1930s, shifted their votes to the Democrats as FDR turned the Democrats into the party of the underprivileged. Farmers and urban workers also flocked to the Democratic Party at this time. In the meantime, the Democrats lost the support of the white South, which switched its allegiance to the Republicans.

64. (D) Industrial Revolution — *Fact Question*

George wrote *Progress and Poverty* in response to the growing gap between the rich and the poor. In his book, he argued that the government should use tax income to pay for social programs for the poor.

65. (A) The Colonial Period — *Trend Question*

Bacon's Rebellion is an example of the tensions between the rich and the poor in colonial America. In 1676, Nathaniel Bacon accused the governor of Virginia of failing to protect poor farmers from Native American attacks. Bacon rallied a large group of poor farmers, who then attacked the Native Americans. When the governor branded them rebels, Bacon and his men attacked and looted the colonial city of Jamestown.

66. (C) The 1950s — *Map Question*

The shaded countries were charter members of the North Atlantic Treaty Organization, which formed in 1949. NATO was designed to contain communism, and it included a collective security provision to protect all member-nations.

67. (B) World War I — *Trend Question*

Wilson correctly perceived that a punitive settlement against Germany would create resentment and animosity, so he called instead for a peace without victory. The other Allied countries ignored Wilson's suggestion, and his fears were confirmed when Germany rearmed and World War II exploded throughout Europe.

68. **(B)** Cultural Trends *Trend Question*
Slave owners sent their slaves to church on Sunday, hoping that the services would teach the slaves obedience and contentment. The sermons made no reference to liberation and emphasized that slaves should be content with their fates and faithful to their masters.

69. **(C)** 1970s–2000 *Except Question*
The Reagan Doctrine emphasized a renewed American presence and active engagement in third world countries. The Cambodian incursion occurred in 1970, before Reagan became president in 1980.

70. **(D)** The Colonial Period *Except Question*
The Molasses Act had little real impact on the American colonies, since it was laxly enforced and since the colonists could avoid the tax by smuggling (B). The act was passed primarily to assuage the grievances of British sugar planters in the West Indies (A), and these sugar planters supported its passage (C). The British did not vigorously enforce the act, though, in keeping with its policy of salutary neglect, which stated that trade laws that hurt the colonial economy would not be enforced (E).

71. **(C)** The Roaring Twenties *Trend Question*
During his campaign, Harding promised a return to normalcy. After the upheavals of industrialization, modernization, and World War I, most Americans longed for a period of tranquillity. Harding capitalized on that desire in order to win the election.

72. **(E)** Revolution & Constitution *Except Question*
Due process does not provide financial compensation for defendants who are found innocent. Trial by a jury of one's peers, assistance from a lawyer, the ability to call a witness, and knowledge of the charges one faces form the basis of due process, as described in the Sixth Amendment.

73. **(B)** The Progressive Era *Quotation Question*
Roosevelt was determined to break up corrupt trusts that restrained trade or commerce. He did not want to break up all trusts, though. He allowed good trusts to remain in business as long as they adhered to government regulations.

74. **(B)** Cultural Trends *Except Question*
The Turner Rebellion occurred in 1831, fourteen years before Douglass wrote his *Narrative*. The rebellion inspired many abolitionists to begin their crusade against slavery.

75. **(A)** Industrial Revolution *Fact Question*
Alger was a proponent of the Gospel of Success, which claimed that any man could achieve wealth through hard work. To illustrate his beliefs, Alger wrote fictional stories about young men who went from rags to riches based on their determination and talent.

76. **(C)** The Colonial Period *Trend Question*
Indentured servants provided the American colonies with their initial labor force. In exchange for passage to the colonies, indentured servants agreed to work for free for a certain period of time (often seven years). At the end of this period, their masters gave them some clothing, seed, and perhaps a little plot of land for farming.

77. **(C)** The Age of Jackson *Trend Question*

Jackson and the Supreme Court clashed over the Indian Removal Act of 1830. The act granted Jackson the authority to remove Native Americans to assigned western regions. Jackson wanted to clear the land that tribes occupied in order to make room for American settlers. In 1832, the Supreme Court ruled in *Worcester v. Georgia* that the Cherokee were a "domestic dependent nation" with a right to be protected from forced migration and other harrassment. Jackson scoffed at this ruling, reportedly saying, "John Marshall has made his decision; now let him enforce it." The Supreme Court was powerless to enforce its decision, and the Cherokee removal continued unchecked.

78. **(A)** The Roaring Twenties *Fact Question*

In 1925, the Tennessee legislature banned the teaching of evolution in schools. In response, the American Civil Liberties Union offered to defend any Tennessee teacher willing to break this law and teach his students evolution. John Scopes accepted this offer, and Clarence Darrow defended him at his trial. Although Scopes was found guilty, Darrow managed to humiliate the anti-evolution proponents, significantly weakening the anti-evolution cause in the U.S.

79. **(C)** Revolution & Constitution *Map Question*

The shaded states were created under the Northwest Ordinances of 1784 and 1787. The Ordinances prohibited slavery in all of the shaded states, which lie north of the Ohio River, and they established the process by which regions in the territories could become states in the Union.

80. **(A)** Industrial Revolution *Fact Question*

Carnegie believed that as a steward of society, he had an obligation to give back to his society. Rather than give money directly to the poor, he chose to build educational institutions that could teach the poor to compete on their own in society.

81. **(D)** The Colonial Period *Except Question*

Chicago was not founded until after the colonial period. Philadelphia, New York, Boston, and Charleston were the principal centers of economic and political activity in the colonies.

82. **(B)** Industrial Revolution *Trend Question*

Small farmers struggled financially throughout the late eighteenth century, as crop prices fell and land prices rose. Farmers' groups, such as the Grange and the Farmers' Alliance, lobbied for political reform that would help small farms. In 1892, members of the Farmers' Alliance formed the Populist Party. The Populists' agenda focused on policies that would improve the situations of small famers and urban laborers. One of the major items of this agenda was the free coinage of silver, which would create inflation, easing debt repayment and raising crop prices.

83. **(B)** The Age of Jackson *Trend Question*

During Jackson's administration, most strikes were about the issue of wages. Suffering from the period's frequent economic downturns, workers wanted to increase their wages in order to meet their everyday needs.

84. **(A)** A New Nation *Chart Question*

Federalists advocated a loose reading of the Constitution. They supported a strong federal government with the power to create all laws beneficial to the country. Anti-federalists, or strict constructionists, believed that the federal government's powers should be confined to those enumerated in the Constitution in order to prevent a tyrannical centralized government from developing. According to the chart, lawyers tended to vote with the Federalists, suggesting that lawyers tended to support a loose reading of the Constitution.

85. **(A)** The 1950s *Trend Question*

During the presidential campaign of 1948, Truman invoked the Smith Act to prosecute eleven leaders of the Communist Party in the United States. This prosecution was supposed to demonstrate his aggressive actions against communism.

86. **(C)** The 1960s *Fact Question*

Black Power was the name given to militant civil rights groups in the late 1960s. Advocates of Black Power argued for separation from white society and sometimes preached violence against whites in order to achieve equality "by any means necessary."

87. **(A)** The Colonial Period *Fact Question*

The First Great Awakening was a religious revival movement that gained support during the 1730s and 1740s. Revival ministers urged their listeners to repent immediately in order to avoid divine punishment and to renounce material trappings. Their sermons, such as Jonathon Edwards's "Sinners in the Hands of an Angry God," often terrified audiences to near hysteria with stories of human corruption and sin. The Great Awakening was a response to Englightenment thought, which encouraged skepticism and logical reasoning.

88. **(A)** World War II *Fact Question*

The America First Committee, which consisted of industrialists, senators, and influential owners of media outlets, opposed American involvement in World War II. Supported by large segments of the Republican Party, the committee frequently criticized FDR's prewar measures. The committee endorsed Wendell Willkie for the presidency in 1940 because of his isolationist position.

89. **(C)** Industrial Revolution *Trend Question*

The sharecropping system kept African Americans in debt and tied to the land. The system prevented African Americans from making enough money to pay their bills and migrate north; as a result, they were forced to remain in the South, where they provided a cheap labor force for whites.

90. **(B)** A New Nation *Trend Question*

During Monroe's presidency, Secretary of State John Quincy Adams wrote the Monroe Doctrine, which stated that the United States was the dominant power in the western hemisphere. Adams wrote this doctrine out of fear that Russia was interested in establishing colonies in the Northwest and that Spain would try to regain its North American colonies.

SAT II U.S. History Practice Test 5

UNITED STATES HISTORY TEST 5 ANSWER SHEET

UNITED STATES HISTORY TEST 5

Directions: Each of the questions or incomplete statements below is followed by five suggested answers or completions. Select the one that is best in each case and then fill in the corresponding oval on the answer sheet.

1. In *On the Road*, Jack Kerouac depicted the

    (A) attitudes of the Beat Generation
    (B) building of the interstate highway system
    (C) phenomenon of family car trips in the 1950s
    (D) relocation of city dwellers to the suburbs
    (E) devastation caused by environmental pollution

2. All of the following issues caused the United States to support the Allies in World War I EXCEPT

    (A) Germany's use of submarine warfare
    (B) anti-German propaganda
    (C) a fear that Germany would help Mexico regain Texas, Arizona, and New Mexico
    (D) Germany's alliance with Russia
    (E) the sinking of the *Lusitania*

3. The Progressive Party supported

    (A) decreased government involvement and increased industrial responsibility
    (B) increased government involvement and increased industrial regulation
    (C) increased participation by the Supreme Court to check the excesses of both government and big business
    (D) desegregation and antilynching legislation
    (E) social Darwinism

4. The decision by the United States to join the North American Treaty Organization in 1949 was

    (A) in keeping with its foreign policy throughout the twentieth century
    (B) motivated solely by a desire to increase trade with Europe
    (C) an attempt to continue the Good Neighbor Policy in Latin America
    (D) a direct contradiction of the country's historical fear of collective security
    (E) a requirement of the Marshall Plan

5. Which of the following was the largest immigrant group between 1860 and 1890?

    (A) Africans
    (B) Chinese
    (C) English
    (D) Northern and western Europeans
    (E) Southern and eastern Europeans

6. In 1863, Abraham Lincoln issued the Emancipation Proclamation in order to

    (A) declare that he would free all slaves at the end of the war
    (B) let the Confederate states know that their return to the Union depended on emancipation
    (C) free slaves in the western territories only
    (D) free slaves in the Union
    (E) free slaves in areas under Confederate control

GO ON TO THE NEXT PAGE

UNITED STATES HISTORY TEST—Continued

7. This political cartoon, which appeared in 1754, emphasizes the necessity for the American colonies to unite in response to the

(A) Sugar Act
(B) Stamp Act
(C) Coercive Acts
(D) French and Indian War
(E) Navigation Acts

GO ON TO THE NEXT PAGE

UNITED STATES HISTORY TEST—*Continued*

8. Which of the following events led to the passage of the Embargo Act in 1807?

    (A) The failure of the Non-Intercourse Act to stop trade with foreign ports
    (B) An alliance between Britain and France
    (C) War with Britain
    (D) The *Chesapeake-Leopard* affair
    (E) Britain's abolition of slavery

9. In 1951, General Douglas MacArthur was relieved from duty because he

    (A) failed to defeat North Korea in the Korean War
    (B) was denounced as a communist by Senator Joseph McCarthy
    (C) publicly criticized the Truman administration's policies
    (D) refused to lead the American occupation of Japan
    (E) flouted regulations established by the United Nations

10. England established its first permanent colony in North America at

    (A) New York
    (B) Philadelphia
    (C) Jamestown
    (D) Plymouth
    (E) Roanoke

11. Which of the following was the primary cause of the Great Depression?

    (A) The stock market crash in 1929
    (B) Overseas investment by American corporations
    (C) The Stimson Doctrine
    (D) Strikes organized by the American Federation of Labor
    (E) An imbalance in supply and demand in the domestic market

UNITED STATES HISTORY TEST—*Continued*

**Union Troops
Available for Duty**

1862	527,204
1863	698,808
1864	611,250
1865	620,924

12. Which of the following best accounts for the rise in the number of Union troops in 1863?

 (A) Disheartened by Confederate losses, many Confederate troops decided to defect to the Union.
 (B) In support of Lincoln and his policy on slavery, Britain and France sent reinforcements to the Union army.
 (C) At the end of 1862, Nebraska became a state in the Union, and its citizens joined the Union troops.
 (D) After the Emancipation Proclamation, the Union began to enlist freed slaves in conquered Confederate territories.
 (E) In 1863, Maryland and West Virginia, which had seceded, decided to rejoin the Union.

GO ON TO THE NEXT PAGE

UNITED STATES HISTORY TEST—Continued

13. In the aftermath of the French and Indian War, the British levied all of the following taxes on the American colonies EXCEPT the

    (A) Molasses Act
    (B) Stamp Act
    (C) Sugar Act
    (D) Townshend Duties
    (E) Tea Act

14. A central feature of the economic program enacted by the Reagan administration in the 1980s was

    (A) the lowering of interest rates in order to raise inflation
    (B) government subsidies for working class families
    (C) an increase in federal spending on education and public transportation
    (D) increased government regulation of industry
    (E) tax cuts designed for the wealthy and intended to have a "trickle down" effect

15. Congress created the Civil Service Commission in 1883 in order to

    (A) give official support to the "spoils system"
    (B) train bureaucrats
    (C) give the civil service authority to regulate industry
    (D) create a civil service
    (E) prevent the practice of patronage in government jobs

16. After the United States entered World War II, the Allied powers collectively decided to

    (A) focus their attention on defeating Japan
    (B) focus their attention on defeating Germany
    (C) divide responsibilities, with Britain and the United States fighting Japan, while Russia dealt with Germany
    (D) force Italy's surrender immediately
    (E) push the Germans out of Latin America

17. John Calhoun made all of the following arguments in support of nullification EXCEPT

    (A) states' rights were supreme
    (B) tariffs levied by Congress must benefit all states equally
    (C) the central government was sovereign
    (D) protective tariffs raised in 1816, 1824, and 1828 damaged the Southern economy
    (E) states had the authority to decide the constitutionality of laws that affected their citizens

18. The philosophy of transcendentalism

    (A) instructed individuals to turn inward in order to escape the materialism of the world
    (B) argued that the poor could overcome poverty through hard work
    (C) advocated westward expansion
    (D) supported the women's rights movement
    (E) rekindled religious fervor and prompted many Americans to attend church

19. In the Freeport Doctrine, Stephen Douglas proposed that slavery

    (A) could be prohibited in the territories if the new states did not pass protective slave codes
    (B) was inevitable and that Congress should allow it to expand into the western territories
    (C) would soon end because it was growing increasingly unprofitable
    (D) should not impede the development of a transcontinental railroad
    (E) was too difficult a political issue for quick resolution and proposed a five-year moratorium on debate over it

20. Passed in 1933, the Twenty-first Amendment to the Constitution

    (A) outlawed communism in the United States
    (B) mandated that presidents balance the federal budget
    (C) repealed prohibition
    (D) set a two-term limit on the presidency
    (E) gave states new powers to regulate commerce

21. Anne Hutchinson was banished from Massachusetts Bay colony because she

    (A) agitated for women's rights
    (B) was an atheist
    (C) was a dissenter
    (D) refused to sign the Mayflower Compact
    (E) was convicted of witchcraft

GO ON TO THE NEXT PAGE

UNITED STATES HISTORY TEST—Continued

22. "The United States assumes no obligation to preserve the territorial integrity or political independence of any other country . . . under the provisions of article 10, or to employ the military or naval forces of the United States under any article of the treaty for any purpose, unless in any particular case the Congress, which . . . has the sole power to declare war . . . shall . . . so provide."

    This statement, made in 1919, reflects the view of the Senate in rejecting

    (A) the Washington Naval Treaty
    (B) membership in the League of Nations
    (C) the Kellogg-Briand Pact
    (D) the Neutrality Acts
    (E) the Open Door policy

23. Which of the following politicians was most responsible for designing the Compromises of 1833 and 1850?

    (A) Henry Clay
    (B) John Quincy Adams
    (C) John Calhoun
    (D) Thomas Jefferson
    (E) James Monroe

24. During the 1950s and 1960s, American politicians who believed in the "domino theory" argued

    (A) for a gradual transition from tariff barriers to free trade
    (B) that if a foreign country fell to communism, neighboring countries would likely become communist as well
    (C) that two-year terms in the House of Representatives would create instability
    (D) that the civil rights protests were creating public support for integration
    (E) that the exploration of outer space would give the United States an advantage over the Soviet Union during the Cold War

25. Henry Clay's American System proposed all of the following measures EXCEPT

    (A) internal improvements in the West
    (B) the abolition of slavery in the North and the West
    (C) high protective tariffs
    (D) the Second Bank of the United States
    (E) federal land sales

26. "We hold these truths to be self-evident: that all men and women are created equal; that they are endowed by their Creator with certain inalienable rights; that among these are life, liberty, and the pursuit of happiness; that to secure these rights governments are instituted, deriving their just powers from the consent of the governed. . . . The history of mankind is a history of repeated injuries and usurpations on the part of man toward woman, having in direct object the establishment of an absolute tyranny over her."

    The statement above was most likely made at the

    (A) United Nations
    (B) Hartford Convention
    (C) Seneca Falls Convention
    (D) Annapolis Convention
    (E) Potsdam Conference

27. Which of the following authors wrote novels that romanticized frontier life?

    (A) James Fenimore Cooper
    (B) Washington Irving
    (C) Herman Melville
    (D) Walt Whitman
    (E) Mark Twain

28. All of the following were true of the Suffolk Resolves EXCEPT

    (A) they declared the Intolerable Acts invalid
    (B) they called for a boycott of English goods until the Intolerable Acts were repealed
    (C) King George viewed them as a serious threat that could result in an English war with the American colonies
    (D) the American colonists used them to signal their desire for independence
    (E) they indicated that the colonies were still loyal to the king

29. Which of the following people was nicknamed the "Wizard of Menlo Park"?

    (A) J. P. Morgan
    (B) Cornelius Vanderbilt
    (C) John D. Rockefeller
    (D) Thomas Edison
    (E) Alexander Graham Bell

GO ON TO THE NEXT PAGE

UNITED STATES HISTORY TEST—Continued

30. African Americans and women entered the American workforce in record numbers during

    (A) Reconstruction
    (B) industrialization
    (C) World War I
    (D) the New Deal
    (E) the 1950s

31. Enlightenment thought in eighteenth-century America held that

    (A) religion was the most important aspect of daily life, and it guaranteed eternal happiness
    (B) the universe was created rationally, and humans could use reason to determine how it operated
    (C) involvement in the slave trade was a fundamental sin against God
    (D) English control was retarding economic growth in the American colonies
    (E) all residents of the American colonies should be able to participate in the political process

32. "It is emphatically the province and duty of the judicial department to say what the law is. Those who apply the rule to particular cases, must of necessity expound and interpret that rule. If two laws conflict with each other, the courts must decide on the operation of each. So if a law be in opposition to the constitution; if both the law and the constitution apply to a particular case, so that the court must either decide that case conformably to the law, disregarding the constitution; or conformably to the constitution, disregarding the law; the court must determine which of these conflicting rules governs the case. This is of the very essence of judicial duty."

    In this 1803 decision, the Supreme Court, under the leadership of John Marshall, ruled

    (A) to strike down the South Carolina nullification threat
    (B) that the Court had the power of judicial review
    (C) that the abolition of slavery was unconstitutional
    (D) in favor of congressional control of interstate commerce
    (E) to give the president the authority to interpret the Constitution

33. During his presidency, William Howard Taft argued that global stability could be achieved through

    (A) gunboat diplomacy
    (B) American investment abroad
    (C) isolationism
    (D) free trade
    (E) peace without victory

34. The growth of journalism in the 1840s had important consequences for American society primarily because

    (A) politicians exploited newspapers as a new means to campaign for office
    (B) newspapers exposed the conflicting views of the North and the South over the issue of slavery
    (C) newspapers played an important role in expanding religious evangelicalism
    (D) journalists promoted traditional family values
    (E) average people were able to express their political opinions in letters to newspapers

35. In the early 1870s, Granger organizations transformed from being predominantly social and cultural to being political because

    (A) their membership was declining as farmers abandoned their homes and moved to cities
    (B) other farm organizations began to compete for members by offering farm education lectures and events
    (C) of their grievances against the railroads
    (D) they were ridiculed in the eastern press for being old-fashioned
    (E) of their increasing support for segregation

36. During the Civil War, England refrained from entering into an alliance with the Confederacy for all of the following reasons EXCEPT

    (A) mill owners in England wanted to replace southern cotton with Egyptian cotton
    (B) England relied more heavily on wheat purchases from the North than on cotton purchases from the South
    (C) France had already allied with the North, and England did not want to start a war against another European nation
    (D) antislavery sentiment in England was strong
    (E) the North's victory at Antietam convinced Britain that the South could not win the war

GO ON TO THE NEXT PAGE

UNITED STATES HISTORY TEST—*Continued*

37. Which of the following prompted the meeting of the First Continental Congress?

    (A) The Battle of Saratoga
    (B) The Battle of Lexington and Concord
    (C) The Coercive Acts
    (D) The Stamp Act
    (E) The Intolerable Acts

38. William Randolph Hearst contributed to the Spanish-American War by

    (A) practicing yellow journalism
    (B) providing Cuban nationalists with financial backing
    (C) winning public support for the Spanish after publishing articles that cast the Cubans in a negative light
    (D) lobbying President William McKinley to support the Spanish
    (E) representing the United States in negotiations with Spain

39. Which of the following individuals played a major role in the development and operation of the underground railroad?

    (A) Harriet Tubman
    (B) Frederick Douglass
    (C) Nat Turner
    (D) David Walker
    (E) Gabriel Prosser

40. In the Monroe Doctrine, the United States was

    (A) asserting its intention to dominate its hemisphere without European interference
    (B) advocating the settlement of the West
    (C) announcing its desire to be actively involved in European political affairs
    (D) reacting to an economic downturn by trying to increase trade
    (E) hoping to avoid costly wars with Native American tribes in the West

41. The Tuskegee Institute was established in order to provide African Americans with

    (A) a lobbying group
    (B) liberal arts education
    (C) practical education
    (D) an archive of the African-American experience
    (E) healthcare in the rural south

42. Which of the following provided the initial source of wealth in the Jamestown colony?

    (A) Gold and precious metals
    (B) The slave trade
    (C) Timber
    (D) Tobacco
    (E) Cotton

43. Franklin D. Roosevelt was unsuccessful in his attempt to pack the Supreme Court in 1937 because

    (A) his brain trust was ineffective in persuading Congress to support the idea
    (B) his identification with organized labor damaged his image
    (C) packing the court was unconstitutional
    (D) the Depression was receding and no one was focused on politics
    (E) most Americans did not want to alter the balance of power in government

44. All of the following were examples of American nativism and xenophobia in the post–World War I era EXCEPT the

    (A) Palmer Raids
    (B) National Origins Act
    (C) rebirth of the Ku Klux Klan
    (D) Chinese Exclusion Act
    (E) executions of Sacco and Vanzetti

45. Social Darwinists in the United States argued that Americans who suffered financially and socially from industrialization

    (A) required the assistance of the federal government through welfare programs
    (B) should be assisted by their churches
    (C) should be exempt from taxes
    (D) would not survive and should be left alone to face extinction
    (E) only required some luck and honest effort to succeed in society

GO ON TO THE NEXT PAGE

46. King Philip's War of 1675 was a conflict between

   (A) Native Americans and settlers in the Plymouth colony
   (B) French and English settlers in western Pennsylvania
   (C) the Spanish and Native Americans in Florida
   (D) the English and Native American slaves in Virginia
   (E) the French and Native Americans on the Canadian border

47. The Northwest Ordinances of 1784 and 1787 resolved the issue of

   (A) regulation of Native-American affairs
   (B) competing colonial land claims
   (C) control of interstate trade
   (D) design of a uniform currency
   (E) organization of national armed forces

UNITED STATES HISTORY TEST—Continued

48. The poster above refers to

   (A) women's attempt to win the right to vote
   (B) the government's effort to end the depression
   (C) women's participation in defense plants during World War II
   (D) Progressive era politics concerning women and prohibition
   (E) the fight against communism in the post–World War II era

UNITED STATES HISTORY TEST—Continued

49. By protesting in 1965 at Selma, Alabama, Martin Luther King Jr. hoped to

    (A) extend the 1964 Civil Rights Act into the private sector
    (B) secure voting rights for African Americans
    (C) support an economic "bill of rights" for African Americans
    (D) stop the extensive drafting of African Americans to fight in Vietnam
    (E) promote racial harmony in the AFL-CIO

50. France's initial interest in the New World stemmed from a desire to discover

    (A) gold and silver
    (B) a route to Asia
    (C) a religious safe haven
    (D) slave labor
    (E) rare spices

GO ON TO THE NEXT PAGE

UNITED STATES HISTORY TEST—Continued

51. The shaded area on the map indicates the land

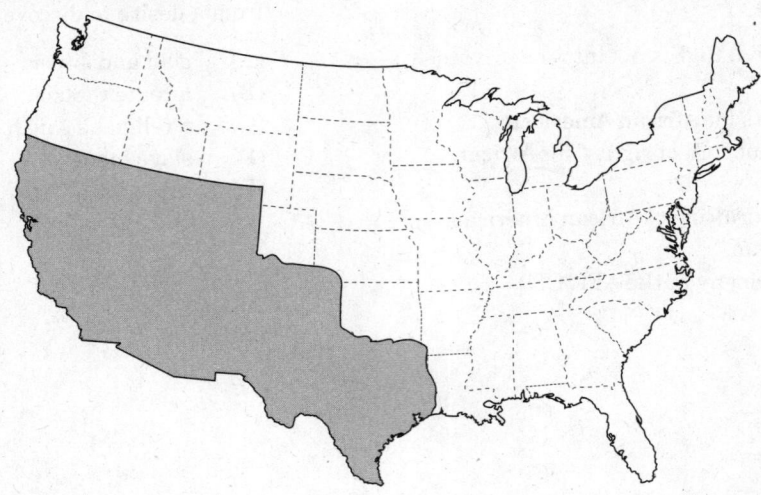

(A) in which slavery was permitted by the Missouri Compromise
(B) that was purchased from the French in 1803
(C) that was the focus of the Wilmot Proviso
(D) that was set aside for Native American reservations
(E) in which slavery was prohibited by the Compromise of 1850

UNITED STATES HISTORY TEST—*Continued*

52. Huey Long opposed the New Deal, arguing that it did not sufficiently address the

    (A) plight of banks
    (B) demands of labor unions
    (C) complaints raised by the American Liberty League
    (D) conservation of the Tennessee Valley
    (E) suffering of the poor

53. According to English mercantile theory, the American colonies were

    (A) not a relevant priority
    (B) a source of raw materials and a marketplace for finished goods
    (C) a hindrance that needed to be controlled
    (D) a potential source of cheap labor
    (E) a good military base for impeding the commerce of other nations

54. Dwight Eisenhower's policy of dynamic conservatism proposed all of the following measures EXCEPT

    (A) tax cuts
    (B) the desegregation of public education
    (C) government-funded public works projects
    (D) farm subsidies
    (E) polio immunization

55. The "Era of Good Feelings" refers to

    (A) James Monroe's presidency
    (B) the period following the establishment of the First Bank of the United States
    (C) the War of 1812
    (D) the period immediately following the adoption of the Constitution
    (E) the period following the Louisiana Purchase

56. Historians have called 1866 "the critical year" in the process of Reconstruction because

    (A) Andrew Johnson took control of Reconstruction after Abraham Lincoln's assassination
    (B) most of the southern states had already returned to the Union under Abraham Lincoln's ten percent plan
    (C) all former Confederate states ratified the Fourteenth Amendment
    (D) Radical Republicans won enormous majorities in the congressional elections
    (E) the Supreme Court declared the Black Codes unconstitutional

57. The Specie Circular of 1836 mandated that

    (A) government lands could be purchased only with gold or silver
    (B) all citizens pay an income tax
    (C) slave sales be confined to major slave markets in Washington, D.C., and Charleston
    (D) the Second Bank of the United States pay all government debts immediately
    (E) paper money was no longer legal currency in the United States

58. In the 1840s, American nativists accused new immigrants of all of the following EXCEPT

    (A) creating slums in urban areas
    (B) taking jobs away from American citizens
    (C) bringing dangerous revolutionary ideas into the country
    (D) conspiring to give the Catholic Church influence in American politics
    (E) trying to replace slaves as a free labor force in the south

59. The main weakness of the government created by the Articles of Confederation was

    (A) the lack of a president
    (B) insufficient attention to foreign policy
    (C) Congress's inability to coin money
    (D) Congress's inability to tax
    (E) land policy restrictions

60. The Gospel of Success preached the idea that

    (A) welfare was necessary for the poor
    (B) the wealthy deserved success
    (C) the poor should seek spiritual solace in religion
    (D) only the fittest would survive in society
    (E) religion and business shared similar goals

61. All of the following individuals were involved in the Watergate scandal EXCEPT

    (A) Gerald Ford
    (B) E. Howard Hunt
    (C) G. Gordon Liddy
    (D) John Mitchell
    (E) Robert Haldeman

GO ON TO THE NEXT PAGE

UNITED STATES HISTORY TEST—Continued

62. In *Schenck v. The United States* (1919), the Supreme Court ruled that

    (A) socialism was unconstitutional and should be banned
    (B) civil liberties could be restricted in times of national crisis
    (C) prohibiting women from the franchise violated the Fourteenth Amendment
    (D) the League of Nation's collective security clause violated the Senate's enumerated power to declare war
    (E) Congress did not have the authority to regulate immigration

63. The Haymarket riot of 1886 resulted in all of the following EXCEPT

    (A) waning public support for unions
    (B) violent clashes between striking workers and the police
    (C) the formation of the Knights of Labor
    (D) the detonation of a bomb
    (E) the imprisonment of several people accused of inciting the riot

64. "If a nation shows that it knows how to act with reasonable efficiency and decency in social and political matters, if it keeps order and pays its obligations, it need fear no interference from the United States. Chronic wrongdoing, or an impotence which results in a general loosening of the ties of civilized society, may in America, as elsewhere, ultimately require intervention by some civilized nation, and in the Western Hemisphere the adherence of the United States to the Monroe Doctrine may force the United States, however reluctantly, in flagrant cases of such wrongdoing or impotence, to the exercise of an international police power."

    Which aspect of American imperialist thought does this excerpt from the Roosevelt corollary to the Monroe Doctrine reflect?

    (A) The search for new economic markets
    (B) The white man's burden
    (C) The Open Door policy
    (D) Dollar diplomacy
    (E) Manifest destiny

65. The adoption of the Three-fifths clause during the framing of the Constitution settled the issue of how

    (A) to select delegates to the electoral college
    (B) new states would enter the Union
    (C) slaves would be counted in the population
    (D) the Supreme Court would be represented
    (E) to pay state debts

66. The War for "Bleeding Kansas" had all of the following repercussions EXCEPT

    (A) John Brown's murder of a group of pro-slavery settlers
    (B) the drafting of the Lecompton Constitution, which proposed establishing slavery in Kansas
    (C) an attack by a pro-slavery groups from Missouri on an antislavery group in Lawrence, Kansas
    (D) Kansas's entrance to the Union as a slave state in 1861
    (E) interference in the Kansas election by "border ruffians" from Missouri

67. The efforts of the Agricultural Adjustment Administration during the New Deal resulted in

    (A) the strict enforcement of farm production quotas under threat of imprisonment
    (B) a decrease in the price of farm products
    (C) an increase in the production of staple crops
    (D) the migration of many poor farmers from the dust bowl to California
    (E) the increasing importation of staple crops from overseas

68. At the end of the 1763 French and Indian War, all of the following occurred EXCEPT

    (A) Britain took Florida from Spain
    (B) France gave Louisiana to Spain
    (C) Britain had a substantial war debt
    (D) the American colonies became self-governing
    (E) France gave Canada to Britain

GO ON TO THE NEXT PAGE

UNITED STATES HISTORY TEST—Continued

69. The Montgomery Bus Boycott helped shape future civil rights strategies because it

    (A) was the first time nonviolent protest had been employed in the cause of civil rights
    (B) relied on extensive media exposure
    (C) combined direct action protest with litigation in the courts
    (D) convinced most white southerners to change their attitudes toward African Americans
    (E) met with no hostility from local southern authorities or townspeople in Montgomery

70. The pace of industrialization in post–Civil War America was greatly enhanced by

    (A) the consolidation of the railroads
    (B) technological innovations
    (C) the utilization of steam power
    (D) southern focus on factory building
    (E) the Granger movement

71. Franklin D. Roosevelt's "Good Neighbor" policy stated that the United States would not intervene in the affairs of

    (A) Europe
    (B) Africa
    (C) Canada
    (D) Latin America
    (E) South America

72. In response to the Supreme Court's decision to integrate public schools, one hundred southern Congressmen

    (A) swore to uphold the new law despite criticism from their constituents
    (B) filed an appeal in the federal courts
    (C) issued a southern "manifesto" that urged defiance of the ruling
    (D) requested federal funds to facilitate the integration process
    (E) agreed to follow the law, but only if it could be implemented gradually

73. The strike by the American Railway Union against the Pullman Sleeping Car Company was organized and led by

    (A) John Altgeld
    (B) Samuel Gompers
    (C) Terrence Powderly
    (D) Eugene Debs
    (E) A. Philip Randolph

74. Before entering the war in 1941, the United States contributed to the Allied effort by

    (A) starting work on the Manhattan Project
    (B) establishing the Committee to Defend America First
    (C) providing lend-lease aid
    (D) signing the Tripartite Pact
    (E) selling arms to rebels in Italy

75. Helen Hunt Jackson wrote *A Century of Dishonor* (1881) in order to

    (A) encourage people to attend church
    (B) argue for women's rights
    (C) raise support for the abolition of slavery
    (D) attack the actions of the American government since the end of colonial rule
    (E) describe the suffering of Native Americans at the hands of the government

76. John T. Scopes was involved in the

    (A) presidential campaign of 1920
    (B) monkey trial in Dayton, Tennessee
    (C) 1919 Black Sox scandal
    (D) Washington Naval Conference
    (E) growth of the advertising industry

77. The American Federation of Labor was established in order to

    (A) organize factory workers nationwide into one large powerful union
    (B) lead a socialist revolution that would put workers in control of factories
    (C) create a powerful interracial union that would fight race discrimination in southern factories
    (D) unionize only skilled workers who could deal with employers from a position of strength
    (E) shut down the Knights of Labor, which Gompers considered anti-Catholic

GO ON TO THE NEXT PAGE

UNITED STATES HISTORY TEST—Continued

78. Which of the following was a point of contention between strict constructionists and loose constructionists?

    (A) The establishment of political parties
    (B) The elastic clause of the Constitution
    (C) The balance of power between large states and small states
    (D) The morality of slavery
    (E) The central government's response to the Whiskey Rebellion

79. Which of the following events was a major catalyst in the secession of southern states from the Union in 1860 and 1861?

    (A) Abraham Lincoln's election to the presidency
    (B) The Tariff of Abominations
    (C) Northerners' condemnation of slavery
    (D) The South's relative poverty compared to the North
    (E) The Supreme Court's ruling that popular sovereignty was unconstitutional

80. When the Populists joined the Democrats in supporting William Jennings Bryan for the presidency in 1896, they abandoned all of their former demands EXCEPT

    (A) a graduated income tax
    (B) free silver
    (C) the abolition of national banks
    (D) direct election
    (E) secret ballot voting

81. The Quaker belief that individuals could experience the "inner light" of God for themselves made Quakers

    (A) controlling and nonreligious
    (B) abandon the concept of priests and ministers
    (C) critical of Puritans and Pilgrims
    (D) advocates of slavery because slaves were heathens
    (E) unwilling to allow women to worship with men

82. All of the following contributed to the expansion of the American economy in the 1950s EXCEPT

    (A) government spending
    (B) baby boomers
    (C) technological progress
    (D) suburban growth
    (E) the end of the Korean War

83. The Supreme Court decision in *Plessy v. Ferguson* (1896) gave constitutional legitimacy to

    (A) industrial rebates
    (B) Jim Crow laws
    (C) women's right to vote
    (D) sharecropping
    (E) trusts and monopolies

84. When it was formed between 1854 and 1855, the Republican Party was united in its stance

    (A) against immigration
    (B) against the existence of slavery
    (C) against the extension of slavery
    (D) in favor of the Kansas-Nebraska Act
    (E) in favor of popular sovereignty

85. In 1920, the women's suffrage movement gained popular support that resulted in the Nineteenth Amendment, which enfranchised women, because

    (A) the Supreme Court ruled that women's disenfranchisement was unconstitutional
    (B) women's contributions in World War I convinced Americans that they deserved to vote
    (C) the Republican Party had always supported women's suffrage and backed the amendment
    (D) nativists wanted to increase the number of native voters in order to keep political power out of the hands of foreigners
    (E) a sufficient number of women had been elected to Congress to push the amendment to a vote

86. Supporters of the eugenics movement would most likely call for

    (A) aggressive foreign policy focused on colonization and economic imperialism
    (B) states' rights
    (C) improvements in secondary education
    (D) an end to immigration
    (E) political and corporate reform

UNITED STATES HISTORY TEST—Continued

87. The federal government's approach to business during the 1880s can be best described as

    (A) hostile
    (B) regulatory
    (C) laissez-faire
    (D) exploitative
    (E) nonexistent

88. The Bill of Rights was added to the Constitution because

    (A) prominent opponents of the Constitution demanded more civil rights protections as a condition for ratification
    (B) Federalists wanted to emphasize the importance of civil liberties by describing them in a separate document
    (C) the framers of the Constitution wanted to test the efficiency of the amendment process
    (D) the Bill of Rights effectively balanced the power of the federal government with that of the states
    (E) pro-slavery forces wanted to distinguish free people from slaves

89. William Lloyd Garrison argued that slavery should be

    (A) gradually abolished over a ten-year period
    (B) continued until slaves could purchase their freedom
    (C) subject to a political referendum regarding abolition
    (D) abolished immediately without compensation to slaveowners
    (E) subject to judicial review by the Supreme Court

GO ON TO THE NEXT PAGE

UNITED STATES HISTORY TEST—Continued

AFTER THE FEAST.
THE WORKING MAN GETS WHAT IS LEFT!

90. Which of the following best summarizes the point of the cartoon above?

   (A) The wealthy earn their success through hard work, whereas the poor are lazy and wait for handouts.
   (B) Working men are not fit to survive in society, so they will die from starvation.
   (C) In the United States, wealthy robber barons outnumber workers.
   (D) In American society, the wealthy control all the money and leave nothing for the average working man.
   (E) The wealthy are stealing from the poor, who are left with nothing.

S T O P

IF YOU FINISH BEFORE TIME IS CALLED, YOU MAY CHECK YOUR WORK ON THIS TEST ONLY.
DO NOT TURN TO ANY OTHER TEST IN THIS BOOK.

SAT II U.S. History Practice Test 5 Explanations

Calculating Your Score

Question Number	Correct Answer	Right	Wrong	Question Number	Correct Answer	Right	Wrong	Question Number	Correct Answer	Right	Wrong
1.	A			31.	B			61.	A		
2.	D			32.	B			62.	B		
3.	B			33.	B			63.	C		
4.	D			34.	B			64.	B		
5.	D			35.	C			65.	C		
6.	E			36.	C			66.	D		
7.	D			37.	E			67.	D		
8.	D			38.	A			68.	D		
9.	C			39.	A			69.	C		
10.	C			40.	A			70.	B		
11.	E			41.	C			71.	D		
12.	D			42.	D			72.	C		
13.	A			43.	E			73.	D		
14.	E			44.	D			74.	C		
15.	E			45.	D			75.	E		
16.	B			46.	A			76.	B		
17.	C			47.	B			77.	D		
18.	A			48.	C			78.	B		
19.	A			49.	B			79.	A		
20.	C			50.	B			80.	B		
21.	C			51.	C			81.	B		
22.	B			52.	E			82.	E		
23.	A			53.	B			83.	B		
24.	B			54.	B			84.	C		
25.	B			55.	A			85.	B		
26.	C			56.	D			86.	D		
27.	A			57.	A			87.	C		
28.	D			58.	E			88.	A		
29.	D			59.	D			89.	D		
30.	C			60.	B			90.	D		

Your raw score for the SAT II U.S. History test is calculated from the number of questions you answer correctly and incorrectly. Once you have determined your composite score, use the conversion table on page 19 of this book to calculate your scaled score. To calculate your raw score, count the number of questions you answered correctly: _____
$$A$$

Count the number of questions you answered incorrectly, and multiply that number by $\frac{1}{4}$:

$$\underline{}_{B} \times \frac{1}{4} = \underline{}_{C}$$

Subtract the value in field C from value in field A: _____
$$D$$

Round the number in field D to the nearest whole number. This is your raw score: _____
$$E$$

1. **(A)** The 1950s   *Fact Question*

Many people consider *On the Road* to be the bible of the Beat Generation. Kerouac's novel centers on a group of traveling youths who rebel against the conformity and conservatism of American life in the 1950s.

2. **(D)** World War I   *Except Question*

Russia did not enter into an alliance with Germany during World War I. After the Russian Revolution, Russia dropped out of the war and signed a punitive peace treaty with Germany.

3. **(B)** The Progressive Era   *Trend Question*

Progressives demanded an interventionist government on all levels—national, state, and local. They also believed that the government should hold big business accountable for its corrupt practices. The Progressive Era lasted roughly from 1901 to 1917.

4. **(D)** World War II   *Trend Question*

America's participation in NATO represented a shift in the nation's foreign policy. At the end of World War I, the Senate rejected membership in the League of Nations on the grounds that the collective security clause in the League's charter could force the United States into future wars. After World War II, however, the fear of communism began to dominate foreign policy, and the United States decided to join NATO as part of its strategy of containment.

5. **(D)** The Industrial Revolution   *Fact Question*

Between 1860 and 1890, most immigrants to the United States came from northern and western Europe. In the mid-nineteenth century, there was also significant Chinese immigration to the West, but in 1882, the government excluded Chinese immigration for a ten-year period, after anti-immigrant sentiments (often directed against the Chinese) arose among the public. During the 1890s, "new" immigrants, southern and eastern Europeans, began arriving in the United States in large numbers, and many of them settled in the Northeast.

6. **(E)** Civil War & Reconstruction   *Fact Question*

The Emancipation Proclamation freed slaves under Confederate control. It did not free slaves in the Union or in parts of the Confederacy that were under Union control. Because the Confederacy did not acknowledge Lincoln's authority, the proclamation in fact freed almost no slaves.

7. **(D)** The Colonial Period   *Cartoon Question*

This cartoon depicts a snake divided into eight sections. The abbreviations stand for South Carolina, North Carolina, Virginia, Maryland, Pennsylvania, New Jersey, New York, and the New England colonies. The slogan "Join, or Die" refers to Benjamin Franklin's 1754 Albany Plan, which advocated the unification of the colonies in the face of French and Native American threats. The Albany Plan proposed the creation of a single government that would rule all the colonies, but the colonies, not ready for unification, rejected the plan.

8. **(D)** A New Nation   *Trend Question*

In 1807 the British HMS *Leopard* first attacked and then boarded the American USS *Chesapeake*. On board, the British hanged four men they accused of deserting the Royal Navy. Thomas Jefferson responded to this event by passing the Embargo Act, which put an end to American importation and exportation. He hoped that the act would end Britain's continual violation of American neutrality at sea, but instead the act's primary effect was to damage the American economy.

9. **(C)** The 1950s *Fact Question*

MacArthur was relieved from duty for publicly criticizing the Truman administration. Frustrated by the military stalemate in Korea, MacArthur wanted to bomb North Korean munitions reserves in Manchuria, but Truman refused to grant him permission. In response, MacArthur criticized Truman's effectiveness as commander-in-chief of the Army. This criticism outraged Truman's military advisors, who then urged Truman to fire the general.

10. **(C)** The Colonial Period *Fact Question*

England's first permanent colony in North America was established at Jamestown in 1607. England's earlier attempt to settle Roanoke failed when storms and a dearth of supplies forced the settlers to abandon the colony around 1590.

11. **(E)** The Great Depression & New Deal *Trend Question*

Overproduction and underconsumption were the fundamental causes of the Great Depression. Corporations continued to produce goods, but American consumers were unable to purchase them because wages did not keep up with rising prices. The stock market crash in 1929 was a symptom of the depression—not its cause.

12. **(D)** Civil War & Reconstruction *Chart Question*

Lincoln's Emancipation Proclamation of 1863 freed slaves in Confederate-held territories. Because the Confederacy refused to recognize the Union's authority, the proclamation in practice freed very few slaves at the time it was issued. But as the Union troops conquered Confederate territories, they began to enlist the freed slaves in those areas. By the end of the war, African-American soldiers made up almost ten percent of the Union troops.

13. **(A)** Revolution & Constitution *Except Question*

The Molasses Act was passed in 1733, before the outbreak of the French and Indian War. In keeping with England's policy of salutary neglect at the time, the act was never rigorously enforced because it was detrimental to the colonial economy. It was levied in order to calm British sugar merchants' concerns about competition from the French, but American colonists easily evaded it by smuggling.

14. **(E)** 1970–2000 *Fact Question*

Reagan cut taxes for the very wealthy, hoping that these tax cuts would have a "trickle-down" effect. This policy was based on supply-side economics, which held that tax cuts for the very rich would trickle down to the poor, since tax cuts would free up more money for the rich to invest in the economy. Reagan's tax cuts resulted in a major recession in the middle of the 1980s and in an increase in the federal deficit.

15. **(E)** Industrial Revolution *Fact Question*

Congress created the Civil Service Commission under the Pendleton Act in order to create a meritocratic civil service. Until the creation of the Civil Service Commission, government jobs were distributed to the administration's supporters and allies. The commission was created in order to restrict this practice of patronage and to prevent the massive turnover in government jobs that occurred with each new presidential administration.

16. **(B)** World War II *Fact Question*

The Allies agreed that Germany posed the greatest threat in World War II. Accordingly, they resolved to defeat Germany before dealing with Japan.

17. **(C)** The Age of Jackson *Except Question*

Calhoun, a native of South Carolina, was outraged by the protective tariffs Congress levied in 1816, 1824, and 1828. In response to the 1828 "Tariff of Abominations," Calhoun argued that the tariffs were unconstitutional because they protected regional interests, and he urged southern states to nullify the tariffs within their borders. The nullification argument depended on the argument that states' rights were supreme. The supporters of nullification did not believe that the central government was sovereign.

18. **(A)** Cultural Trends *Fact Question*

A challenge to rationalism and materialism, transcendentalism was a spiritual movement that focused on the individual. Transcendentalists believed that individuals could acquire an understanding of God by turning inward; they emphasized intuition and emotion. Ralph Waldo Emerson and Henry David Thoreau were leading figures in the transcendentalist movement.

19. **(A)** Westward Expansion & Sectional Strife *Fact Question*

In the *Dred Scott* decision, the Supreme Court ruled that popular sovereignty was unconstitutional because it violated the Fifth Amendment. Douglas, a supporter of popular sovereignty, devised the Freeport Doctrine as a way of getting around the Supreme Court's ruling. Douglas suggested that territories could effectively abolish slavery by not enacting slave codes. He argued that slaveholders would not risk bringing their slaves into areas without laws that protected their slaveholding rights.

20. **(C)** The Great Depression & New Deal *Fact Question*

The Twenty-First Amendment, ratified in 1833, repealed prohibition.

21. **(C)** The Colonial Period *Fact Question*

John Winthrop and other influential members of the community believed Hutchinson's teachings were an attack on Puritanism. In 1637, they banished her from Massachusetts Bay for being a dissenter.

22. **(B)** The Roaring Twenties *Quotation Question*

The quotation is from a statement made by Henry Cabot Lodge to the Senate when it was deliberating joining the League of Nations. Lodge opposed participation because he thought the collective security clause (article 10 of the League's charter) would commit the United States to fighting its allies' wars. The Senate agreed with Lodge and rejected membership in the League of Nations.

23. **(A)** A New Nation *Fact Question*

Henry Clay, a congressman from Kentucky, designed the Compromise of 1833 and the Compromise of 1850. Known as the "Great Compromiser," Clay also helped negotiate the Missouri Compromise of 1820 and resolve many sectional tensions in Congress.

24. **(B)** The 1960s *Trend Question*

According to the domino theory, if a nation falls to communism, the nations surrounding it will likely fall to communist rule as well. This theory played a crucial role in justifying the policy of containment that the U.S. government employed in the 1950s and 1960s. Dwight Eisenhower relied on this theory when deciding to intervene in Vietnam. He believed that if communists took over Vietnam, they would soon control most of Southeast Asia.

25. **(B)** A New Nation *Except Question*

Clay's proposed American System was designed to achieve economic self-sufficiency for the United States by linking regions of the country together commercially. His proposal included internal improvements in the West, high protective tariffs, the creation of the Second Bank of the United States, and federal land sales to raise revenue for the government. Clay made no mention of slavery in his proposal.

26. **(C)** Cultural Trends *Quotation Question*

This excerpt is from the Declaration of Sentiments, which stated that men and women are created equal. The Declaration was issued in 1848 at the Seneca Falls Convention, where the members of the women's rights movement met under the leadership of Lucretia Mott and Elizabeth Cady Stanton.

27. **(A)** Cultural Trends *Fact Question*

James Fenimore Cooper became famous for writing novels that presented romantic visions of the American frontier. He is credited with creating the first western hero in such novels as *The Pioneers* (1823) and *The Last of the Mohicans* (1826).

28. **(D)** Revolution & Constitution *Except Question*

The colonists issued the Suffolk Resolves as a strong protest against the Intolerable Acts, but they refrained from demanding independence. Instead, the colonists pledged continued loyalty to the king. The main purpose of the Suffolk Resolves was to state the colonists' intention of boycotting British goods until the British government repealed the acts. Despite the pledge of loyalty, King George viewed the resolves as a serious threat to peace and feared that violence would ensue.

29. **(D)** Industrial Revolution *Fact Question*

In his research laboratory in Menlo Park, New Jersey, Thomas Edison invented the phonograph, the moving picture projector, and the incandescent light bulb, thus earning him the nickname the "Wizard of Menlo Park."

30. **(C)** World War I *Trend Question*

African Americans and women entered the workforce in record numbers during World War I. The war stimulated the domestic economy, increasing factory output. In order to meet new production levels, the workforce swelled by a million people.

31. **(B)** The Colonial Period *Fact Question*

Enlightenment thought, which spread through Europe and the United States in the eighteenth century, promoted the idea that the universe was grounded in rationalism and logic. Enlightenment thinkers revised traditional religious beliefs and advised looking to science and logic for proof of religion. Most of these rational thinkers believed that the world's natural order implied the existence of a rational creator. Benjamin Franklin and Thomas Jefferson are two examples of famous American rationalists.

32. **(B)** A New Nation *Quotation Question*

The Supreme Court's decision in *Marbury v. Madison* established the principle of judicial review, extending the power given to the Supreme Court by the Constitution. The principle of judicial review holds that the Supreme Court has the authority to declare an act of Congress unconstitutional.

33. **(B)** The Progressive Era *Fact Question*

Taft advocated a foreign policy of "dollar diplomacy." According to Taft, American investment abroad would promote global stability in addition to aiding American economic interests. Dollar diplomacy was a marked contrast to Theodore Roosevelt's "big stick" policies, which called for an aggressive approach to international affairs. Taft's efforts at investment failed in China and met with little success elsewhere in the world. Eventually, he was forced to use military force in Nicaragua in order to suppress a revolt.

34. **(B)** Civil War & Reconstruction *Trend Question*

Newspapers publicized the growing conflict between the North and the South over slavery. They reported on the marked differences between life in the slaveholding states and life in the free states, and northern papers published abolitionist editorials, which exacerbated tensions.

35. **(C)** Industrial Revolution *Trend Question*

The Grange was formed by midwestern farmers in 1867. It hosted biweekly social functions where farmers could get an education, bond, and voice their complaints. The organization became increasingly political as the railroad companies began to hike up prices for short-distance shipments. In response to the railroads' practices, the Grangers lobbied Congress, and the Interstate Commerce Act was passed in 1887.

36. **(C)** Civil War & Reconstruction *Except Question*

France did not enter into an alliance with the North. For a brief time, the Confederacy flirted with the idea of allying with France or England, but neither of these alliances came to fruition.

37. **(E)** Revolution & Constitution *Fact Question*

The Intolerable Acts of 1774 provoked the colonies into unified action for the first time and led directly to the meeting of the First Continental Congress in Philadelphia in 1775.

38. **(A)** The Age of Imperialism *Trend Question*

Hearst's newspaper, the *New York Journal*, engaged in yellow journalism, exaggerating and sometimes inventing accounts of Spanish atrocities against the Cuban rebels. Responding to these sensationalist reports, the American public gave increasing support to the Cuban nationalists and called for American intervention in the revolt.

39. **(A)** Westward Expansion & Sectional Strife *Fact Question*

Harriet Tubman helped more than 300 slaves escape to freedom using the Underground Railroad, a loosely organized network of shelters and "conductors" who led the escaped slaves through the North.

40. **(A)** A New Nation *Trend Question*

The Monroe Doctrine asserted U.S. supremacy in the western hemisphere and warned foreign nations against colonization or interference in that region. In exchange, the United States promised to refrain from interfering in European political affairs.

41. **(C)** Cultural Trends *Trend Question*

Booker T. Washington founded the Tuskegee Institute in order to provide African Americans with an education. The institute focused on providing a practical rather than a liberal arts education. Washington believed practical education would help African Americans achieve economic independence from whites.

42. **(D)** The Colonial Period — *Fact Question*

The original settlers in Jamestown hoped to find gold and precious metals, but the colony's initial source of wealth came from tobacco. After several years of disease, starvation, and death, the colony began to flourish when John Rolfe, who later married Pocahontas, introduced a strain of West Indian tobacco to the colony. The crop grew well, and the Virginia Company made a huge profit exporting tobacco.

43. **(E)** The Great Depression & New Deal — *Trend Question*

The Court Packing scheme tarnished FDR's reputation. In 1937, FDR attempted to reform the Supreme Court by introducing a bill that would allow the president to appoint an additional justice for each sitting justice over seventy years old. Many Americans accused FDR of trying to change the system of checks and balances by diluting the power of conservative justices on the Supreme Court.

44. **(D)** The Roaring Twenties — *Except Question*

The Chinese Exclusion Act, which banned Chinese immigration for ten years, was passed in 1882, not in the post–World War I era.

45. **(D)** Industrial Revolution — *Trend Question*

Social Darwinists applied Charles Darwin's "survival of the fittest" theory to human society. They argued that the very poor were not "fit" to survive and that the government should not prolong their misery by giving them relief.

46. **(A)** The Colonial Period — *Fact Question*

Metacomet, called King Philip by the colonists, led Native Americans in an attack on Plymouth in 1675, after Plymouth colonists had executed several members of Metacomet's tribe for the murder of a settler. Metacomet and many of his followers were killed during the war.

47. **(B)** Revolution & Constitution — *Fact Question*

By establishing a system for admitting new states to the Union, the Northwest Ordinances resolved the competing land claims held by existing states. The ordinances created the states of Michigan, Illinois, Wisconsin, Indiana, and Ohio from the Northwest territory.

48. **(C)** World War II — *Cartoon Question*

The poster shows a determined-looking woman under the slogan "We can do it!" Posters like these were designed to encourage women to join the domestic war effort during World War II. Since the production of war materials increased while the number of male factory workers decreased, employers increasingly sought female workers.

49. **(B)** The 1960s — *Fact Question*

At Selma, King protested for voting rights, which previous civil rights legislation had not obtained for African Americans. Although historians disagree about the impact his protest had on reform, that same year Lyndon B. Johnson proposed a law that became the Voting Rights Act of 1965.

50. **(B)** The Colonial Period — *Fact Question*

The hope of finding the Northwest Passage initially spurred the French to explore the New World. France hoped that a water route to Asia existed somewhere in North America.

51. **(C)** Westward Expansion & Sectional Strife *Map Question*

The shaded area on the map represents the land the United States acquired during the Mexican War. This territory was the subject of the Wilmot Proviso, which proposed banning slavery in all lands acquired during the war. The proviso failed to win support in the House of Representatives.

52. **(E)** The Great Depression & New Deal *Fact Question*

A champion of the lower classes, Huey Long criticized the New Deal for failing to alleviate conditions for the poor. Long proposed an alternative to the New Deal, called the Share Our Wealth program, which would focus on income redistribution and benefits for the poor.

53. **(B)** The Colonial Period *Trend Question*

Mercantilist theory held that a country could amass great wealth by increasing exports and collecting raw and precious materials in exchange. The American colonies were important to England because they provided both a marketplace for finished English products and a source for raw materials used by English manufacturers.

54. **(B)** The 1950s *Except Question*

Although Eisenhower criticized many aspects of the New Deal, he continued some of its most important programs and practices, including the public works projects and farm subsidies. While he upheld the Supreme Court's decision in *Brown v. Board of Education*, desegregation was not a component of his dynamic conservatism, and he considered the *Brown* ruling to be a mistake.

55. **(A)** A New Nation *Fact Question*

The Era of Good Feelings centers on Monroe's presidency (1817 to 1825). From the end of the War of 1812 to the rise of Andrew Jackson in 1828, the American political scene was dominated by a one-party system, with little opposition or controversy.

56. **(D)** Civil War & Reconstruction *Trend Question*

The 1866 election was an overwhelming success for Radical Republicans. The huge majorities they won in both houses of Congress allowed them to override presidential vetoes and to control the Reconstruction process.

57. **(A)** The Age of Jackson *Fact Question*

The Specie Circular was an executive order issued by Andrew Jackson in order to cool down the rampant speculation that threatened to destabilize the economy. The order required that government lands be purchased with only gold or silver instead of with credit or paper currency. Financial panic and economic depression gripped the country, as speculators who could not pay their government debts were forced into bankruptcy.

58. **(E)** Cultural Trends *Except Question*

Nativists did not believe that immigrants were trying to replace slave labor in the south. Their main fear was that continued immigration would swamp and destroy "American" values and culture. Nativist groups, such as the Know-Nothings, gained support in northern cities during the 1840s and 1850s in response to increasing levels of immigration during those decades.

59. **(D)** Revolution & Constitution *Trend Question*

The Articles of Confederation did not give Congress the authority to tax. As a result, the central government could not raise operating funds or afford to raise an army. In order to raise funding, the government continued to print paper money, thus lowering the currency's value and creating serious economic problems.

60. **(B)** Industrial Revolution *Fact Question*

The Gospel of Success preached that anyone could become wealthy through hard work and determination. According to this belief, wealthy Americans deserved their success and should be praised for it. The Gospel of Success represented one of the ways that elite Americans justified the growing gap between the rich and the poor during the industrial revolution.

61. **(A)** 1970–2000 *Except Question*

Gerald Ford was not involved in the Watergate scandal; at the time, he was a Republican congressman from Michigan. After Spiro Agnew resigned, Richard Nixon selected Ford to be his new vice president. When Nixon resigned in 1974 as a result of the Watergate cover-up, Ford became president and pardoned Nixon for his role in the scandal.

62. **(B)** World War I *Fact Question*

In the *Schenck* decision, the Supreme Court ruled that Americans' civil liberties, such as the right to free speech, could be denied or curtailed by the government in time of "clear and present danger." This precedent-setting case brought into question the applicability of the Bill of Rights in times of war and national crisis.

63. **(C)** The Industrial Revolution *Except Question*

In 1886, workers in Chicago protested the use of police brutality against strikers. The protest became violent when a member of the Knights of Labor threw a bomb, and the police retaliated. The police arrested several leaders of the Knights of Labor, who were then convicted for inciting the riot. Public support for the unions quickly fell afterward, and the Knights of Labor were effectively destroyed.

64. **(B)** The Age of Imperialism *Quotation Question*

The Roosevelt corollary functions on the assumption of the "white man's burden." Roosevelt believed that many nations in the western hemisphere were hanging on to the "ties of civilized society" and that these countries needed the United States to keep them "civilized." The corollary proposed that the United States intervene whenever "inferior" people proved themselves unfit to govern their own nations.

65. **(C)** Revolution & Constitution *Fact Question*

During the framing of the Constitution, southern states argued for the inclusion of slaves in population counts to determine the number of representative seats a state would have in Congress. Northern delegates objected to this inclusion, since it would give the South an unfair advantage. In the end, the delegates compromised and agreed on the Three-fifths clause, which would count slaves as three-fifths of a free person for representation and taxation purposes.

66. **(D)** Westward Expansion & Sectional Strife *Except Question*

Kansas was not a slave state. It entered the Union as a free state in 1861 after the crisis over "Bleeding Kansas."

67. **(D)** The Great Depression & New Deal *Trend Question*

The Agricultural Adjustment Administration was designed to regulate farm production in the United States. Its goal was to decrease farm production and increase farm prices by paying subsidies to farmers who agreed to produce under certain quotas. While the AAA benefited many large farmers, its efforts hurt small farmers in the rural Midwest. Many of these farmers ended up migrating west, hoping to find employment in California.

68. **(D)** The Colonial Period *Except Question*

The American colonies did not become self-governing as a result of the French and Indian War. Trying to raise revenue to pay its large debt from the war, the British government began to levy harsh taxes on the colonies after 1763, and Britain moved away from its former policy of salutary neglect to one of tight control.

69. **(C)** The 1950s *Trend Question*

The boycott successfully used two civil rights strategies: community protest and litigation. The Montgomery Improvement Association, led by Martin Luther King Jr., organized a boycott that crippled the Montgomery City Lines bus company. At the same time, the National Association for the Advancement of Colored People sought legal redress through the courts. The combination of direct action and litigation led to success in Montgomery and provided a useful model for future civil rights protests.

70. **(B)** Industrial Revolution *Trend Question*

Rapid technological innovation throughout the nineteenth century fueled industrial development in the United States and expanded the American labor force.

71. **(D)** The Great Depression & New Deal *Fact Question*

In the Good Neighbor policy, FDR declared that no nation had any right to interfere in another nation's affairs. The policy specifically stated that the United States would refrain from interfering in Latin-American affairs.

72. **(C)** The 1950s *Trend Question*

One hundred southern congressmen signed a southern "manifesto" condemning the *Brown v. Board of Education* ruling, which called for the integration of public schools, and urging states to nullify it. The call for nullification recalled the struggle in the nineteenth century between the states and the federal government. By issuing the manifesto, the congressmen demonstrated that integration would not proceed smoothly in the South.

73. **(D)** Industrial Revolution *Fact Question*

Debs organized the railway workers' strike after Pullman ordered a twenty-five percent cut in the workers' wages. The strike was unsuccessful. It destroyed the union and resulted in Debs' incarceration for failure to obey court procedure.

74. **(C)** World War II *Trend Question*

Although FDR wanted to wait for public support before entering World War II, he assisted the Allies through other means before 1941. Several months before the United States entered the war, FDR passed the Lend-Lease Act, which gave the president the authority to lend or lease supplies to nations if he deemed them "vital to the defense of the United States." FDR started by providing lend-lease aid to Britain and later extended the aid to the Soviet Union.

75. (E) Westward Expansion & Sectional Strife — Fact Question

Jackson wrote *A Century of Dishonor* in order to raise public awareness of the Native American situation. In the book, she blames the plight of the Native Americans on the U.S. government and on American citizens.

76. (B) The Roaring Twenties — Fact Question

Scopes was arrested for teaching evolution in violation of a Tennessee law that prohibited the teaching of evolution in public schools. Although he was found guilty and forced to pay a fine, the anti-evolution forces suffered humiliating blows during the trial, and the anti-evolution cause was significantly weakened across the United States.

77. (D) Industrial Revolution — Fact Question

Samuel Gompers founded the AFL as a union for skilled craftsmen. He believed that skilled workers had an advantage in labor negotiations, since employers could not easily replace them if they went on strike.

78. (B) Revolution & Constitution — Trend Question

Strict constructionists and loose constructionists disagreed over the elastic clause. Strict constructionists believed that the powers of the federal government should be confined to those expressly stated in the Constitution. Loose constructionists favored a strong central government that could do anything not expressly forbidden by the Constitution. The elastic clause gave Congress the power to create all laws "necessary and proper" in order to keep the country operating. Strict constructionists argued that the elastic clause gave the federal government too much power, but loose constructionists believed the clause was necessary in order to have an effective central government.

79. (A) Westward Expansion & Sectional Strife — Trend Question

In 1828, South Carolina threatened to secede from the Union after the passage of the "Tariff of Abominations," but the southern slaveholding states viewed Lincoln's election as a much greater threat, even though Lincoln promised not to interfere with slavery in the South. Shortly after his election in 1860, a South Carolina convention unanimously agreed to secede. A year later, six other states followed suit. These seven states formed the Confederate States of America and elected Jefferson Davis their president. In 1861, four other slaveholding states seceded and joined the Confederacy.

80. (B) Industrial Revolution — Except Question

The Democrats and Populists united in support of bimetalism during the 1896 election. Bryan argued that "free silver" (the unlimited coinage of silver) would benefit farmers and the poor by easing debt repayments.

81. (B) The Colonial Period — Trend Question

The Quakers did not have priests or ministers because they believed that people communicated on an individual level with God.

82. (E) The 1950s — Except Question

During the Korean War, the United States increased its military spending, thus stimulating economic growth during the first part of the 1950s. The end of the Korean War brought military spending back down to peacetime levels; it did not aid in the expansion of the economy in the 1950s.

83. **(B)** Industrial Revolution *Fact Question*

In the 1896 *Plessy* decision, the Court stated that Jim Crow laws, which institutionalized segregation in the south, were constitutional as long as the facilities available to whites and Africans Americans were equal. The "separate but equal" doctrine established in this decision was overturned in 1954 in the *Brown v. Board of Education* case.

84. **(C)** Westward Expansion & Sectional Strife *Fact Question*

The Republican Party formed as a coalition of groups opposed to the extension of slavery. Although the groups that formed the Republicans had disparate aims, they were united in their stance against slavery's extension into the Western territories. Their "free soil" campaign sought to ban slavery in the territories, but it did not seek to ban slavery where it already existed.

85. **(B)** The Roaring Twenties *Trend Question*

Women's contribution to the war effort during World War I won them the respect of many Americans and ultimately helped them win the right to vote. During the war, women worked as volunteers in the armed forces, performing clerical duties and serving as nurses. Many women worked in defense industries, filling in vacancies left by men who were fighting overseas.

86. **(D)** The Progressive Era *Trend Question*

The eugenics movement represented an extreme form of progressivism. Supporters of eugenics wanted to turn the United States into a white, Protestant nation, completely free of the "impurities" of other races and religions. The eugenics movement was virulently anti-immigration, and a eugenics supporter would have wholeheartedly wished for an end to immigration.

87. **(C)** Industrial Revolution *Trend Question*

During the 1880s, the government took a hands-off approach to business. According to the government's laissez-faire approach, the market should be free of any government intervention because free markets would produce competition, which would in turn produce goods of fair quality at fair prices. Regulatory legislation that was passed during this period was only laxly enforced.

88. **(A)** Revolution & Constitution *Trend Question*

The Bill of Rights was added to the Constitution because critics, such as Thomas Jefferson and James Madison, worried that the Constitution did not adequately protect individual civil liberties. Those critics, who were generally Anti-federalists, demanded the addition of civil liberties protections in exchange for ratification of the Constitution.

89. **(D)** Cultural Trends *Fact Question*

Garrison, the most famous white abolitionist in the 1830s, advocated the immediate abolition of slavery, arguing that slavery was an unjustifiable and immoral system.

90. **(D)** Industrial Revolution *Cartoon Question*

This cartoon highlights the disparity of wealth between the wealthy and the working class during the "Gilded Age." On the right, luxuriously dressed and well-fed men enjoy their cigars, while a skinny working man timidly stands in the room on the left. The caption says, "After the feast, the working man gets what is left," but what's left is nothing—just the skeleton of the bird that the rich men devoured for dinner. The cartoon criticizes the wealthy for growing fat off their wealth while leaving nothing behind for the poor workers.

Take the NEXT STEP in TEST PREP

SparkNotes™ interactive online test preparation system will raise your scores on the SAT, ACT, and SAT II subject tests in Biology, Physics, U.S. History, Math IC and IIC, and Writing.

testprep.sparknotes.com

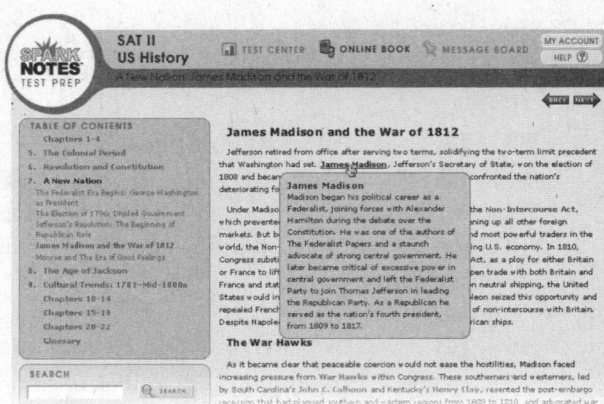

Our Entire Book Online Get a fully searchable, hyperlinked version of the SparkNotes book we sell in stores for each test.

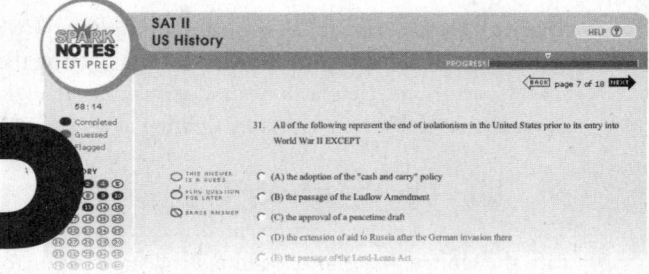

Practice Tests Make Perfect Up to 5 interactive practice tests with complete explanations for each question.

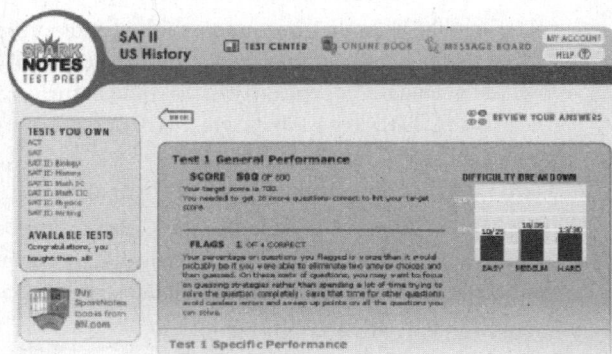

Instant Diagnostic Feedback Get instant results: overall score, strengths, weaknesses, progress. Then see a personalized study plan that links back to the book.

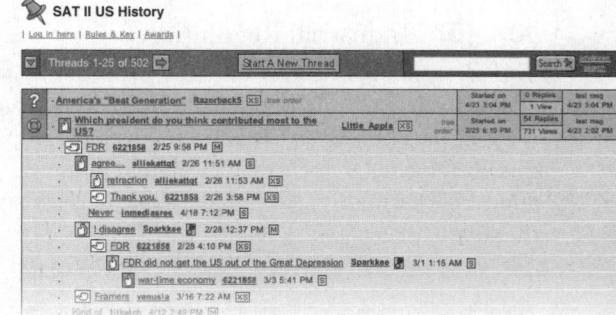

Don't Go It Alone Message boards connect you to other students taking the same test you are.

Awesome and Affordable We've made test prep dynamic, interactive, and affordable. At $14.95 it's the best deal online or off.

SPARKCHARTS™
EVERYTHING YOU NEED TO KNOW
in Just Four Pages!

Imagine if the top student in your course organized the most important points from your textbook or lecture into an easy-to-read, laminated chart that could fit directly into your notebook or binder. SparkCharts are study companions and reference tools that cover a wide range of subjects, including Math, Science, History, Business, Humanities, Foreign Language, and Writing. Titles like Presentations and Public Speaking, Essays and Term Papers, and Test Prep give you what it takes to find success in high school, college, and beyond.

Outlines and summaries cover key points, while diagrams and tables make difficult concepts easier to digest. All for the price of that late-night cappuccino you'll no longer need!

- Accounting
- Algebra I
- Algebra II
- Calculus II
- Chemistry
- Circulatory System
- Digestive System
- English Composition
- English Grammar
- Essays & Term Papers
- Finance
- French Grammar
- French Vocabulary
- General Anatomy
- Geometry
- Macroeconomics
- Math Basics
- Microbiology
- Microeconomics
- Muscular System
- Mythology
- Periodic Table with Chemistry Formulas
- Philosophy
- Physics
- Physics Formulas
- Pre-Calculus
- Psychology
- Reproductive System
- Resumes & Cover Letters
- SAT Math
- SAT Verbal
- SAT Vocabulary
- Shakespeare
- Skeletal System
- Spanish Grammar
- Spanish Vocabulary
- Statistics
- Trigonometry
- U.S. Constitution
- U.S. Government
- U.S. History 1865–2002
- Weights & Measures
- Western Civilization
- World History
- …and more.

Time to cut standardized tests down to size.

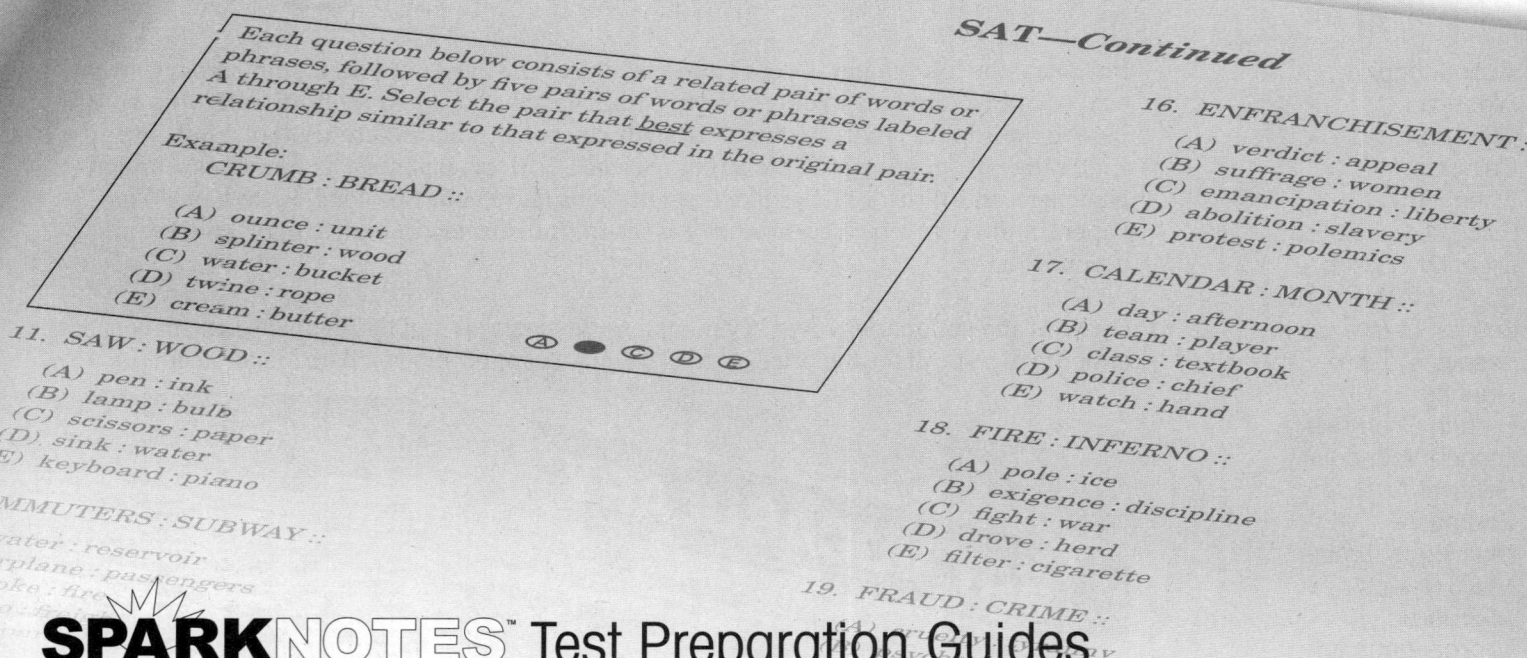

SPARKNOTES™ Test Preparation Guides

Smarter Packed with critical-thinking skills and test-taking strategies that will improve your score.

Better Fully up to date, covering all new features of the tests, with study tips on every type of question.

Faster Our books cover exactly what you need to know for the test. No more, no less.

SparkNotes Guide to the SAT & PSAT — DELUXE INTERNET EDITION
SparkNotes Guide to the SAT & PSAT
SparkNotes Guide to the ACT — DELUXE INTERNET EDITION
SparkNotes Guide to the ACT
SparkNotes SAT Verbal Workbook
SparkNotes SAT Math Workbook
SparkNotes Guide to the SAT II Writing
5 More Practice Tests for the SAT II Writing
SparkNotes Guide to the SAT II U.S. History
5 More Practice Tests for the SAT II History
SparkNotes Guide to the SAT II Math IC
5 More Practice Tests for the SAT II Math IC
SparkNotes Guide to the SAT II Math IIC
5 More Practice Tests for the SAT II Math IIC
SparkNotes Guide to the SAT II Biology
5 More Practice Tests for the SAT II Biology
SparkNotes Guide to the SAT II Physics